HUMAN PROBLEMS and How to Solve Them

by Donald Curtis

YOU can be as happy as you want to be. You have every right to all the happiness you want. *And, with the help of this book you can achieve it.*

No matter what it is you want—health, happiness, security, love, peace of mind, recognition, job advancement—all of these things and more are within your grasp. You have only to reach out and take hold of them.

With this book there will be no limit to what you can accomplish. For here, with the loving help of God, you will learn how to re-channel your creative power into those constructive paths which bring everlasting happiness and tranquillity.

You are shown how to cast out of your thinking all destructive negative mental and emotional states of mind. The 5 negative attitudes that cause difficulties and unhappiness are pointed out and you are given 5 positive attitudes to replace them.

Based on hundreds of case histories and the author's long experience in helping people with all kinds of problems, this book is a master guide to releasing the powerful, God-given forces within you. It will help you to become the whole person you are meant to be, to become attuned to the Universal Mind, to unify yourself with your ideal, to overcome the limitations of self, condition and experience and think with a larger awareness.

All of these things are documented with actual problems of real people. There is the story of George Wilson who found himself with only a $1.33 and no job. There is the story of George Elton who in gaining material wealth had lost his zest for living. There is the story of the rising young actress who lost her health because she couldn't resolve her inner conflicts.

You will see how all of them not only solved their immediate problems but kindled a new inner spark, a renewed confidence, a new meaning for their lives that moved them to an even higher plane. *And you will be shown how to apply the principles they used to enrich your own life.*

You are at the beginning of the path to a new life, brimming with a glorious inner radiance. Step forward!

by Donald Curtis

An outstanding leader in New Thought and metaphysics for over twenty years, Dr. Donald Curtis is the senior minister of the Unity Church of Dallas where he ministers to thousands in person and through his regular radio and television programs.

In addition to his major books,

Your Thoughts Can Change Your Life

Human Problems and How To Solve Them

Daily Power For Joyful Living

Science of Mind in Daily Living

New Age Understanding

he is the author of many inspirational booklets which are widely read by Truth students everywhere. He has written hundreds of articles which have appeared regularly over the years in **Science of Mind, New Thought Quarterly,** and Unity periodicals. He is a District President of the International New Thought Alliance and speaks and teaches regularly at the INTA Congress each year.

Dr. Curtis speaks and conducts classes at Unity and other metaphysical churches throughout the United States and abroad. His seminars based upon his books are widely attended everywhere.

His writings are used as textbooks in healing, meditation, and spiritual education at many churches and centers. Dr. Curtis' sales and executive and leadership training seminars are popular in the business and professional fields, and he is in great demand as an after-dinner and convention speaker. He appears regularly before service clubs, speaking on his favorite theme, "The Unlimited Potential Within You." He presents techniques for developing this potential, releasing the free, full flow of life through the individual as his consciousness expands and he experiences richer, fuller living. Through the Spiritual Unity of Nations and other organizations throughout the world, Dr. Curtis works tirelessly for human understanding, international cooperation, and world peace.

He carries on a large correspondence with readers, teachers, and students all over the world. An extensive traveler, he has spoken in England, Switzerland, Germany, Ghana, South Africa, Greece, India, Japan, Hawaii and in the Caribbean Islands. A deep student of world religions, Dr. Curtis has studied with the yogis and holy men of India, spending time in their ashrams, as well as seeking out the counsel and instruction of Buddhist monks, and Tibetan lamas. In Japan, he studied Oriental techniques of healing, studied Zen, did research in the traditional older religions, and spoke at the centers of many of the "new religions" there, including an extensive lecture tour for Seicho-No-Ie founded by Masaharu Taniguchi.

Dr. Curtis' broad background and universal approach to spiritual matters make him welcome by religious groups of all denominations.

HUMAN PROBLEMS
AND HOW TO
SOLVE THEM

by Donald Curtis

Published by
Melvin Powers
WILSHIRE BOOK COMPANY
12015 Sherman Road
No. Hollywood, California 91605
Telephone: (213) 875-1711

To my son Christopher

Library of Congress Catalog Number 62-17777

ISBN 0-87980-298-7

Printed in the United States of America

Printed by

HAL LEIGHTON PRINTING COMPANY
P.O. Box 3952
North Hollywood, California 91605
Telephone: (213) 983-1105

PREFACE

What's your problem? Chances are you have one—or several. There's no disgrace in that; problems are necessary for growth. Finding the answers to life's problems is one of the privileges of living. The important thing is not to let the problem get bigger than you are.

Our difficulties arise when we subconsciously accept two opposing ideas. Unless this conflict is resolved, there will be nothing but trouble inside and out. The battleground is within our minds and hearts. Failure, disease, unhappiness, poverty, and all human ills are the result of negative forces winning out in this subconscious war. This book is designed to help you solve your problems by reconditioning the subconscious mind with constructive thoughts and attitudes whereby the destructive negative attitudes will be dissolved.

False beliefs cause separation and limitation. When we get our inner attitudes in line, our lives straighten out. It is not hard to succeed in life when we get our spiritual, mental and emotional equipment working properly. Every one of us is here for a purpose. Discover that purpose, determine to fulfill it, identify yourself with it, build a strong conviction of success in your consciousness, and flow with the main stream. Obstacles drift away as we dissolve them in our minds.

This book presents specific techniques to help you solve your problems and attain your goals.

Donald Curtis

CONSCIOUSNESS CONDITIONERS
IN THIS BOOK

CONTENTS

CHAPTER ONE

YOU CAN BE AS HAPPY
AS YOU WANT TO BE

"There's nothing wrong with me that a good job won't cure."
"If I could only get married."
"A few hundred dollars would take care of all my problems."
"I'd be all right if I just had more time."
"All I need is a little more rest."
"Business will be picking up soon. Then I'll be out of the woods."
"As soon as I finish this new course, I'll be ready to get underway."
"I'm in line for a promotion. Then I'll have it made."
"Things will be a lot different when we move to a better neighborhood."
"If I just had some friends, I wouldn't be so lonely."
"Nobody understands me. If they only knew what I'm really like."
"Why don't we go away for a trip? Give us a chance to find ourselves."
"I'm going to a psychiatrist. He'll straighten me out."
"I need a new doctor. I know the right one could do wonders for me."
"I'll be fine as soon as this pain stops."
"I'm going into the hospital for surgery. I'm sure this will make all the difference."
"I need a pick-me-up."
"Gimmee a cupacoffee!"
"Gimmee a cigarette!"
"Gimmee a drink!"
"Gimmee a fix!"
"Gimmee!"

1

HAVE YOU A PROBLEM?

Everyone thinks he understands his problem and how to overcome it. The parade goes on. We are all searching for something—usually the answer to a specific need or the solution to a certain situation. If we can get over just this one hurdle, we think we will have it made. Such, however, is hardly ever the case. Situations are met, but the basic problems remain because our approach is backwards. In this book, we will try to put first things first.

Everyone has a certain amount of trouble. Obstacles are necessary for growth, for we learn from our mistakes and we progress by triumphing over difficulties. Struggle strengthens. Unhappiness starts when we resist these natural exigencies of life and see them only as problems. What we call the problem could preferably be labeled the symptom. The problem lies much deeper: in the realm of the human psyche; in the mental and emotional adjustment; in the spiritual values; in the conditioned responses and daily activities; in our habitual actions and reactions.

HERE IS HELP FOR YOU

There are guides to help you solve your problems at the point of cause. Based upon the case histories of several hundred men and women whom I have counseled, this book will unveil the drama of human experience and bring to the fore specific ideas and techniques to help each of us with our own particular brand of trouble.

This book is about you. You see, there is a basic pattern in all human problems. They repeat themselves over and over again with persistent regularity. Only the details vary. Therefore, in the stories that follow, you may feel that you are reading case histories of your own problems rather than those of the persons about whom I am writing. You see, the people who come to me for help do so in strictest confidence. I respect it always; I have a sacred obligation to do so. However, the lessons which my students and I have learned together in dealing with their problems are now shared with you.

THE DESTRUCTIVE POWER OF NEGATIVE THINKING

There is no law of error, no principle behind problems, no definitely predictable condition or disease. But this we know: *all negative* mental and emotional states are destructive. Inner trouble always produces outer trouble. Causes and conditions always match, even though we may have trouble in unravelling them. A person who has one kind of problem usually has several. When one problem is healed at the point of cause, all of the others can be healed at the same time. In spiritual mind treatment the focus is never upon the problem. We focus upon the solution. A problem has no independent existence. It is merely an effect caused by something—invariably negative inner attitudes.

A sustained feeling of inner happiness is the only known cure for human travail, no matter what particular form it may take—suffering, illness, frustration, lack, loneliness—or just plain unhappiness. This state of inner happiness is the kingdom of heaven which Jesus talks about in the Bible.

GEORGE ELTON HAD IT MADE

"Well, what's your problem?" I queried the prosperous looking businessman as he sat across my desk lighting a Corona-Corona. I'm not usually that abrupt in counseling, since most people haven't the slightest clue to their own problem even though they can vividly describe the thousand and one symptoms it has produced. But in this instance I decided on the direct approach.

My patient looked at me quizzically, then leaned back and puffed meditatively upon his cigar for a few moments before finally bursting into a rather rueful laugh.

"I haven't any, Dr. Curtis."

I joined in with the laughter.

"That's the most refreshing thing I've heard today," I observed. "Most people who come to see me aren't quite so blessed."

"I'm not sure I am either," the man we'll call George Elton continued.

"Oh?"

"You see, that's my problem."

"What?"

"Just what I said before. I haven't any."

"Oh come now . . . ," I remonstrated.

"I'm serious," Mr. Elton continued. "You remember the story of the dejected greyhound who caught the rabbit at the dog track? Well, that's my fix exactly. I don't have any reason to keep running either. To put it quite simply, I've got it made. I haven't a problem in the world, and I'm bored stiff."

"Tell me more about it," I encouraged, sensing that there was more here than met the eye. "How long has this been going on?"

"Just about three years now. Ever since I was forty. You look surprised. I know my middle-age spread makes me look a lot older. That didn't start until about three years ago either."

"What happened three years ago?" I asked.

"Now look, I've never told this to another living soul . . ."

"Go on," I encouraged as he paused. This wasn't the first time I had heard an exclusive; I listen to them between twenty and thirty hours every week.

"I don't want to brag," George Elton continued, "but three years ago I had made my first million. From the time I had been hungry as a kid, and had gone out to become the breadwinner for my mother and brothers and sisters when I was just twelve, I vowed to become a millionaire by the time I was forty."

"And you made it?"

"With three months to spare. And that isn't all of it. All my other dreams have come true, too. I own my own business. It's going so well, I've made two more million since the first one. I have the most wonderful wife in the world, and four beautiful kids. I have two Cadillacs and a Mercedes-Benz, a home which is the front porch to heaven, and I've been around the world twice. Everybody thinks I'm wonderful."

"You must be," I conceded. "The evidence shows it."

"Then why aren't I happy?"

Here was a man who had gained the whole world but had lost track of his own soul. He had proved that happiness is not guaranteed by money or things. It isn't even provided by success, esteem, love, family or pleasant diversion. George Elton was unhappy because he had failed to provide himself with new incentives when his original one—to make a million dollars—was achieved. It was a fairly simple matter to help him solve his problem. We just provided him with new goals, new ideas, a new sense of values, and some new patterns of action. He was a sensitive and highly intelligent man, and with a little spiritual orientation, he saw that he had become one-sided. He had centered his attention upon outer accomplishment and accumulation, and neglected to develop himself as a whole person. As with so many big businessmen, he knew how to make it, but not how to enjoy it.

Re-Channel Your Creative Power

George Elton knew how to use the creative power within him—otherwise he could not have achieved what he did. All that was necessary was for him to re-tool his sense of values and re-channel his energies. He went to work on the following suggestions, which will help you find happiness just as they did him.

1. Fall in love with life and live it fully.
2. Get interested in people.
3. Give yourself wholeheartedly to an idea.
4. Dedicate your time, your talent, and your money to helping others.
5. Explore the Great Unknown through thought, study, discussion, prayer, meditation and worship.

George Elton threw himself into the program of rehabilitation with all the fervor with which he had made his millions. He rediscovered himself and had a whale of a time doing it. He started by checking himself out on each of the five points:

1. *Fall in love with life and live it fully.* He found that he had not been nearly as much interested in life as he was in what he could get out of life. Although he was a go-getter, he didn't know what to do with it after he got it. Recognizing his self-centeredness and one-sidedness, he began to approach life differently. He started having fun, developing new interests, forgetting himself and living a more balanced existence. For the first time, he experienced happiness.

Now, I don't imagine you have George Elton's outer problem—that of having too much and not knowing what to do with it—but chances are some of your unhappiness arises from failing to balance yourself out on these five points. As you examine them carefully, you will find that they encompass the five major areas of our being and experience: Spiritual, Mental, Emotional, Physical, Material.

A human being is a complicated thing, but with a little effort you can understand a lot more about yourself than you do now. You can classify everything about you in one of these five major groupings. A little self-analysis will reveal in which level your problem lies. The basic problem is always somewhere in the inner nature—the spiritual, mental and emotional—which we know as the soul. Unhappiness, illness, want, suffering, disappointment, frustration and other human difficulties arise from soul sickness. Heal your soul and you won't have any more problems. Once that is done you will know how to deal with physical and material experience. George Elton did it. So can you.

2. *Get interested in people.* George Elton discovered that he had never been interested in people—not even the members of his family whom he loved very much, in his own way. He dealt with many people, but had never taken the time to know them, seeing them only as different units in his experience. He identified them with himself and his purposes, but he failed to identify himself with them. His interest was a reflected self-interest. He used, collected, possessed people; but he neither understood nor loved them.

Now, our hero was not a bad man. He was simply thoughtless, unfeeling and unaware—just like most of us. His subconscious attitude was, "What can this fellow do for me?", not "What can I do for him?" Even his wife and children were little more than possessions. He liked to have them around; they were a most necessary part of the picture which he had projected of himself, but he didn't think of them as individuals. He was somewhat like the minister, noted for his love for children, who one day became incensed when a group of neighborhood youngsters ploughed through his freshly poured cement sidewalk during a game of follow-the-leader. As he started to chase them with a club, an astonished neighbor remonstrated, "Why, Reverend Smith, I thought you loved children."

"I do love children in the abstract, Mrs. Brown," he fumed, "but not in the concrete."

That will hardly suffice. We either are interested in people or we are not. When we are interested in them, we will love them, and one of the most important avenues of human happiness is opened to us.

George Elton had the time of his life getting to know the people he had been merely acquainted with for years. His employees, his customers, and his family became a source of inspiration and joy. He found himself in other people. Why don't you try it?

3. *Give yourself wholeheartedly to an idea.* George Elton had done this all right, but he found it was the wrong idea. He had become pretty much like the disgruntled character in a recent magazine car-

toon who was sitting glowering, alone and unhappy, with a deep scowl upon his face.

"He struggled, he slaved, he sacrificed, and he worked," his wife explained to a friend, "He spent years fighting his way to the top. And now he doesn't like it at the top."

Make sure your goal is worth attaining. The journey is just as important as the destination. Work to express yourself, give what you have to give, do what you have to do, live your life the way you think it should be lived. Formulate an inner image, marry yourself to noble goals and purposes, and go full speed ahead, never worrying about recognition or material rewards. Rudyard Kipling summed it all up in his great poem, "L'Envoi:"

> But each for the joy of the working, and each, in his separate star,
> Shall draw the Thing as he sees It for the God of Things as They Are!

What is the most important thing in the world to you? Examine it carefully and ask yourself: "Is this a good thing for me to do? Does it express what I really am? Is it contributing anything? Is it for the best interests of everyone concerned—does it work toward the greatest good for the greatest number? Will this objective provide the accomplishment with which I want to be identified?"

If you can answer, "Yes" to these and similar questions, then go all the way with your dream. Jesus instructed, "Whosoever shall compel thee to go a mile, go with him twain." (Matt. 5:41) Life only pays off when we follow through.

George Elton took another look at the business empire which he had built. He saw a tremendous opportunity for service to humanity in it. He found a much bigger idea than just making money, and gave himself wholeheartedly to it. Losing himself in something bigger than egoism, he found happiness.

What is the biggest idea in your life? This idea is God's desire to express Himself through you in that way. Clear the decks, and go to work serving it, for you will never rest until you do. The world is strewn with the wrecked lives of those who have abandoned their dreams.

The riches of the kingdom are showered upon those who faithfully carry out what God has given them to do. Let's do it.

4. *Dedicate your time, your talent, and your money to helping*

others. George Elton faced the hard fact that he had never really thought about anyone but himself. That's why he got bored and went stale. He had drawn his circle too tight. He hadn't allowed room enough in which to move and express himself. Giving everything he had to making his first million, he never gave one thought to what he would do when his goal was achieved. The more successful he became, the more time he had on his hands. With the lessening of his incentive, he allowed his talents and energies to go unused.

George Elton was a race horse who had been put out to pasture too soon. He decided to get back in the race. He started to look for things to do for others. He applied himself to public service with the same zeal he had previously shown in just making money.

"Do you know something?" he laughed. "The harder I work to give myself away, the more I have to give. I've been so busy helping other people that I haven't any time to take care of my business. It's been running itself. But here's the funny thing: It's doing better than ever—seems to have gotten a shot in the arm."

Of course. George Elton, his business, and his whole life got a shot in the arm when he channeled his time, talent and resources into doing good for others. He discovered potentials in himself and in his work that he had never dreamed of. He turned over all of the responsibilities of his original business to a general manager. Then Mr. Elton formed a foundation, devoted to the idea of doing good for others. It was set up on a non-profit basis, but because of his genius for organization and management, it too became profitable, providing more resources to apply to doing good in the world. George Elton couldn't help being successful. Now, however, he was a *happy* success, and everyone else was happier as a result.

Have you tried giving yourself away lately?

5. *Explore the Great Unknown through thought, study, discussion, prayer, meditation and worship.* George Elton discovered that there was much more to this business of living than he had ever dreamed of. His new approach to himself, to his work, to other people, and to life in general, opened up vast new vistas. He started to really think, using his mind for something other than adding up profits. He comes to me regularly, sometimes several times a week, to discuss the principles back of our scientific spiritual approach to life. He has enrolled in my classes in the Science of Mind, and has outlined a program of reading and study which is providing that bal-

ance and understanding which he lacked when he was interested only in making money.

"About all I ever used to ask was 'how much?' " he remarked recently. "Now I find that there are a lot more interesting and pertinent questions which can be discussed. In fact, we've formed a discussion group down at the plant. A bunch of us get together every Friday afternoon. And do you know what we discuss? Now get this—not costs, not sales methods, not manufacturing problems, or stuff like that. No sir! We talk about God, the meaning of life, the nature of Truth, and how we can understand each other better. We got going so hot and heavy last week that we almost forgot to go home to dinner. And you should see what a difference it's making in all of us. Nearly everyone has started going to church, and several are taking evening classes in philosophy, psychology—and I think several of them are now studying with you, Dr. Don."

"That's right," I agreed. "You're doing a great job, George. I'm proud of you."

"But that's not half of it. I've discovered how to pray. Your classes and our private sessions have given me an entirely new approach to this business of prayer. I hadn't really prayed in years—just went through the motions at church—but now I get right down to business. I believe that prayer is talking to God in language which we both can understand. I believe everything you think and feel is a prayer—either constructively or destructively. I am saying a prayer inwardly whether I actually speak it or not. As a matter of fact, I often feel closest to God when I don't say anything—when I just sit there and enjoy the fact that I'm alive. Meditation, I guess you call it. Dr. Curtis, I guess I didn't ever believe in God before. I guess it was because I didn't understand the whole idea. Now, thanks to you and some of these ideas you got me started working on, at least I think I'm beginning to get an inkling of what it is all about."

FIND YOURSELF AND YOU FIND HAPPINESS

What exactly happened to George Elton? He started to find himself, that's all. When he changed on the inside, the outside took care of itself. He proved that happiness is not a myth. When we establish spiritual, mental, emotional, physical and material balance, we will be happy. This is the business of living. We are supposed to be happy.

Happiness indicates wholeness. "Behold, thou art made whole," (John: 5:14) Jesus commanded as he healed the people. When we become whole, balanced, happy, we will be healed of whatever is bothering us, from physical illness on up to the most subtle of psychological and spiritual problems.

This book proposes to explore the spectrum of the human make-up and experience so that you may find yourself and do something about becoming a happier person. Let us consider the following topics:

1. Happiness
2. Health
3. Prosperity and Success
4. Order and Balance
5. Right Action
6. Integration and Coordination
7. Guidance and Protection
8. Unfoldment and Growth
9. Love
10. Faith and Confidence
11. Meaning and Purpose
12. Peace and Freedom

Here are the main areas in which our difficulties are most likely to arise. There are obvious overlaps, but we have here a useful guide for helping us check our make-up and find ourselves. One chapter will be devoted to each category, and self-help techniques will be given. The over-all purpose is to assist in solving those inner problems which produce the troublesome outer difficulties. When you follow the suggestions as given, you cannot help but be a better person. Isn't that what we are all striving to become?

When George Elton embarked upon his program of finding himself, he needed to rid himself of the conditioning of five negative attitudes that were causing his difficulties and making him unhappy:

1. Haste
2. Personal Ambition
3. Greed
4. Competition
5. Self-Centeredness

We eliminated these harmful attitudes by changing them into more constructive ones. The process is called "treatment," or "consciousness-conditioning." Just as George Elton did, you may re-condition your inner states of mind. Use the following treatments.

Haste. "Haste makes waste. I learn to take my time. There is no reason to hurry. I have all the time there is. All urgency is dissolved as I cooperate with the timelessness of the creative process. All anxiety is removed as I flow with the main stream of life. I am quiet and calm. I move purposefully and efficiently through life. I accomplish all things in the proper way and at the proper time. I am at peace with myself and my world now. And so it is."

Personal Ambition. "I know I am important, but I also know that there are things that are more important. I assume my rightful place in the scheme of things. I learn to get 'my bloated nothingness out of the way.' I know that God wants me to have all good things. I know that I have what I need at the moment I need it. I dissolve all desire for recognition or reward. I seek only to do a good job and to be the best person I know how. I let the great law of life take care of the rest. I practice humility and release now. And so it is."

Greed. "I desire no more than I need. I have no interest in accumulating money or other material things. I abundantly produce and joyously use all good things. I do not try to hold on to everything. I praise and bless the Source from which all things flow. I know that money is for spending, so I spend it wisely. I know that things are to be used, so I use them well. I know that abundance is to be shared, so I give generously of my substance to whomever needs it. I share. I give. And so it is."

Competition. "No one is against me. I am not competing with anyone. There is more than enough good for all. I want everyone to be happy, prosperous and successful. No one can take my good from me. I do not desire to take anything away from anyone else. I believe in 'all for one, and one for all.' I work with life and life works with me. I work with people and people work with me. I am for everyone and everyone is for me. I cooperate, I share, I help. I give thanks for everyone's good today. And so it is."

Self-Centeredness. "I extend the area of my interest today. I forget my little self. I am interested in everything and everybody. I give unstintingly of myself. I am aware of what is going on around me. I lose myself in the wonder and beauty of life. My attention is always upon things that are bigger than I. I am centered in my true self— the Presence of God within me. This realization gives me compassion and love. In forgetting my little self, I find my real Self. I am one with my true Self now. And so it is."

As we get rid of these and other harmful inner conditionings, we release our natural creative energies for constructive purposes. To develop that efficiency in living which leads to true happiness, we must learn to understand and use our mental tools. Here are the five most important ones:

1. Thought
2. Imagination
3. Will
4. Attention
5. Concentration

Thought. Your mind is made for thinking: for receiving and formulating ideas, for selecting and arranging, for reasoning and reaching conclusions, for choosing procedures, for initiating action. Get your mind in order. Clean house. Arrange your thoughts. Learn to examine ideas and reflect upon them. Apply logic and common sense. Avoid set points of view and preconceived notions. Keep your mind open. Let the Larger Intelligence fill your mind and instruct you. Bring your mind into focus with the One Mind.

Imagination. Imagination is the creative faculty within you. Use it freely and wisely. Give color and form to your goals and objectives. Visualize; see your life the way you want it to be. See the completed objective and action. Create the entire experience inwardly. Bring the inner senses into play; they are more real than the outer ones. See, hear, touch, taste and smell with your imagination. Feel what you want to feel. Immerse yourself in the idea you want to bring into expression. Mentally and emotionally become the thing you want to be. Find your imagination; understand it and trust it. Control your imagination and use it with purpose and intelligence.

Will. Will power is certainly more important than "won't" power, but there is a far greater power than human will. The human will is for the purpose of making decisions and choices—of focusing the attention upon the desired objective. The main function of the human will is to cooperate with the creative forces within. Will power is not to be used for making things happen. Use your will for the purpose of choosing your objectives, applying your imagination, focusing your attention, and coordinating your energies. Make your personal will the instrument of the Divine Will which works through you.

Attention. "Power flows to the focus of attention." We can literally do anything we put our mind to. Observation, perception, awareness, interest, enthusiasm and identification are all part of the capacity of your mind to focus upon and absorb an idea. As we have said, use your will to focus your attention. Bring all of your mental powers to bear upon the thoughts, ideas and situations which confront you. Hold your attention steady so that a complete impression may be formed before releasing it and going on to something else. This will give the subconscious intelligence something to work on. Return to it at intervals to renew and strengthen the flow of intelligence and creative energy. You can control your attention. Do so, and it will keep you in contact with the creative power within you.

Concentration. "To concentrate" means literally, "to bring to the center." Use your will to concentrate your attention upon the object of your thought and imagination. This gives us the proper relationship of these fine mental tools. There should be no effort or beetle-browed strain involved in proper concentration. Concentration is merely holding the mind steady upon one central idea. Concentration also involves bringing all of your faculties and powers to bear upon that which is most important at the time. Concentration is centering. Concentration provides the channel of strength and power. A single bullet has more impact than a load of scattered shot. A magnifying glass can focus light at such intensity that it will burst into flame. Stand a sheet of paper on end, and it is not strong enough to support anything; roll it up and it will bear considerable weight. These illustrations are indicative of the concentrative powers of the mind. Learn to concentrate, and all of the power of the universe is at your command.

FIVE STEPS TO HAPPINESS

There is not set formula for attaining happiness, but there are many things we can do to help bring it about. Every time you inject affirmative ideas into your mind, and adopt constructive habits and patterns of action, you are solving the problems which block the attainment of happiness, health, prosperity, success, and all the other desirable goals on our list.

Here are some positive suggestions for thought and action:

1. *Always act from; never react to.* Establish a strong center of confidence and strength within yourself, and relate all things to it. This will enable you to face all manner of outside difficulties without being upset.

2. *Erase all belief in difficulty.* Nothing is against you except the false beliefs within yourself. Nothing is difficult to the person who

knows how. You have the capacity within you to handle anything that comes up. Know it.

3. *Learn to say, "So what?"* Once you get over letting outer things bother you, you can put things in proper place by saying, "So what?" Loss, gossip, difficulty, failure—none of these have any real power to affect the real you. Pull the fuses from the trouble bombs by adopting an attitude of "So what?"

4. *Always work for the greatest good of the greatest number.* There is no personal good without general good. If we are in a deal, it must work out well for both of us, or it won't be good for either of us. Say, "I honestly desire that which is for the best interests of everyone concerned." Work for good and you will receive the best.

5. *Live each moment as if it were both your first and your last.* Right now, this instant, is the only moment of eternity that you need to be concerned with. The past and the future will both take care of themselves if you take care of the present. Live each moment fully. Together, they form the span of your life.

FIVE THINGS TO BE

It is what you are that determines what happens to you—whether or not you are to be prosperous, successful, or healthy. If you would be happy, try being these things, and see the difference it makes:

1. *Be kind.* Never hurt another living thing.

2. *Be aware.* Know that God is the only reality. Spend regular time in contact with this reality.

3. *Be interested.* Wake up and appreciate the wonderful things around you.

4. *Be awake.* Be alert to your abilities and potentialities and constantly keep the channel open for the free, full flow of life through you.

5. *Be thankful.* Praise, bless, appreciate, compliment, and commend. "Thank you, Father, for the abundance which is mine."

FIVE BASIC REQUIREMENTS FOR THE FULL LIFE

There are five basic requirements for the complete and happy life. Develop them and you will conquer all problems, inside and out, as you move steadily forward toward becoming the person you really are.

1. *Faith in a Higher Power.* Whether you call it God, life, nature, science, philosophy or principle—there is a Supreme Power. There is one intelligence behind all things. Everything bears eloquent evidence of it. It is not a person, but is extremely personal to each one of us. Faith in this Great Power is the starting point for anything and everything we want to achieve. Without faith, there is no hope. With faith, there is no obstacle. Faith is the basic affirmative attitude. Start with faith in God—the All-Good.

2. *Confidence in Yourself.* If you don't believe in yourself, no one else is going to. Confidence releases the flow of life-giving spiritual energy through you. Confidence in yourself is evidence that you have made God your partner. Believe in yourself! Know that you can do whatever you need to do! Know that you have within you the capacity to solve any problem, to achieve any goal. There is no limit to what you are and can become. Believe you can and you can. Know that you are and you will be. Recognize, praise and bless the magnificent power within you.

3. *Dedication to Purpose.* There is nothing which can block or resist the person who knows who he is and where he is going. The will to succeed is an expression of the will to live—the most powerful force there is. People are often kept alive solely by their determination to finish a project or accomplish a purpose. When we dedicate ourselves to something greater than we are, we become as great as it is. As we lose ourselves in aims, ideals, goals and purposes we find our own souls, resident in the kingdom of God which is within us.

4. *Lively Interest in Everything and Everybody.* "No man is an island." By the mere fact of being alive, we are automatically a part of everything that is. We are constantly giving and receiving life to and from the people and the things around us. As Emerson said, "Our atmospheres mingle." Interest is the key to discovery, and discovery is growth. We grow by participating in the experiences of others. We learn from the glories of nature, and from the wonders which are people. Interest releases the dynamic flow of creative energy. Interest is recognition of life. Life fulfills life. Deep answers deep. Get interested in living today!

5. *Mastery of One Field of Endeavor.* Man is universal by nature—individual by expression. We are specialists rooted in a great common garden. Each of us is here for a purpose. We must serve and fulfill that purpose. In Shakespeare's *Hamlet*, Polonius says:

> *To thine own self be true,*
> *And it must follow as the night the day,*
> *Thou canst not then be false to any man.*

Be true to yourself by being true to your talent. Find what you are here to do, and do it well. Learn your trade. Steep yourself in your profession. Sharpen your tools. Apply yourself diligently. Learn what you need to learn. Know what you are doing at all times. Apply yourself skillfully. Master your job. Master yourself, and you will master the world.

Consciousness Conditioner For Happiness

I fulfill the requirements for happiness. I earn it by applying myself diligently and well. I know that I can be as happy as I want to be. I want to be completely happy. I believe that I am supposed to be. I know that the kingdom of happiness is within me. I let nothing interfere with its complete expression in my world.

All unhappy thoughts and feelings are dissolved from my mind. I remove the road-blocks to happiness. I cut through the underbrush of confused thinking. I am clear in mind—warm in heart. I cleanse my consciousness of all unworthy content. I have no place for the shoddy, cheap or second-rate. I constantly contemplate the facts of life from the highest point of view. I pray without ceasing. I affirm the magnificence of life. I glory in the wonder of being. I am happy because I am whole. I am whole because I seek to give expression to the God-nature within me.

Quietly now, I release all concern for outer things. I dwell in the kingdom of heaven. I live and move and have my being in the great love and intelligence which has created all things. I exult with the joy of living. My heart sings out the glad tidings of joy and happiness. I laugh and shout with the sheer exuberance of being alive. Light indwells me and emanates from me. God is the source of my happiness. I share this happiness with others by making my life an example which all may follow. I spread joy and happiness throughout my world today. *And so it is.*

CHAPTER TWO

HOW TO STOP HURTING

"That gives me a pain."
"I can't stand it."
"Oh, my aching back."
"I can't go on."
"I don't see it."
"I won't hear of it."
"I'm slowing down."
"I won't put up with this any longer."
"Life has lost its meaning for me."
"I'm dead!"
"I'm sick to death of it."
"I could just die."
"I'm fed up."
"I can't stomach this."
"That gripes me."
"This always upsets me."
"I can't swallow that."
"I'm all choked up."
"I'm snowed under."
"He makes me sick."
"I'm just miserable."
"I'm worried sick."
"Everything's a mess."
"That bugs me."
"I'm bothered."
"I don't know which way to turn."
"I'm confused."
"I can't understand it."
"I don't know what to do with myself."

"This drives me crazy."

"I can't take it."

"I can't stand the pressure."

"I just want to run away from everything."

"That burns me up."

"I get hot under the collar every time that happens."

"He's a real itch."

"I'm scared to death."

"I'm running around in circles."

"This wears me out."

"I'm worn out!"

"I'm tired!"

"I'm pooped!"

Do any of these cries of woe have a familiar ring? Quite likely, because we are either saying them or hearing them all the time—often unconsciously. There is no limit to our capacity for making ourselves sick. Every time we say, think or feel anything similar to the above statements, we are ordering pain, illness or trouble of some sort. A negative thought, feeling or word is an order to the subconscious mind to produce a problem.

These problems first appear as symptoms in the physical body. Obviously, the first step toward health is to rid ourselves of negative thoughts and feelings. The second step is to learn to think and feel in a healthy, positive manner. It is just as simple as that. The purpose of this book is to teach us how to solve all of our problems by this process. The purpose of this chapter is to apply the principle to physical health.

HEALTH IS YOUR NATURAL STATE

Actually, there is no such thing as physical health apart from mental and emotional health. Health means "wholeness." The "whole man" is made up of spirit, mind and body. Any attempt to heal the body must deal first with the inner consciousness of the individual. The body will be healthy when the mind and emotions are attuned to the natural spiritual wholeness—to the life force within each one of us. Health is our natural state. Any belief to the contrary is just another one of the many factors which make us ill. *You are health.* Firmly implant that in your mind. Start with this major conviction and relate everything else to it. Accept no fear, opinion or evidence to the contrary. Constantly affirm: "I am healthy, I am strong, I am whole, *I am health.*" Re-educate your mind so that it accepts and, therefore, produces health.

Of course, in the attainment of mental, emotional and physical wholeness health is more than just a matter of affirmation. It is also a matter of complete understanding and of constant practice of the mental and physical principles which produce and maintain health. Spiritual awareness and mental and emotional balance must be accompanied by obeying the laws of diet, rest and exercise on the physical level. There isn't much point in doing spiritual and mental treatment for a stomach-ache if one continues to stuff himself with hot dogs, popcorn and soft drinks. It won't help to pray for energy and strength if you stay up all night. You won't produce a vital, well-formed, and well-coordinated body unless you exercise and use it properly. You can't just think away flab. You start with thought and feeling, but then you must follow through and do something about it. There are many excellent books about diet, rest and exercise. Read them. There is also common sense. Exercise it as well. What we are dealing with here is the spiritual principle back of health.

You are interested in your health. Start where you are. It doesn't matter what your current condition is or your past illnesses may have been. You can be healthy if you want to be, and if you are willing to do what is necessary to produce and maintain health. Don't be like the patient who once said, "I don't want to be good, I just want to stop hurting." You will be healthy when you become good. It's up to you. No one can do it for you. But once you start the ball rolling you will have unlimited help from the abundant natural resources within your mind and body. Remember, "The thing that makes you sick is the same thing that makes you well." It is all a matter of how you use it. Let's decide to use it for health. Harry Gaze, an early pioneer in the New Thought field, used to say, "Of course you have to die, but you don't have to die sick!" Let's go on from there.

Take Control—Cause Health Now

What is the state of your health right now? Is it as good as you would like it to be? Are you in control of your body or is it controlling you? Are you in command of yourself or are you at the mercy of things that happen to you? Are the things you are doing—spiritually, mentally, emotionally, physically, socially, occupationally—a benefit or a detriment to your health? Be honest with yourself. Everyone has something to correct. Don't hide your faults and mistakes. Get them out into the open and correct them. They'll only cause trouble if you cover them over. Be willing to change. Remember, if you are sick, the cause is somewhere within you. Let's start causing health now.

Review the negative statements given at the beginning of this chapter and rephrase every statement to a constructive one. For instance, instead of, "That gives me a pain," say, "That makes me feel good." Or instead of, "Oh, my aching back," say, "My fine, strong back." Form new habits of looking at things. When your mind responds constructively, the release of inner energy and power will heal you. If any of the statements give you particular trouble, do special drill upon them until the mental and emotional attitude changes from negative to positive. In addition, make up your own list of personal negative expressions and go to work systematically to eliminate them and establish constructive ones.

Here is a list of the most common inner attitudes which cause ill health. Let's change them as follows:

Negative Attitude or False Belief	Change To	Constructive Attitude and True Belief
1. Fear	⟶	Assurance
2. Hostility	⟶	Love
3. Anxiety	⟶	Quiet
4. Worry	⟶	Serenity
5. Jealousy	⟶	Empathy
6. Escapism	⟶	Responsibility
7. Confusion	⟶	Order
8. Rejection	⟶	Acceptance
9. Resistance	⟶	Cooperation
10. Pressure	⟶	Release
11. Tension	⟶	Relaxation
12. Self-Condemnation	⟶	Self-Appreciation
13. Disappointment	⟶	Understanding
14. Irritation	⟶	Harmony
15. Agitation	⟶	Tranquility
16. Resentment	⟶	Compassion

Negative Attitude or False Belief	Change To	Constructive Attitude and True Belief
17. Antagonism	⟶	Peace
18. Stupidity	⟶	Knowledge
19. Envy	⟶	Gratitude
20. Thoughtlessness	⟶	Thoughtfulness
21. Limitation	⟶	Expansiveness
22. Selfishness	⟶	Selflessness
23. Greed	⟶	Generosity
24. Indecision	⟶	Decision
25. Lack of Faith	⟶	Faith
26. Guilt	⟶	Forgiveness
27. Nervousness	⟶	Calm
28. Insecurity	⟶	Security
29. Frustration	⟶	Expression
30. Grief	⟶	Joy

We could go on and on, but this will cover most of them. Work on each point as shown in the following sample treatment. We'll dissolve "Resistance" and affirm "Cooperation":

"I cooperate with life and life cooperates with me. All resistance is dissolved as I flow with the mainstream of life. There is no difficulty; there is only ease, order and right action. There is no immovable object; there is only freedom and fluidity. The only irresistible force is the flow of spirit through me. All obstacles and blockages are removed as I work with life instead of against it. Nothing is hard to do for That which knows how to do it. There is That within me which knows how to do all things. 'My yoke is easy, and my burden is light.' (Matt. 11:30) I am filled with dynamic and vital energy now. And so it is."

Negative attitudes definitely tend to produce unhealthy conditions in the body. Back of every illness or disease is a disordered state of mind. Since the body is a projection of consciousness and is acted upon by the mind (thought, feeling, beliefs, attitudes), it is helpful to know which mental states cause what conditions. Although these correspondences do not always hold true, a trained practitioner can usually find the cause back of a negative condition by analyzing the attitudes of the patient. You can do this yourself. Your body is a score-board. Your ailments are points which you must correct. The nature of the disease will indicate the attitude that needs correction.

Then, correct it! Or—if you know you have certain negative or destructive mental and emotional tendencies—dissolve them, and you will eliminate present difficulties and prevent possible future physical trouble as well. *All destructive mental and emotional states are destructive to the body. All constructive mental and emotional states tend to heal and maintain the body in health.*

Whenever any single mental or emotional fault is corrected, it not only tends to heal the specific physical condition immediately, but it reflects favorably in the entire body.

JOHN STANTON: A CASE HISTORY

John Stanton had been troubled with constipation and dyspepsia for years. He had periodic blinding headaches, and his energy level was very low. He was constantly in financial difficulty and was having trouble with his business. Twice-divorced, he was estranged from his children and had difficulty getting along with everyone. He had the disposition of a wounded bear.

It wasn't difficult to find the cause of Mr. Stanton's ailments and difficulties. He was almost completely negative. Name a negative attitude and he had it. He was filled with fear; afraid of himself, of failure, of others, of life—of practically everything. He was resentful, vindictive, greedy in money matters, and completely ruthless in his business dealings.

John Stanton sounds terrible, doesn't he? He seemed to be, even to himself, but he really wasn't. He was just caught up in a lot of two-way problems he couldn't understand. His bad disposition was causing his headaches, and his headaches were giving him a bad disposition. His greed and fear were causing his constipation, and the resulting toxic condition caused his personality problems. He revolved in several vicious circles at once.

When Mr. Stanton first came to see me for spiritual mind treatment he was blaming everybody but himself for his troubles. This, of course, is a common tendency with all of us—but an intelligent approach to solving our problems will soon set us straight.

"Do you like yourself?" I asked him.

"No," he replied.

"Why not?"

He told me, and in so doing, did a beautiful job of enumerating the negative attitudes already described.

"What are we going to do about it?" I asked him.

"We're going to get rid of them. Dr. Curtis, will you help me?"

Naturally I agreed, since this is my business. Together, we took John Stanton apart, and with God's assistance in scientific spiritual mind prayer treatment we put him back together again. John Stanton was sick of being sick—the first step in getting well. And he was diligent in correcting those inner attitudes which had made him sick. When they were corrected his body began to function normally, his disposition improved, he was reconciled with his family, and he became successful and free from money worries for the first time in his life. Health—wholeness—was established not only in John Stanton's body, but in all of these departments. You see, you can't heal even your little toe without improving everything else in your life. This is the principle back of our scientific spiritual approach to all human problems. Man is naturally happy, healthy, successful and free. It is only when he gets in his own way that difficulties arise. When we get out of our own way, we re-establish contact with the power that heals.

Our treatment for John Stanton went something like this:

"This is a personal treatment for John Stanton of Los Angeles, California. John Stanton is whole in spirit, mind and body. He is one with the One source from which he came. He is one with the Power that created him. This Presence and Power is whole, complete, un-conditioned in every way. This Divine Potential is present and functioning within John Stanton right now. Anything unlike the nature of God is removed from his consciousness. He is 'perfect even as his Father in heaven is perfect.'

"All fear is dissolved and complete and perfect faith is established in John Stanton's mind and heart. He has assurance that all is well. He has faith in God, trust in life, belief in other people, and confidence in himself. John Stanton rests in blessed assurance now. He is calm and confident at all times. He is pleasant, kind and forgiving to other people. He understands other people, including all members of his own family; he forgives them and himself; he loves them and all people.

"John Stanton is fair in his dealings with other people. He is established in fair and constructive business enterprise. He works to be of service at all times in every possible way. God is the Source of his supply, and he is established in abundance and plenty. All good things are flowing into his experience now.

"These statements are true of John Stanton right now. They are now firmly impressed upon the Deeper Mind, from which they come forth in full and perfect expression. It is already done now. And so it is."

Notice that the treatment is specific in every area where the patient had a problem. By systematically dissolving the false, negative attitudes and beliefs, we cleared the way for the natural action of wholeness to establish itself. By affirming definite and specific constructive attitudes, we assisted the healing process.

PSYCHOLOGICAL CAUSES OF PHYSICAL ILLS

The following table will indicate the probable psychological causes underlying some of the most common physical ailments. Remember, true healing can take place only when the cause back of the condition is removed. These correspondences, while not exact, will help you be more specific in your treatment.

Ailment	Probable Psychological Cause	Treatment
1. Anemia	Lack of interest in life	Enthusiasm, Interest, Joy
2. Appetite (loss of)	Rejection, Revulsion	Acceptance, Assimilation
3. Arteries (hardening)	Resistance, Tension	Relaxation, Cooperation
4. Arthritis	Bitterness, Resentment	Forgiveness, Compassion
5. Asthma	Oversensitivity, Fear of hurt	Freedom, Expressiveness
6. Backache	Burden-bearing, Money problems	Ease, Release
7. Bladder Trouble	Anxiety, Inferiority	Calm, Confidence
8. Blood Pressure (high)	Fear, Emotional Upset	Peace, Order
9. Blood pressure (low)	Depression, Sorrow	Joy, Uplift
10. Cancer	Deep emotional hurt, Intense Disappointment	Wholeness, Control, Love
11. Colds	Confusion, Emotional Upsets	Order, Clearance, Perfect Circulation
12. Colitis	Oppression, Heaviness, Defeatism	Freedom, Peace
13. Constipation	Greed, Limitation, Hanging on to the past	Generosity, Release, Freedom

Ailment	Probable Psychological Cause	Treatment
14. Coughs	Nervousness, Annoyance, Criticism	Serenity, Understanding
15. Deafness	Rejection, Isolation, Stubbornness	Faith, Balance, Participation
16. Diabetes	Lack of love, Emotional turbulence	Love, Individuality, Belonging
17. Drinking Problems	Inferiority, Self-Rejection, Need for Love and Assurance	Confidence, Love, Discipline
18. Epilepsy	Violence, Rejection, Rebellion	Peace, Security, Love
19. Exhaustion	Resistance, Effort, Dislike for Work	Cooperation, Relaxation, Re-filling with spiritual energy
20. Eye Problems	Lack of Perception, Bondage to details, Inability to see spiritually	Perception, Discrimination, Vision
21. Foot Problems	Lack of stability, Overload, Uncertainty, Lack of Understanding	Stability, Adjustment, Surety, Understanding
22. Fevers	Fear, Hate, Irritability, Instability	Faith, Love, Tranquility
23 Glandular Disturbance	Imbalance, Lack of Order, Poor Distribution	Balance, Harmony, Order, Proper Function
24. Growths	False sense of values, Wrong ideas, Shock, Hurt	Truth, Right Place, Integration
25. Hemorrhoids	Burden, Pressure, Tension, Fear	Ease, Release, Faith
26. Hair (baldness)	Inferiority, Rejection, Anxiety, Weakness	Strength, Confidence, New Ideas
27. Halitosis	Fear, Impure Thoughts, Disturbed emotions, Impure motives	Calmness, Purity, Wholesomeness
28. Headache	Confusion, Emotional Upsets, Sexual Problems	Peace, Quiet, Adjustment
29. Heart Trouble	Strain, Pressure, Tension, Hurt, Lack of Emotional Fulfillment	Confidence, Love, Strength, Security, Encouragement

30. Hernia	Strain, Burden-bearing, Heaviness, Self-punishment	Cooperation, Teamwork, Lightness, Self-Acceptance
31. Indigestion	Fear, Apprehension, Dread, Anxiety	Peace, Faith, Understanding, Assimilation
32. Influenza	Unrest, Response to mass negativity, Reaction to world problems	Strength, Spiritual understanding, Protection
33. Insanity	Hysteria, Escapism, Disturbed Relationships, Separation	Faith in One Mind, Perfection, Wholeness, Balance
34. Kidney Trouble	Frustration, Sensitivity, Jealousy, Confusion, Impurity	Fulfillment, Peace, Purity, Adjustment
35. Liver Trouble	Melancholy, Despondency, Repression, Depression, Emotional Disturbance	Joy, Aspiration, Circulation, Participation
36. Nervousness	Struggle, Rushing, Wrong thinking, Confusion	Peace, Proper timing, Order, Love
37. Obesity (over-weight)	Self-rejection, Lack of Control, Greed, Frustration	Self-acceptance, Control, Fulfillment
38. Pain	Congestion, Blockage, Bondage	Freedom, Circulation, Spiritual Contact
39. Paralysis	Fear, Escape, Resistance, Shock	Faith, Incentive, Participation, Right Action
40. Pneumonia	Tired of Life, Lack of spiritual understanding, Emotional wounds, Desperation	Spiritual awakening, Joy of living, Interest, Acceptance
41. Prostate Trouble	Defeatism, Carelessness, Life rejection, Giving up	Energy, Life, Freedom, Incentive
42. Rheumatism	Irritation, Chronic unpleasantness, Bitterness, Revenge	Pleasantness, Pleasing personality, Goodness, Forgiveness
43. Sinus	Frustration, Agitation, Hurt, Over-sensitivity	Peace, Protection, Adjustment, Quietude

Ailment	Probable Psychological Cause	Treatment
44. Skin Diseases	Over-sensitivity, Lack of self-identification, Need for Love, Touchiness, Rebelliousness	Protection, Proper Self-image, Love
45. Strokes	Resistance, Violence, Pressure, Desire to die	Ease, Divine energy, Will-to-live
46. Teeth	Inattention to details, Inability to analyze and assimilate ideas	Carefulness, Application, Perceptiveness, Attention
47. Throat Trouble	Lack of expression, Emotional hurt, Loss, Sadness, Tension	Expression, Joy, Exultation, Gaiety
48. Tuberculosis	Selfishness, Self-satisfaction, Possessiveness, Cruelty	Humility, Oneness, Freedom, Kindness
49. Ulcers	Anxiety, Tension, Fear, Pressure, Irritation	Peace, Confidence, Relaxation, Humor
50. Varicose Veins	Negativity, Resistance, Discouragement, Disappointment	Release, Freedom, Joy, Purpose

This table is presented as a guide to help you be more specific in treating your own problem. It will enable you to get to the root of the trouble. It is not exact, because tendencies and causes vary with the individual, but it will show you what type of thought and feeling tends to produce certain physical ailments. In later chapters we will give correspondences for other human problems. Again, we must state the principle: *The primary cause back of all problems is within yourself.* Of course, there are many secondary causes which often make it difficult to find the real cause, but it is always there.

For instance, you might get your feet wet and catch cold. You would say, "I caught cold because I got my feet wet." That, however, is the secondary cause. Back of that is the false belief that wet feet cause colds. They don't. Colds are caused by congested and confused states of mind resulting from emotional upsets. These, together with neglect of the care of the body, lower resistance, cause toxins to accumulate, change the blood chemistry, and generally make the physical organism a favorable climate for the growth of cold germs. All of the factors—wet feet, negative suggestion that wet feet cause colds, mental confusion, emotional disturbance, neglect of the body, low resistance, and an acid and toxic condition—caused the cold. The mental and emotional state was the primary cause. The others are secondary.

Our work is with primary causes. They may be hard to find, but our table will help. I want to repeat, however, that *there is no law of disease*. A person may have a disease which does not match the cause indicated, or he may find that he has a certain negative mental or emotional state, but there is no apparent disease. This does not change the principle that every effect must have a cause and every cause must produce an effect. Disease is always an effect. A disturbed mental or emotional state is always the cause back of the disease even though you may not be consciously aware of it. Causes operate at the subconscious level. Our job is to become consciously aware of our hidden, destructive disease and problem-producing mental and emotional states, so that we may get rid of them and put constructive, health-giving causes into creative operation. In your affirmative treatment, deny the cause back of the condition by stating, "*Anything unlike the nature of God is removed from my consciousness. I am free from all negative and destructive tendencies. I am whole in spirit, mind and body. Only constructive causation is working through me now.*"

One thing you can be sure of: *Something* causes negative conditions, and that something is always within us. Even though we may sometimes miss the mark with our analysis as to specific cause, we can always be effective with our mental and spiritual treatment. No good is ever lost, and when you are pouring affirmative spiritual thoughts, feelings and statements into your consciousness you are doing good and assisting the healing process. Make a habit of your affirmative spiritual mind treatment work. It is a matter of "eliminating the negative and accentuating the positive." Positive, constructive states of mind produce health.

The foregoing table was developed over many years of professional practice, during which time I have counselled and treated untold numbers of people with all manner of ailments, diseases and problems. The correspondences are based upon this experience. You will find it helpful in treating yourself into the constructive states of mind which will heal you. Be your own doctor, psychiatrist or practitioner. Wake up and find out about yourself. Start manufacturing health and happiness instead of illness and problems. This book shows you the way, but you must do it. Follow the suggestions given and you will be amazed.

DEVELOP AND AFFIRM POSITIVE ATTITUDES

The basic affirmative attitudes are love, faith, peace and understanding. Develop these and you will be practicing the best preventive medicine there is. Get a sense of the continuity of life. Establish spiritual dominion within your mind and heart. Align yourself with the mighty forces of the Universal Mind. Control your own life. Learn to live!

If you would enjoy health, then you should:

1. Think and speak constructively at all times.
2. Develop inner feelings of love, faith, peace and understanding.
3. Learn to pray and live as a "whole person": in spirit, mind, and body.
4. Obey the laws of diet, exercise and rest.

Your health is a direct reflection of your way of life. Join with the thousands of others who are using common sense in daily living. Think of yourself as a whole being. Everything you say, think, feel and do contributes to your total well-being. Keep yourself in tune with life through:

Serenity

Regularity

Temperance

Exercise

Rest

Go to work consciously to develop the following health-giving program:

1. Quiet your mind.
2. Balance your emotions.
3. Rejuvenate your body.
4. Harmonize your world.
5. Develop your soul.

TEN COMMANDMENTS FOR BETTER HEALTH

Apply these principles to specific actions, as follows:

1. *Sleep every chance you get.* Learn from your pets. When a dog or a cat doesn't have anything to do, he goes to sleep. He is ready for

anything because he is always fresh and rested. Take "cat-naps" several times during the day. The natural healing forces of life take over when you go to sleep and stop resisting them. Find out how much sleep you need and be sure you get it. Sleep "knits up the raveled sleeve of care."

2. *Hang onto your temper.* Anger destroys. Control your feelings. Emotional outbursts are destructive. Stop upsetting yourself. Develop yourself into the kind of person you can live with. Forgive yourself. Get rid of resentment. Correct mistakes. Be tolerant of the short-comings of others. Dissolve resentment. Cleanse yourself of irritation. Learn to say and mean, "It doesn't matter just because it doesn't matter."

3. *Never worry.* Your worst troubles never happen, so stop worrying about them. You will never be confronted with a situation you are not capable of handling. Worry is bondage to the past or the future. Forget the past. Plan for the future, but don't worry about it. Live in the present and do the best you can with whatever comes up. Use your head for sensible creative planning. Nothing can happen that you and God together can't handle. So why worry?

4. *Learn to laugh.* Laughter is the song of the soul. "A merry heart doeth good like a medicine but a broken spirit drieth the bones" (Pr. 17:22). Get happy inside and let your laughter come bubbling out. Laughter starts the flow of the healing juices in your body. Why live unless you can have a good time doing it? Get a bang out of life, and infect others with your laughter. Laughter is the best outlet for pent-up feelings. Your laughter can heal you. Laugh out loud today.

5. *Organize your time and always give your best.* Stop running around in circles. Decide what you are going to do, set aside time for it, then go ahead and do it. Wasted time is wasted life. Use your time constructively. Even learn to do nothing purposely. What you do with every moment affects your health. Get with it. If you are going to do a thing, do it well. You owe it to yourself and everyone else to always give your best. It will keep getting better.

6. *Eliminate harmful habits.* This means all of them—mental, emotional and physical. They include the sins of omission as well as those of commission. Everyone knows that little good can come from smoking or drinking in any degree, and that they can do serious damage when indulged in to excess. Moderation is the key in all things, of course, but if we know something is harmful, why do it at all? Get rid of the corrosion of criticism, irritability and a bad disposition.

7. *Eat sensibly.* Again, use moderation. Overeating is a form of suicide. Digging your grave with your teeth may be slow, but it is certain. Eat to live; don't live to eat. You are not meant to be a human garbage pail. Learn about foods. Most of the junk we put in our stomachs is not fit to eat. Help your body maintain itself by finding out what it needs, then provide it in sensible quantity and with good quality. The next time you take a bite of something, remember that in a certain sense, "you are what you eat."

8. *Exercise regularly.* Your body is meant to be used, so use it. You'll feel better when you do. Your health depends upon it. Your life depends upon proper circulation. Exercise provides it. Your legs are for walking. So stop kicking and use them for the purpose for which they were intended. Climb a mountain. Go swimming. Find a game you like and play it. Get rid of your inner aggressions with some intensive physical activity. Lead a vigorous life. It's good for you.

9. *Love people.* People are wonderful. Get to know them; develop an affection for them. No one can live without love. We all have more love inside of us than we could ever use, but let's try. The more love we give, the more returns to us. Understanding, interest, compassion and empathy all produce health. Talk to people; encourage them. Give yourself to them. Help them, and there will always be someone there to help you. Love is life in action. Love people.

10. *Learn to pray.* Prayer is affirmation. Prayer connects you with the source of life. Prayer is participation with the creative process. Prayer is the process of making ourselves bigger and better than we think we are. Prayer is renewal. Prayer stimulates the flow of life through us. Prayer brings our entire being into focus with the source of all life. Prayer transforms you by renewing your mind. Prayer renews your body. Prayer produces health.

SPECIFIC TREATMENT FOR HEALTH AND HEALING

Whether your purpose is to maintain your body in perfect health, or to bring healing power to a specific condition, affirmative spiritual mind treatment is the starting point. Take time each day to treat yourself to health. We will have much to say about treatment and how to do it in the later chapters, but let's start right now practicing a technique of treatment for health.

There are five basic steps.

1. Relax the body.
2. Quiet the mind.
3. Cleanse your consciousness of all resentment, fear and anxiety.
4. Visualize wholeness in every part of your body.
5. Thank God that healing is taking place and that health is established.

TREATMENT FOR HEALTH

Relax your mind and body and speak these statements aloud with clarity and conviction. Later on you will want to formulate your own. Begin with these affirmations.

(1) "Quietly now, I relax and let God take over. As I become still in my mind and body, I become one with the Great Source of all Life. I attune myself to wholeness. I cooperate with God, the First Cause of all things. God's health is my health now. I feel the flow of life through every part of my being. I am relaxed and ready for great experience.

(2) "My mind is quiet and receptive as I focus my attention upon that which is greater than I. I am at peace. I give thanks for the blessings of life. Good is flowing into me. The healing action of spirit is cleansing me of all negative thoughts, feelings and attitudes.

(3) I am free from resentment or hostility of all kinds. I am filled with love. Perfect love casts out all fear. I am filled with faith. I am calm and quiet. All anxiety is dissolved as I experience 'the peace of God, which passeth all understanding.' (Phil. 4:7) I have deep inner peace and wholeness.

(4) "As I am whole inside, every cell of my body expresses this wholeness. I am a complete person. I enjoy perfect health. I am organically and functionally whole. I am a total being. God's health is my health now.

(5) "The healing action of life is taking place through every part of me right now. All negative causation is dissolved as I express good in all ways and at all times. The pattern of health—wholeness—is established in my mind and heart. Complete and perfect health is therefore expressed in my body. I give thanks that this is so. And so it is."

TREATMENT FOR A PARTICULAR AILMENT

Refer to the chart on causes (page 25). Determine the underlying cause of the particular condition that you wish to be rid of, and then give yourself a definite treatment for healing by affirming the constructive mental states as indicated. Be definite and specific in your denials and affirmations. Dissolve the negative attitude causing the condition and firmly plant the healing affirmative one. Here is a healing treatment for a headache. Use it as a model for treating any other condition. Of course, your affirmations and denials will be based upon those applicable to that condition.

"I am filled with the consciousness of peace and goodness. The free, full flow of abundant life circulates through me now. I am free from all confusion. I am quiet, calm and peaceful. My feelings, urges and desires are all under control. I am in command of my consciousness. I am well adjusted. I am balanced, I am free, I am whole. I am myself at my highest and best. I experience only good now and always. And so it is."

Note that the condition is never mentioned—only the cause of it. When the negative cause is systematically dissolved, and the new affirmative attitude established, the healing takes place automatically.

In this chapter we have given you specific techniques for integrating the spiritual, mental, emotional, physical and material aspects of your make-up so that you may stop hurting and start living.

In Proverbs 4:23 we are told to "Keep thy heart (your subconscious mind) with all diligence; for out of it are the issues of life." Here is the way to do it:

1. Keep your head cool. (mental)
2. Keep your heart warm. (emotional)
3. Keep your words kind. (spiritual)
4. Keep your body pure. (physical)
5. Keep your actions controlled. (material)

Consciousness Conditioner For Health

I am health. I am a healthy person on every level. I am whole and complete in every way. I am a balanced, integrated individual. I am constantly in tune with the Source which created and maintains me in perfect health. I am nourished by the rich substance of Spirit. I am vital, alert and energetic. I am whole.

The words of my mouth and the meditations of my heart are above reproach. My thoughts are clear and pure. My ideas are noble and constructive. My head represents the glory of God's Intelligence present within me. I am conscious of my divinity. I am aware of my spiritual identity. I am attuned to the glorious flow of divine energy and inspiration as it surges through me now. I am filled with light.

I feel wonderful. I respond to the wonder and glory of life. I am one with all good things. There is nowhere that I leave off and God begins; I am an expression of the Divine Fact. Whatever God is, I am. Whatever is true of God is true of me. I am perfect even as my Father in heaven is perfect.

My voice sings out the praises of the Most High. I praise the wholeness and unity of all life. I marvel at the wonders which God has wrought. My words are kind and loving. My word has the power to create. My word goes forth out of my mouth and accomplishes all good things. My word returns to me as health on every level. My health comes from within. I am a perfect expression of complete health now.

I give thanks for my glorious health. I revel in the magnificence of complete harmony and balance. I thrill to the surge of dynamic life through my veins. I exultantly proclaim the kingdom of health. I give thanks for my perfect health now. *And so it is.*

CHAPTER THREE

THE RICHEST MAN IN THE WORLD

"I don't know what we're going to do, Dr. Curtis. We have exactly a dollar and thirty-three cents between us. I don't even know what we are going to eat tonight. There isn't a thing in the refrigerator and the cupboard is bare."

The attractive middle-aged woman broke down in sobs as her husband put his arm disconsolately around her. They were the picture of dejection and despair. As far as they could see, they had reached the end of the line. They were unemployed, lonely, hungry and broke. One could hardly blame them for feeling defeated.

These two had come to my office in search of help. They had exhausted every other possibility, and had come to me because they had heard my radio broadcast that day in which I discussed the laws of prosperity and success.

"There isn't anything wrong with us a few dollars won't cure," the man blurted out. "All we need is something to tide us over until I can find a job."

"But George, it's been nearly four months! Dr. Curtis, I don't think he'll ever get a job—not the way he's going. Please—isn't there something that can help us?" The wife certainly expressed their desperation.

"Yes, there is something and someone that can help you," I replied. "Let's talk about it. The someone who can help you is yourself, and the something is the creative power of life within you. You need money; you need a job. But these are only surface needs. These will be met. Let's know that. But there is something you must know first: *God is the Source of your supply.*"

I wasted no time in explaining the spiritual principle involved in the couple's problem. There was no doubt they were in great need. Their supply lines had broken down. They were disconnected from the source. Money was essential to meet their human needs, but lack of money was not their problem. Being broke was merely the symptom of a larger problem within their minds and hearts.

A Strange Kind of Poverty

After a period of quiet prayer treatment, I explained how negative attitudes and false beliefs are responsible for all of our difficulties, including financial ones.

As is always the case, this proved to be true with this couple. The roots of their problem were of long duration, and included broken marriages on both sides, a drinking problem, a failure pattern, frequent job changes, a bankruptcy, and consistent inability to get along with other people. The man had held several good sales positions, but invariably became dissatisfied and moved on to something else. Four months previously he had quit his job in another state and had brought his wife to California, the land of golden opportunity. He immediately secured a fine position, but was let go shortly after a run-in with his boss, and hadn't been able to find anything else over a period of months. With their money gone, having borrowed from every available source, evicted from their apartment, they had taken a job as superintendents of an apartment house in return for an apartment. All this happened to a man who had at various times made over $25,000 a year. Something was obviously wrong.

Treasures Greater Than Gold

The couple readily admitted it. They were willing to do anything to correct the situation. "Man's extremity is God's opportunity," I pressed on. I could have given them money; the need was certainly there. But I decided not to. If I was really going to help this couple, I was going to have to give them something more valuable than money. I explained this to them. We decided to work solely with principle. Our treatment was as follows:

"This is a specific treatment for Jean and George Wilson of Los Angeles, California. They are secure in their knowledge that God is the source of their supply. Perfect order and right action are taking place in their lives right now. The infinite law of abundance is flowing through every part of their consciousness and experience. Every need is instantly and fully met. Jean and George Wilson are in their right place, going through those experiences which are necessary for their growth and fulfillment. There is no lack; there is only the fullness of supply flowing through them right now. They have sufficient money to meet all needs. The channels are open and the flow is constant. All discouragement and unhappiness are removed as this couple gives thanks for the riches of the universe. Their cup is filled to overflowing and they joyously give thanks that this is so.

"This so-called emergency is met from within. There is a rebirth of understanding. Jean and George Wilson are transformed by the renewing of their minds. There is nothing they cannot be. There is nothing they cannot do. George Wilson is pleasantly and profitably employed in the one right job, at a salary sufficient to meet all of his obligations and requirements. This job is looking for *him*. This job wants George as much as he wants it. George accepts himself, he accepts his right place, he accepts this job. The law of attraction brings them together in complete and permanent union.

"Together we completely accept these affirmative ideas. We place this treatment in the Law of Mind where it is an already completed fact in the experience of Jean and George Wilson. We give thanks that this is so. And so it is."

When we finished our period of prayer treatment I put my arms around the sobbing couple. "God bless you," I said. "Everything is going to be all right." I sent them on their way. Even though they still had only the same $1.33 between them, they were facing the future with heads up, eyes shining, and a spring in their steps. They were all *right*.

Later that evening they called to give me two pieces of good news. First, when they returned home there was a special delivery letter with a check for $50 from a relative who sent it because "she thought it might be needed." There was also a phone call for a job interview the next morning with a company to which George had made application some months before but had never heard from. We gave thanks together on the telephone, and I included a treatment which stated:

"We give thanks for good received. We give thanks for this money which is now put to good use. All feeling of emergency is dissolved as all situations are met with courage and understanding.

"We give thanks for this job interview. If this is the right job for George Wilson, it is automatically his. We accept this job, its *equivalent* or *better*. The right person is in this job. George Wilson is in his right job. Everything is accomplished with perfect order and right action. And so it is."

Did the first prayer treatment produce the check for $50 and the job interview? What do you think? In this case, as in many others of a similar nature, despair turned to hope, and when this transformation of the inner attitude was made, the outer problem was solved. In this case, as always, it may seem like coincidence, but the fact remains that the emergency was met. It is an unfailing law that when there is a change in thoughts and feelings, environment and experiences change. Things do not happen to us; they happen through us. Scientific prayer treatment, such as the one we gave for Jean and George Wilson, establishes new causes. New causes produce new effects. In this case despair changed to hope, confidence and expectancy, with the result that need changed to fulfillment, and lack to plenty. It always happens. Details are unimportant. We need merely to build the mental equivalent of what we expect to receive. We'll discuss the Law of Mental Equivalents more fully a little later on.

GOOD FROM EVERY DIRECTION

George Wilson got his job. In fact, he got two jobs. He went to work immediately after his interview the next day. The job was exactly what he wanted and the salary was right. However, within a week, before he had become established in the job, he received a better offer from another firm. Torn between loyalty to his present employer, and the desire to accept the new job, George again found his way to my office.

"What should I do, Dr. Curtis?" he asked.

"I don't know, George."

"Oh, I thought you would help me decide."

"I will, but I don't know the answer any more than you do. But I do know that there is Something which does know the answer. Suppose we start there," I suggested.

Again we treated—this time for guidance and confidence that George would handle the situation properly and make the right decision. He left my office with inner confidence that he would do the right thing and that everything would work out in the right way.

It did. He decided to tell his employer about the new offer. The employer was delighted in his good fortune, and not only did he not stand in the way, he actually helped George by providing an excellent reference and personally calling the head of the other company. George Wilson was established in the best job he had ever had, within a week of the time he and his wife had only $1.33 between them. Now, nearly two years later, he is with the same company, happy, prosperous and successful, and with two promotions to his credit.

George Wilson got well, but that's not the whole story. It took some doing. I don't want you to think that I just waved a magic wand and everything happened like magic. That is not the way spiritual mind therapy works. Spiritual mind treatment re-conditions the deeper mind so that normal action can take place. Lack, failure, suffering, pain and unhappiness are sick, abnormal states, resulting from disturbed states of mind and the emotions. Prayer treatment dissolves the negative and strengthens the positive aspects of consciousness. There was a great deal to be changed within George Wilson.

Opening New Accounts of Mind and Soul

He readily saw that his original sad situation was the result of inner conflicts, and would probably recur unless he did something about them. He came to see me once a week for over a year, in addition to attending lectures and classes regularly, and becoming an active member of the Science of Mind Church. George took personal inventory and found out what needed to be changed if he was ever going to be successful.

He got to know himself, and with self-knowledge, he saw that he needed to change. Here are the steps which put George Wilson in command of his own life for the first time. Use them to establish dominion over yours:

1. Get a clear picture of yourself the way you would like to be.
2. Examine yourself to see how you are different from the way you want to be.
3. Realize that the reason for this difference is within yourself. So is the power to correct it. Be willing to change.
4. Stop doing those things which are keeping you from being the way you want to be.
5. Start doing those things which will make you the person you want to be.

There was no doubt that George Wilson had ability and the stuff from which success is made. Then why wasn't he a success? Why had he been unemployed and broke at an age when most men are at the peak of their productiveness? A little digging turned up the causes for George Wilson's failure. The correction of them strengthened his conviction of success, and produced resultant success and prosperity in his world.

ROAD BLOCKS TO SUCCESS AND PROSPERITY

Correct the following inner weaknesses and you will find new and abundant circumstances appearing in your world just as George Wilson did.

1. *Limitation*. Think big and you will be big; think small and life will respond accordingly. Get rid of all piddling, second-rate ideas. Don't let details and trivia weigh you down. Free yourself from the bondages of early childhood conditioning, environment and experience. You can be whatever you want to be, and have whatever you want to have if you develop the consciousness of that thing and believe that it can be true for you. Develop a larger picture of things and expand your attitudes to accept new experience and greater expression.

2. *Inferiority*. The world is going to accept you at face value. People will accept you and believe in you in the exact measure with which you accept and believe in yourself. Self-depreciation is an order for failure and lack. If you don't believe you can, you can't. Self-rejection keeps you from getting ahead. Reject yourself and so will everybody else. Self-condemnation is the quickest way there is to get blamed for everything by everybody. Praise yourself and mighty powers will go to work to make you successful and prosperous.

3. *Greed*. This includes selfishness, penny-pinching, avarice, miserliness, and the love of money for its own sake. Greed eventually impoverishes a person because it shuts off the flow. Jesus said, "Lay not up for yourselves treasures upon earth, where moth and rust doth corrupt, and where thieves break through and steal: But lay up for yourselves treasures in heaven For where your treasure is, there will your heart be also." (Matt. 6:19-21) Interest yourself in service and in giving something to the world, and you will get your share. We may not always get what we want, but we always receive what we need in

one way or another. Let go. "Your Father knoweth what things ye have need of, before ye ask him." (Matt. 6:8)

4. *Fear.* Fear is lack of faith. You can't succeed at anything unless you have faith that you can. Faith is the substance of prosperity and supply. Believe that you can, and you can. Fear is negative belief. Be ruthless in removing fear from your mind. Dissolve fear; affirm faith. There is no limit to the things we can be afraid of if we let ourselves. Fear of failure, fear of disease, fear of death—all of these must go. Chronic attitudes of fear impoverish and destroy. A truly prosperous and successful person is never afraid of anything.

5. *Hypersensitivity.* The whiner, the martyr, and the thin-skinned individual always have problems with money and success. Many of us are charter members of the "PLOM (poor little old me) Club," smarting and hurting constantly from all kinds of wrongs, real or imagined. It's good to be sensitive; that keeps us in tune. But oversensitivity impoverishes us because all of our energy is used up in reactions and defenses which really aren't necessary. Nobody is trying to hurt you. Get rid of your suspicions and get on with the business of living. Life pays off for the person who is so busy and interested in constructive projects that he doesn't have time to be hurt.

6. *Resentment of Authority.* We have to learn to take orders before we can learn to give them. The proper placement of authority is essential to good organization. Somebody has to lay out the plans and give the orders. The person who says, "Nobody can tell me what to do," is usually trying to tell everyone else what to do. Resentment is another energy-sapper, for it burns up your success and prosperity-making powers. The only way you can climb to a higher position of authority is to do the best possible job where you are, forgetting yourself in the perspective of the larger picture. Nobody is really any more important than anyone else. We just have different jobs to do. Let's help the other fellow do his.

7. *Inability to Get Along with Other People.* A recent survey showed that 70 per cent of job turnovers was attributable to this cause. Granted that some people aren't too easy to get along with, we still must try. "There is so much good in the worst of us, and so much bad in the best of us, that it behooves none of us to talk about the rest of us." In other words, we're all in the same boat. Irritation and unpleasantness cause poverty and failure. When we fight with others

we are really fighting ourselves and taking it out on them. The successful, prosperous person is that way because he loves people—therefore, he gets along with them.

ONE GOOD DEPOSIT AFTER ANOTHER

George Wilson improved steadily as we did concentrated treatment work on each of these major areas. We got rid of tons of negative material that clogged the gears. As George took honest inventory of himself, he saw why he had been a failure. He started to remake himself into the kind of person he wanted to be. He got his faith back, and there was no stopping him. Mrs. Wilson joined in this new approach to life, and their marriage was strengthened as they became true partners instead of just married people. They were going places just as you will when you learn to:

1. Believe in Life
2. Believe in Good
3. Believe in Yourself
4. Believe in Other People
5. Believe in What You Are Doing

O. A. Harris, supervisor of service at the "Tail O' The Cock Restaurant" on famed "Restaurant Row" on La Cienega Boulevard in Los Angeles, puts these principles to work in handling his large staff. He hands each waiter and bus-boy a "Daily Meditation" Card when he comes to work. It says: "I will not willfully pass any task in my line of duty. I will be courteous at all times to guests and workers, no matter what the provocation. I do like my job and I offer honesty, courtesy, efficiency and a smile as proof."

Each person is asked to carry his card with him at all times. If difficulty arises or the worker becomes negligent in his duties, Mr. Harris just asks, "Do you have your card with you?" That is all that is necessary. They get the point, read it over, and endeavor to live up to what it says. As a result, "The Tail O' Cock" has a fine staff with very little turnover, and everyone, management and staff alike, share in the resulting success. We prosper when we do our jobs the way they should be done.

ACTIVE INGREDIENTS IN BUSINESS SUCCESS

During a recent dinner conversation with the general manager of one of the largest manufacturing organizations on the West Coast, I asked, "What do you consider the main deficiencies which keep men from succeeding in business?" He listed these five:

1. Lack of Purpose
2. Lack of Initiative
3. Lack of Imagination
4. Lack of Discipline
5. Lack of Courage

"There's no limit to where a man can go in our organization," he said. "There's always room at the top. At the rate we're expanding, if a job doesn't exist for a fellow who is ready for promotion, we create one for him. Our top men all came up through the ranks in our own company, and everyone of them has developed these five characteristics to a high degree. They have purpose, initiative, imagination, discipline and courage. I don't think anyone can get anywhere in life without them.

"We like a man to know why he is working for us, and what he hopes to achieve by it. The fellows who just put in time to pull down a salary don't last very long with us. In our way of thinking, our organization is only as strong as the people who work for us. Our company objectives are the result of the clarity and strength of purpose of the men who form the company. Success is no accident, and we all know it. Success is the direct result of your purpose and dedication. Our company is prospering and so are our people. We intend to keep it that way."

"What about the other points?" I asked.

"Well, let's take a look at initiative. You've got to be a self-starter. You'll never get anywhere if you wait around for someone else to tell you what to do. Take yourself, for instance. You're a successful man, and you certainly look prosperous. Why? Because you lay out your own work. Who tells you to get up before daylight every morning to write your books? Who tells you to give a class or go on a lecture tour? Who tells you what to do and when to do it, and how hard and how long to work at it?"

"No one," I replied. "If they did, I'd probably rebel."

"Of course. So would I. You and I are where we are because we like what we're doing and we do it because we want to. My job is my greatest pleasure. It's the most fun I know."

"I feel the same way," I agreed.

"Of course you do. That's initiative. We're always looking for fellows who want to take the ball and run with it. We encourage him and give him free rein. Of course, he's bound to make some mistakes, but what of it? You can always correct those. Give me a fellow with some get-up-and-go. I can teach him. But I can't do anything for a deadhead who won't get off his fanny."

"Just running with the ball doesn't guarantee prosperity and success though," I observed. "You have to have something on it too, don't you?"

"That goes without saying. And do you know where that comes from? A fertile imagination. We encourage initiative and imagination in all of our people. In our planning sessions, we lay out the problem, but we never try to get the complete answer right there and then. We usually say, 'Cook on that for awhile and see what you come up with.'

"Every idea and scheme gets a hearing no matter how outlandish it may seem. Some of our standard procedures have been adopted from proposals that seemed completely from left field when they were first brought up. It just took a little more imagination to make them useful. Why, one of our top men was almost let go when he first came to work for us because of what he coughed up out of that imagination of his. Everyone thought he was some kind of a nut or something. Boy, it scares me when I think of how we almost lost out with him. His imagination is a regular gold mine. We pay him to just sit around and dream things up."

"Just pure imagination can get out of hand once in awhile, can't it?" I asked.

"Sure. That's where point number four comes in—discipline. But there has to be something to discipline. Get the raw stuff of purpose, initiative and imagination going first—that's my motto. Then develop your discipline and control so as to give it form. Of course, if a man would be prosperous and successful, he has to know exactly what he is doing at all times. He must have himself under complete control—

on every level: spiritually, mentally, emotionally, physically and materially. A businessman must keep in training just like an athlete. Being able to call upon that extra ounce of reserve may often make the difference between a touchdown and losing the ball on downs. No, neither life nor business has much use for the nervous-nellies and the weak sisters who may have the goods but don't know what to do with it. A man has to whip himself into shape and keep himself in line. Everyone has will-power; we just have to learn how to use it. Start with discipline. I tell my men, 'Be tough with yourself. Get rid of the fat in your head and in your gut! Be a man! That's my idea of discipline."

"There's no mistaking your meaning," I smiled, "Even if you are, well—a bit—"

"Outspoken—plain spoken? Why not? I don't believe in pussyfooting around when dealing with important issues. Let people know where you stand, then they know where they stand. Love people—really care about them, and they'll know it, and feel secure with you. Then you can take a stand on anything you believe in and speak your piece without worrying whether some red-neck is going to get his nose out of joint. And what if he does? Who cares? You can't please everybody. If you try to do that you're really in the soup. That's the quickest way to failure I know. Stick up for what you believe! Be an individual! God knows the world needs a few. Sure it takes guts—courage to you—but the world needs that, too. We talk about prosperity and success, money, fame, power, acclaim—all the things men strive for. What do people think they are? Presents on a Christmas Tree? Hell, no! They have to be earned. Success doesn't just happen to you. You have to create it.

"There, that takes care of courage, along with the rest of what it takes to make a go of it in life." My friend laughed jovially as he summarized his little treatise on success. He gave the impression that he knew what he was talking about. And I'm sure he does, as he continues to live what he believes. He is a big man in business, he accomplishes great things, he makes a lot of money, he is happy and he makes others happy. I'd say he is successful. If you have any doubt of it, reread what he has to say about purpose, initiative, imagination, discipline and courage, and think about it as applied to yourself. It's pretty hard to argue with success, especially when it is expressed by a person who knows what it is and how to get it.

THE MENTAL EQUIVALENT OF SUCCESS

A very capable and personable friend of mine, a man nearing forty, had never made the grade.

Disdaining to enter his father's successful business, he got a good job immediately following college and seemed on his way to making a success on his own. But things never seemed to work out for him. He changed jobs frequently and ten years after college he was getting nowhere fast.

"What do you think is the problem?" I asked as we were discussing the situation one day. "You've got everything. If I had the business ability you have I'd have a million dollars by now."

"I don't know what it is, Don," he replied. "I always start to worry when the going gets a little tough. Everything seems to be going along fine, and all of a sudden I get buck fever. I choke up, and the harder I try the worse it gets. I eventually pull out of it, but by that time some newcomer is in my spot, and I'm looking for another job. Every time I go into something new, I think, 'This is it. This time it will be different. I know I'll make it now.' But it's always the same story. I–I–guess–I–just–haven't got it."

Tears welled up in his eyes and he sobbed with deep hurt and frustration.

"Tell me something about your boyhood, Bill," I urged him. "We'll find the key to this somewhere."

And we did. It all went back to his father who, disappointed that his only son had not come into the family business, was always saying, "You'll never make it. Why don't you come back home where you belong? Why don't you give up? You just haven't got it."

Unsure of himself anyway because his father had domineeringly downgraded him ever since he was a child, Bill succumbed to the suggestion of the negative expectation, and was crippled by subconsciously accepting his father's negative evaluation of him until he became conditioned to failure.

Bill finally gave up and went home, defeated and without hope, where he languished for several years in a subsidiary position under his father's dominance, clinging to the security of a "sure" job, unsatisfactory and humiliating though it was. Finally, however, he regained his old spark, re-evaluated himself and stood up to his father. His wife helped him, by continuing to encourage him down through the years, saying, "You can do it. I believe in you, Bill. I love you. Everything is going to work out all right. I know it is."

Bill made it, because his wife's faith in him led him to expect more of himself. *The more we expect of ourselves, the more we will deliver.* Today, Bill is the head of his father's business, and doing a good job. He changed his mental equivalent from failure to success, and he became successful.

In selling homes, a friend of mine who is a real estate agent starts with the conviction that there is a buyer for every home and a home for every buyer. Knowing that this is true, it then becomes simply a matter of getting the two together. A good salesman never needs to sell anyone anything. He operates on the premise that people will buy what he has to offer because it is what they want. Of course he must make sure that they want what he has to sell. Creating the desire is one of the major steps in salesmanship. My friend matches homes with buyers and vice versa. He never wastes time showing a house to a family unless he knows it is right for them. He goes shopping among houses that aren't listed in his search for just the right house for a buyer. He obtains listings when the people haven't even thought about selling. His conviction that he can find the right house for anyone no matter who it is, and a buyer for any house no matter where or what it is, plus good hard work accounts for his success. He builds an inner mental equivalent of a completed sale, then goes ahead and brings it about. This salesman has a plus factor working for him all the time. You can do the same.

HOW TO BUILD YOUR MENTAL EQUIVALENT

1. Get a clear picture of the object of your desire.
2. Use affirmative statements to strengthen your conviction.
3. Repeat these affirmations out loud as part of your regular daily prayer treatment periods.
4. Completely identify yourself with your desire. Become one with it. Act as though it were already true.
5. Don't talk about it to anyone else. Work upon it quietly, secretly and with deep faith. Give your idea a chance to grow and produce the harvest.

HOW TO RAISE YOUR INCOME

By expanding your mental equivalent, how else? Don't worry about the details of how it is going to come about. Develop your thinking along this line and it will happen:

1. Mentally accept more than you now have.
2. Visualize more money flowing into your hands.
3. Develop unlimited ideas of prosperity.
4. Eliminate all limited and poverty thoughts.
5. Think "plenty" instead of "not enough."
6. Feel rich inside.
7. Praise the power within you and feel it expand.
8. Believe and act as if you already have your new high level of income.
9. Establish harmony in your world.
10. Believe in and live by the spiritual law, "God is the Source of my supply."

THE MENTAL EQUIVALENT OF WHAT YOU ARE

Your success in life and the basis of your prosperity is rooted deeply in what you are as a person. As you build the mental equivalent of yourself as a prosperous and successful person, use the following check-list to measure your progress:

1. Ambition
2. Conviction
3. Vision
4. Integrity
5. Loyalty
6. Persistence
7. Responsibility
8. Self-Confidence
9. Sincerity
10. Tolerance
11. Thrift
12. Will-Power

Consciousness Conditioner For Prosperity and Success

The infinite law of abundance flows through me. I am the channel of love and blessing through which all good things are expressed. I am a prosperous and successful person. I experience plenty of all good things. I am attuned to the inner wholeness which is the source of all supply. I am one with the richness of life. My consciousness expands and I am a productive and useful person. I dedicate myself to doing good works. I give to my world and good is returned to me many times.

"He is a success who has lived well, laughed often, and loved much, whose life is an inspiration, whose memory a benediction." I believe in living well. I strive to be a good person. I put everything I have into life. I do a good job of being myself at my highest and best. I am generous. I am outgoing. I have a mental equivalent of expansion and growth. I praise and bless the inner resources of spirit. I give thanks for my talents and abilities. I am constantly developing. Each day I am one step closer to my goal of fulfillment.

The wealth of the inner kingdom is pouring into my mind and heart at all times. "My cup runneth over." All that the father has is mine. I am completely and permanently connected to the enriching stream of life. I am renewed, refreshed and replenished. I am transformed by the renewing of my mind. The father knows what things I have need of before I ask. It is the father's good pleasure to give me the kingdom. I accept it, I use it wisely, and I increase it and pass it along to others.

I am rich in every sense of the word. I am filled to overflowing. I am a prosperous and successful person now. I praise God from whom all blessings flow. I give thanks for unlimited abundance now. *And so it is.*

CHAPTER FOUR

YOU'RE IN THE DRIVER'S SEAT

In a large eastern city, a number of years ago, a slight sensitive man introduced himself after one of my lectures and asked for help through spiritual mind treatment. We will call him Paul Ardley. This is his story.

The Ardley family had lived for many years in one of the fashionable suburbs of this great metropolis, and were well-known for their business and professional accomplishments, their political influence, and their social standing. They were pillars of society. The founders of the family had built a strong foundation, which had grown into tradition, and the several generations of fine sons and daughters had continued to uphold the family name and standing.

Paul loved his family individually and collectively, and all that they stood for. Although, as a child, he had admired and respected his father and brothers, it was with the feminine side of the family that he felt closest. When his brothers had grown up and left the home, and his father had died, Paul didn't marry, but continued to live with his mother and one sister in the old family home, content in the security of the family position and the close affection which these three had for each other.

Paul ventured out into the world to some extent, and being of a sensitive and artistic nature, found his field of expression in the profession of interior decorating, at which he became quite successful, even though he preferred the quiet reflectiveness of the suburban family life to the bustle of the world of business. The arrangement was satisfactory with all concerned. The other brothers were relieved that there was a male member of the family on hand to look after the mother, and the years passed easily, with the illusion of the subtle conceit that present conditions would last forever. Paul's life was not complete in

51

the usual sense of the word, but he was content and wished for nothing more.

The inevitable, of course, always happens even though we seldom expect it. Paul was not prepared for his mother's passing even though she was well along in years. He had great difficulty adjusting himself to living without her, and his grieving extended far beyond any reasonable or healthy period. He and his sister sought to comfort each other in the musty expanses of the family home, withdrawing even further from a busy world which all but forgot their existence. But they did not seem to mind. Paul carried on only a token activity in his profession, and seemingly devoted his life to his grief and lived mostly in the past, rummaging about the mementos of years gone by. Although only in his forties, he aged rapidly, and naturally slight, he became wizened and dried up in appearance. There was no light in his eyes nor color in his skin, and his frail body was wracked by a persistent cough.

A few years passed and then suddenly the sister died and Paul was left alone in the old house in which he virtually buried himself from the world. He ceased all work, and spent his days in numb grief, seldom bothering to eat, and never even opening the shades so that sunlight might enter the fetid gloom. Thus Paul might have spent the remaining few of his years had not the world begun to move in on him and assert itself. There is a giant pendulum swing in the Universe which is always tending toward normalcy. We mortals are forced into the direction of what is normal for us.

Poor Paul had never been completely normal so he didn't know what it meant, but the Intelligence which created him knew, and acted to jar him out of the subnormal rut into which he had fallen, spiritually, emotionally and physically. First the brothers, partly concerned for Paul and partly for their share of the inheritance, wanted to sell the old house. There were excellent offers because of a new industrial development in the area, and the house could be sold at a sizeable profit, but Paul refused—alienated himself from his family and continued his voluntary withdrawal from life. He turned down all overtures from friends who wished to help him, and from former business associates who wanted to lure him back into the lucrative interior decorating profession, but he refused.

Then one day neighbors who were concerned at seeing no sign of life in the old house, broke in and found him unconscious on the floor. He was taken to a hospital where his case was diagnosed as heart trouble, and he spent long months there undergoing treatment. Finally, with very little improvement, he was released. He had reflected during his long idle hours in the hospital and had come to the conclusion that he must re-enter life and start to live—but he found that he no longer knew how. Now he was worse off than before. He had the desire to live but not the knowledge of how to go about it. He clung to the old house, not because it served his needs any longer, but because he did not know how to break away.

When he came to my lecture and had summoned the courage to tell us his story afterward, it was a desperate effort on his part to align himself with life.

Paul Ardley learned how to use the principles of the Science of Mind and is using them today. But—I am getting ahead of our story. When he finished talking to Mrs. Curtis and me that first evening he was suffering from an intense pain in his chest, which he felt was the beginning stage of a heart attack. We began prayer treatment work immediately, but rather than responding quietly, our patient was seized with a fit of coughing so intense that he had to leave the room. He returned, however, within a half hour to tell us that the pain had completely disappeared. Paul Ardley was like a different person. He said that he felt a great peace within him which he described as a "warm internal bath." At that moment, we both realized that we had witnessed an instantaneous healing!

There is no time element involved when one is dealing with the great Healing Principle. Our good is always at hand waiting to be discovered. For some of us it takes longer, but for this man the healing was instantaneous. A consultation with his physician the next day confirmed this fact. It showed that the cause of the pain had not been due to any trouble in the heart itself, but had been caused by a lung abscess pressing on the heart region. The abscess had broken during our treatment work together and the patient had coughed up the poison. This actually saved his life because if the poison had been released all at once into the blood stream it would have caused great damage.

It is interesting to note that Mr. Ardley was healed physically when he took steps within his own mind to move in the direction of the will to live rather than the withdrawal from life. His intense grieving had caused a congestion in his consciousness, which naturally had to reproduce itself in his body. Understanding the nature of cause we see that this congestion would be in his chest, because the respiratory system has to do with the air which enters our bodies. Air represents spirit, and spirit is life. It is also interesting to note that the abscess was near the heart, which represents love—and that seemingly it was the heart which hurt. Paul loved his mother and sister, but when this natural love was perverted into excess grieving it became poisonous and backed up on itself, thereby stagnating and forming the abscess.

Once we have the key to these matters, as revealed through the larger understanding which comes through treatment, their explanation and cure become mathematical in their scientific certainty. There is nothing left to chance in nature. Everything happens according to natural law. In the Science of Mind we endeavor to discover the nature of all natural Law.

Paul Ardley was not long in getting the rest of his life in order once he had recovered his physical strength. He disposed of the old house shortly thereafter and forever removed the weight of old memories from his life by disposing of the gathered impediments of many years of wrong thinking and incomplete living. His declaration of independence was inside himself. He then took steps to establish the evidence of this freedom in his social affairs, which in turn gave renewed strength to his inner resolves. Everything proceeded consistently. Paul Ardley again became active and re-established himself in his profession, and his interests and circle of friends grew around his completely full and normal life.

Today he is a healthy, happy man, completely in control of himself and the details of his life. Paul Ardley is in the driver's seat. He is living a life of order and balance. You can do the same thing. With minor variation of details, this could be your story or mine. We all have problems to meet in life and adjustments to make. We go through a variety of experiences before we achieve order and balance in our world of affairs. Sometimes these experiences are nearly fatal, as they were in Paul Ardley's case, but we need not wait as long as he did to meet the issues of life. We can start right now—establishing order and balance in our lives.

DISCOVER YOUR LIFE'S PURPOSE NOW

Start where you are—with the experience you are going through right now. Every experience has its place in the larger scheme of things. Life is One. It is only our false beliefs that cause separation and limitation. When we straighten out our inner attitudes, our lives straighten out. That is the purpose of this book. It is not hard to succeed in life when our spiritual, mental and emotional equipment are properly balanced. We are here for a purpose. Our task is to find that purpose, fulfill and identify with it. Build a strong conviction of success in your consciousness, and flow with the main stream. The obstacles drift away as we dissolve them in our minds. As William Shakespeare said:

> "There is a tide in the affairs of men,
> Which, taken at the flood, leads on to Fortune."

Rudyard Kipling's great poem, "If," has been a constant source of strength and inspiration to me since I was a boy. Hardly a day goes by that I don't dip into it for strength and courage. I often read it aloud to a troubled person who comes to me for counseling. It does something. Here it is in its entirety. Read it first silently, then aloud several times. Let its powerful statements sink into your subconscious. Make it a part of you, and let it be your guide.

IF

> If you can keep your head when all about you
> Are losing theirs and blaming it on you;
> If you can trust yourself when all men doubt you,
> But make allowance for their doubting too:
> If you can wait and not be tired by waiting,
> Or, being lied about, don't deal in lies,
> Or being hated don't give way to hating,
> And yet don't look too good, nor talk too wise;
>
> If you can dream—and not make dreams your master;
> If you can think—and not make thought your aim,
> If you can meet with Triumph and Disaster
> And treat those two imposters just the same:
> If you can bear to hear the truth you've spoken
> Twisted by knaves to make a trap for fools,

Or watch the things you gave your life to, broken,
   And stoop and build 'em up with worn-out tools;

If you can make one heap of all your winnings
   And risk it on one turn of pitch-and-toss,
And lose, and start again at your beginnings,
   And never breathe a word about your loss:
If you can force your heart and nerve and sinew
   To serve your turn long after they are gone,
And so hold on when there is nothing in you
   Except the Will which says to them: "Hold on!"

If you can talk with crowds and keep your virtue,
   Or walk with Kings—nor lose the common touch,
If neither foes nor loving friends can hurt you,
   If all men count with you, but none too much;
If you can fill the unforgiving minute
   With sixty seconds' worth of distance run,
Yours is the Earth and everything that's in it,
   And—which is more—you'll be a Man, my son!

                           Rudyard Kipling

YOU MUST DECIDE

In my personal counseling I never influence the choice of an individual in deciding what he should do. I especially refrain from giving people advice about whether or not they should try to get into motion pictures or television in Hollywood. After more than twenty years on the stage and before the TV and motion picture cameras, I know what it takes for a person to make a go of it in that highly specialized field of unique and rigid requirements. Success in show business demands a dedication and a will to succeed in the face of almost insurmountable odds and difficulties. It is a matter of survival of the fittest, and a Hollywood aspirant must see that he is fit or he is licked before he starts.

During the past twenty-five years my life has centered around this fantastic city and the motion picture industry. I have been on the outside looking in, on the inside looking out, and now—by the grace of God—I am in a position to help people in both positions. My personal experience seems to make this of some value. When I first entered my present profession in New York, I said, "I'm going back to Hollywood. I am going to become minister to the motion picture industry. These people need this affirmative spiritual teaching more than anyone else I know. I want to share with them this way of life which has meant so much to me."

There Is A Right Road For You

This was and continues to be my intention and that is the way it has worked out. In the congregation of the Science of Mind Church, among the thousands from every walk of life, is a large representation from the entertainment industry—actors, writers, directors, extras, producers, stage hands, electricians, and the ever-present hopeful hangers-on. Through personal counsel I deal with their hopes and dreams, their successes and failures, their marriages and divorces, their scandals and crimes, their heartbreaks and headaches, their triumphs and tragedies, their alcoholism and their dope addiction, their discouragements and their confusion. They are the most wonderful and most impossible people in the world, just as all the other people from other areas of life, and I love them. I wouldn't trade places with anyone in the world. I love my job, the rewards are many, and I am gratified to see more and more of my friends find their contact with the True Self. The constant schedule of lectures, classes, counseling sessions, and radio and TV broadcasts, are all worth it as I see the changes that come about in people's lives when they use these ideas. It is my prayer that through this book you, too, will find a realization of your true self.

In Krishnamurti's little masterpiece, *At the Feet of the Master*, is an affirmation which will help you achieve inner order and balance:

> "Whatever man has done, man can do.
> I am man but also God in man.
> I can do this thing and I will."

Aim To Reach The Top

The hardy souls who have preceded us on this journey of life have blazed a trail for us to follow. Within each one of us is the potential of greater things than have ever been done. Once someone breaks through a barrier, everyone does it. Babe Ruth hit sixty home runs in one season. The record stood for many years, and will always stand as the high mark for a 154-game season, but when Roger Maris set a new mark of 61 homers in 1961, even though it was for an extended schedule, it had a tremendous psychological effect on every slugger. They had considered Ruth's record inviolable, but when Maris set his record they began to say, "If Maris can do it, I can do it." It is inevitable that someone will. The same thing has been true of the once mythical "4-minute" mile and many other athletic marks which were once thought inviolable. The same principle holds true in every field of endeavor. No boundary is permanent, no horizon limited.

ORGANIZE YOUR INNER RESOURCES

If you want to do something, do it. If you know you can, you can. It's as simple as that. Get right inside. Establish order and balance and go to it. You wouldn't have the idea in the first place unless you could carry it through to completion. Here are five steps which will establish the foundation of inner order and balance enabling you to have the strength to do whatever you will:

1. Choose what you want to do.
2. Know that you can do it.
3. Count your blessings.
4. Know that God is within you and is ready to help you.
5. Act confidently.

Remember, you are more than just an individual person. You are an individual expression of the Universal Power within you. "I am man, but also God in man." "With God, all things are possible (Matt. 19:26). If God be for us, who can be against us?" (Romans 8:31).

PRACTICE THE ART OF SELF-EXAMINATION

Ask yourself some questions as you set about establishing order and balance in your life:

1. What do I want to do?
2. What do I want to be?
3. Where do I want to go?
4. What do I need to do to accomplish these things?
5. What do I want to stand for in my little corner of the world?

Think about these points and formulate answers. Define your objectives and fall in love with them. Develop a strong conviction concerning them. Harness your spiritual, mental, emotional and physical power, and go all out. Use these five steps to help you:

1. Dream your dream and go all the way with it.
2. Direct all of your work and energies toward the achievement of your dream.
3. Don't let people discourage you.
4. Don't let yourself become tired or unhappy in your journey toward accomplishing your objective. You are bound to have set-backs. These are only temporary re-evaluation periods. Never abandon those worthy goals which you have set for yourself.
5. Go into partnership with God. Jesus said, "I and my father are one. He that hath seen me hath seen the father." John 10:30; 14:9)

The establishing of inner spiritual, mental and emotional order and balance is the first step in the creative process. These periods of inner action will set this discipline. It simply must be done. There is no other way, so form the habit now and never neglect it. "Keep thy heart with all diligence; for out of it are the issues of life." (Pr. 4:23)

PLAN YOUR SELF-DEVELOPMENT PROGRAM

The time you spend in this inner work may vary from time to time, but base it roughly on the idea of 10 per cent. Various times during the day you will want to be alone and "talk it over with the Boss." Mohammed worked out a program of daily living, spending eight hours in work, eight hours in rest, and eight hours in developing his soul. Aim for this apportionment of your time. It will balance your life. Salvage the lost hours which we habitually fritter away. Put them to work in a well planned program of self-development. Remember, you are made up of the three main components of spirit, mind and body. This equation must be kept balanced, because we are acting and growing on all three levels simultaneously. Unless we spend time in developing each one we become lop-sided and will be unable to realize our true potential.

The purpose of this book is to show you the basis of the teaching of scientific spiritual truth and to give you some sound working techniques for using it. The techniques of achieving what you want have a sound spiritual basis. There are spiritual laws governing all life, and it is necessary for us to understand and obey these laws. Faith in a Higher Power and an awareness of our individual relationship to It are essential to our happiness and well-being. We can live effectively only when we start from this basis and sustain the action of Love and Faith in everything we do.

We control our own destiny by understanding and personal initiative. There is no point in asking God for things as is all too often done in prayer. We have already been given all things. It is up to us to claim and arrange what we need to most effectively express ourselves and accomplish good in our lives. An understanding of the spiritual and mental laws of causation helps us do this.

CONTINUE THE SEARCH FOR TRUTH

I am not trying to convert you to my way of thinking. I am merely presenting you with a set of tools which work, and some evidence of how they have worked in my life and the lives of others. If you are a religious person, you will find that everything that is said here is compatible with the basic teaching of all religions that *the life of man is the life of God, and our minds are the instruments through which we use the One Mind which is God.* If religion does not interest you— if you are interested only in the scientific basis of mental causation— then you will find what you are looking for in this book also. There is no nonsense about it. It is just common sense. There is much more to know than anyone knows. That which is, is—no matter what anyone says or thinks. Our job in life is to discover as much of the Truth as we can, live it the best that we can, and grant everyone else the freedom to do the same.

The yardstick is the results we achieve. We are known by our accomplishments. Those of us who teach the scientific spiritual approach to life as lecturers, ministers and practitioners can all attest to the results that thousands of people achieve through this means. The blind see, the lame walk, the sick are healed, the poor are made prosperous. Attitudes of love, faith, peace and joyousness replace hatred, fear, anxiety and depression. The timid and inferior gain strength and confidence, and frustrated and aimless drifters find purpose and meaning in the adventure of life. It has happened to me. It can happen to you.

GIVE PRIORITY TO MAJOR GOALS

In my work, as with nearly everyone, there is more to do each day than can possibly be done. This is inevitable. Action begets action. Therefore, we must learn the important principle of selection. Simply do first things—the big important ones—first. Most of the rest will be taken care of automatically when you attune your actions to the larger picture of what you are trying to accomplish. Keep your goal and purpose in mind and work steadily toward it. Eliminate everything that doesn't move you in that direction. It is easy to lose sight of the forest because of the trees. Don't let this happen. Don't do anything that doesn't need to be done. Eliminate unnecessary actions. A good percentage of our energy is squandered on inconsequential details. If something throws you, learn to say, "It doesn't matter just because it doesn't matter," then resume the task at hand and get on with it.

Life is not meant to be difficult, and it won't be when you learn to act intelligently by firmly establishing inner patterns of right action. Most of us scurry around like katzenjammer kids, sunk under the weight of our own disorganization and hypnotized by our own negative beliefs. Let's correct this right now.

Plan intelligently. Pray regularly. Work diligently.

Keep your task firmly in mind, develop strong convictions concerning it, and follow through. Take things as they come and don't be concerned with results. You will get good results when you base intelligent and efficient action upon sound mental and spiritual principles. Balance your work-load by letting the inner power take over for you. It must do what you tell it to. The inner power responds to our thought. Develop the constructive inner attitudes discussed in this book and your life will be one of joy and accomplishment.

RECOGNIZE EXCUSES FOR WHAT THEY ARE

For years prior to the publication of *Your Thoughts Can Change Your Life* in 1961, I had been trying to get a book written, but something always interfered. There was always too much to do, not enough time, or something else which had to be done first. All seemingly legitimate excuses, but they didn't hold water, because they indicate a lack of understanding of the principle of right action. We create our own actions and responsibilities out of our own inner consciousness.

There is no need to have a tiger by the tail unless we have taken hold of it in the first place. Excuses, evasions, deviations and procrastinations all must come home to rest in the individual. We can only change an undesirable situation by changing ourselves.

During the process of writing my first book, I discovered that the only way to write a book is to write it. If you have a strong enough compulsion to do something you will do it, no matter what else is going on. I had been trying to get down to writing *Your Thoughts Can Change Your Life* for years, but in all that time I completed less than two chapters. I seemed to be continually submerged in other work. This was a constant source of frustration to me. I told myself that I would complete the book as soon as other work let up—but it never did; it kept getting heavier.

What was I to do? I carry the equivalent of about five full time jobs in my ministry as pastor, teacher, radio and television broadcaster, practitioner, counsellor and administrator. How could I possibly find time to write? I couldn't have if I hadn't made a very important discovery— the hours spent worrying about the lack of time could have been used for creative purposes. I decided to do something about it. I said to myself: "I know what I have to do and I know how to do it—so I will do what needs to be done when it needs to be done." Then I made it a practice to do and finish one thing at a time without worrying about what was coming next. I got things organized with my staff, laid out a work schedule and then took things as they came. At the same time I sat down and had a little talk with God about the book. I said, "Now, Father, you have given me the idea of this book. I know that you know how to write it. I will do everything I can to cooperate. I am ready."

Believe it or not, things started to happen. I felt more freedom and peace than I had known in years. With it came a feeling of inexhaustible power and energy. I rearranged my schedule, arose an hour earlier, and spent several hours each morning at my desk concerned only with the book. This went on six and sometimes seven days a week. Each morning after a period of quiet meditation and prayer, I started to write. In a few months of steady work, the book was finished.

PLAN AND ACT DECISIVELY

Do you see the importance of sound planning and intelligent and steady action? One activity produces another. All kinds of wonderful things have happened to me since I have been writing regularly. New avenues of expression have opened up all down the line, and everything I do has greater effectiveness. It is all a matter of order and balance. Decide on something, plan it and do it.

Things are not nearly as hard to do as we think they are. Unlimited power and "know-how" are within you, just waiting to be used. Your magnificent potential doesn't know anything about difficulties. It just does what it is given to do. Rid your mind of limitations, and let the larger power come through. The old adage, "Never put off until tomorrow what you can do today," is a pretty good rule of thumb.

The inner idea is the seed from which the tree of action grows, for all action is generated by inner thoughts and feelings. Confusion and waste reign when we reverse the procedure by concentrating on the outer first.

One time I complained that certain conditions and situations were keeping me from doing what I wanted to do. I felt I was being blocked by circumstances beyond my control.

"What does that have to do with you?" a wise counsellor asked me. "Never react to; always act from. Form a solid basis of action within yourself, and then carry it out. Forget about what the world and other people are doing; just be sure that you know what you are doing, then do it. Everything else will take care of itself."

Jesus said, "Judge not according to the appearance, but judge righteous judgment. . . . (John 7:24) In the world ye shall have tribulation: but be of good cheer; I have overcome the world." (John 16:33) The Great Teacher acted from His inner convictions, refusing to let Himself be deviated by outer considerations. He taught by example and stressed the importance of believing in yourself. Jesus is the prototype of the ideal man. We should think of Him as the great example rather than the great exception. He said, "He that believeth on me (your own Higher Self), the works that I do shall he do also; and greater works than these shall he do." (John 14:12) This all adds up to intelligent and purposeful action.

When we realize that compared to the real potential of the human race, hardly anything worth doing has yet been done, we will attune our actions to worthy ideals and noble purpose and do our very best at every moment. Every one of us is here for a purpose. Our job is to find out what this purpose is, and to do our best to fulfill it. Nothing but our best is good enough. Apply yourself completely to expressing your highest and best at all times and the riches of the kingdom will be yours. Paul said, "Whatsoever ye do, do it heartily, as to the Lord, and not unto men." (Col. 3:23) This is the code of good workmanship.

YOU ARE ON YOUR OWN

Pick up the ball and run with it. It was passed to you. It is yours. You'll never know what you can do until you try, and if you don't try to do that which means something to you, you'll be miserable until you do. The creative process can only work effectively when the idea is given clarity and conviction. You must *become* the living embodiment of the idea. When you become the thing you seek, you will attract all the help you need. But until you are sure, you must go it alone. Wise spiritual teachers never give advice. We counsel, we encourage, we pray for guidance, and we help when we are asked and needed, but we never intrude our personalities upon what must be the responsibility of the individual to initiate and carry through on his own life's purposes and projects. More ships have been sunk by advice than have ever been floated by it. Make your own decisions; formulate your own plans. Be intelligent about it, proceed according to principle, but let no one stack your blocks for you. You can only enter the kingdom on your own. You can only find God—success, achievement, growth, fulfillment—within your own heart. You alone can hear the inner voice which speaks to you. You alone can give life to the picture which burns in your mind and heart.

Even though you may be lonely and unsure of your dream, remember the Congressman's definition: "A camel is a horse designed by a committee." You must deal alone with the stuff your dreams are made of. Seek the counsel and guidance of wise friends and teachers, but be prepared to accept their help on the terms in which they give it. Don't depend upon them to supply that which you have failed to do for yourself.

REPLENISH YOUR INNER RESERVES

Constantly strengthen your inner conviction with mental and spiritual disciplines. Keep ever before you that which you want to achieve. Constant affirmation will lead to conviction and acceptance. Clear thinking and strong feeling work together to form a strong subjective pattern of your desired good upon which the creative law may work. There are no shortcuts. Only you can do it.

The directions outlined in this book are specific and definite. If you follow them your life will change for the better and you will get where you want to be. I am not giving advice. I am showing you a way of life which brings results. It has worked for me.

Man is made for victory—not defeat. In our individual minds we win the battles. Our strength comes from the realization that our minds are merely our individual use of the One Mind which is "common to all individual men." In this One Mind is the answer, the means and achievement—"the Kingdom, the Power, and the Glory" of all things.

Daily Guide To Order and Balance

I get my life in order today. I establish inner balance. I am poised and integrated. I arrange all things around a pattern of inner harmony and order. I think clearly, I react calmly, I act definitely and with purpose. All confusion is dissolved. Peace lives in my heart. My mind is quiet and untroubled. I know who I am, why I am here, and where I am going. Nothing can disturb me. I am alive, alert, and awake. I am well coordinated. I know what I am doing, and I do it well.

My life expresses the beauty and symmetry of the universe. I am one with all wonderful things. In unity there is strength. I am unified with the Source of all things now. I am in tune with the celestial symphony of noble purpose, ideal and action. I sing with the angels of love, hope and aspiration. My mind is one with Divine Mind. My soul expresses the One Soul. My body is a masterpiece of manifestation. I am a whole person. Everything is in order. I am perfectly balanced. I maintain the proper relationship among all the components of my being. I am constantly connected to the Source of all life. The elements of nature are mixed in me in perfect proportion. I am a living expression of what man should be.

Infinite Intelligence guides and instructs me. I am in constant contact with the Source of all knowledge, wisdom and understanding. I intuitively perceive the wonder and beauty of the universe. I gaze upon its magnificence and I let myself be formed in the image and likeness of God. I am inspired by the image of wholeness, health, beauty, order, harmony and balance which is firmly established in my deeper mind. All things are in place in my life today. I experience perfect order and balance. *And so it is.*

CHAPTER FIVE

HOW TO MAKE YOUR LIFE A HIT

"Cast on stage! Places! Every one on stage please! Ready for a complete run-through. Places!"

The words were music to my ears. I had heard them hundreds of times, but this time they gave me a special thrill. It was my first Broadway play. I had finally made it! After years of school productions, stock companies and Hollywood "B" pictures, I had finally made it to the Big Street. My fondest dream had come true. I had a good part in a New York play. Heaven could have no more to offer than this.

The rehearsal started. It was the fifth day and we were going through the entire play for the first time. It was rough; characterizations were incomplete and lines were uncertain, but all in all, it was a thrilling experience.

"Eleven tomorrow, ladies and gentlemen. That's all for today. Good night everyone," the director dismissed us following the run-through. I was walking on air as I went out the stage door. What a wonderful profession! How glorious it was to be an actor!

"Oh, Mr. Curtis! Just a moment please." I paused as the stage manager caught up with me.

"Yes?" I inquired.

"Mr. Curtis—uh—I have something for you."

My heart turned over six times. "Oh no!" I exclaimed.

"Look, I'd rather be shot than give you this—I don't understand it. I thought you were great in the rehearsal today, but they want to make a change. I'm sorry, but—well, here it is."

He handed me my pink slip. My services were no longer required and I hadn't really had a chance to offer them!

"But —," I pleaded.

"I can't help it, son. I'm sorry. I wish I could help you, but I can't. Excuse me now, huh? They're waiting for me on stage. Chin up fellah, this isn't the only play this season, you know. Good luck." And he was gone.

The Pain of Rejection

Dazedly, I walked up to the corner of 46th Street and Broadway and stood looking out at this magic street which I had first seen at Christmas time nearly fifteen years before. It had taken me that long to get back with the courage and the conviction that I had what it took to be a New York actor. And now—

I stopped at the nearest bar and mixed bitterness, disappointment, and self-pity with whiskey until the place closed. I wallowed around in the combination for the next few days, so low that I had to reach up to touch bottom.

"What's the use?" I asked myself. "I'll never get any place now. I might as well quit." I played my dismal role to the hilt as if I were the first actor that ever got fired—the first person that ever had a set-back before he got where he wanted to be. I was a mess. If I had known about the Science of Mind I could have pulled myself together and avoided some of the experiences which followed, but I didn't. I had to learn the hard way. Experience is a great teacher, but sometimes a very tough one. I was to find this out.

I couldn't even bring myself to look for another play after my first fiasco, even though this was the only reason I had left Hollywood for New York. By the time I had finally pulled myself together, all casting had been completed for the fall season. It was this experience which precipitated my sojourn in the hospital which I told you about in my earlier book, *Your Thoughts Can Change Your Life.* When I had recovered sufficiently, I went back to Hollywood with my tail between my legs.

It was two years before I had nerve enough to return to Broadway— and I needed the time. I had a lot of work to do on myself. I have been eternally grateful for finding the Science of Mind when I most needed it. But in the years since, during which time I have learned to use these principles, I have discovered that we always find exactly what we need at the exact moment we need it. It is just that we may need adversity to bring us to our senses. You see, Nature insists that we grow. If we don't assist Nature willingly, we will just have to go along for the ride, no matter where it takes us, until we can get ourselves back into the driver's seat. It is getting in the driver's seat and staying there that is the whole business of living. Naturally, it takes some doing, but there is a way, as we are finding out, as we apply constructive spiritual and mental principles to our lives.

Following my crushing disappointment in being fired from the play, I finally came to realize why. It was my own fault. Despite my years of experience, I hadn't yet learned the discipline and control necessary for success. The desire was strong, but I hadn't yet developed a true inner image. I hadn't accepted myself as a successful Broadway actor. I was full of positive thinking and purposeful action but since my inner conviction was lacking, I projected uncertainty and anxiety through subliminal signs in personality and behavior. This made the producers of the play unsure of me, even though they didn't exactly know why, so they decided not to take a chance. The incident was a shattering one at the time, but as I look back upon it I am grateful for the experience, because I would probably never have learned these lessons otherwise. At least not so soon. You see, life presents the lessons. If we don't learn them on our own, experience steps in and teaches them to us, often through suffering and heartbreak.

A Return With Resolution

When I returned to New York two years later I was prepared for what I wanted to do. Evidently, I projected an impression entirely different from my previous one. I had worked diligently to develop more healthy inner attitudes and to gain additional experience and skill in my profession. I had no difficulty in securing employment as an actor and enjoyed a considerable measure of success before I bridged over into my present field.

When you are strong inside, you project an entirely different impression. Even discouragements, failures and disappointments don't phase you. You are able to maintain an indomitable optimism and cheer even in the face of disaster. If this weren't true, no one would ever really succeed in anything.

I experienced plenty of disasters in the years which followed. There are dozens of Broadway flops to every hit. The flops are quite an experience.

"I think I'll mix myself a drink, dear," the character which I was playing muttered for the umpteenth time during the third act of one dreary opus as the opening night audience had long since either gone home or to sleep. It had been a gruesome evening for both audience and actors. The audience could leave, but we on the stage were stuck, and had no choice but to play it out to the last curtain. We kept bravely on.

As I uttered my recurring line, "I think I'll mix myself a drink," one bored spectator was aroused from his nap long enough to remember something.

"Mix me one too!" he shouted toward the stage. Instantly the audience came to life as peals of laughter rang out. There couldn't have been a more perfect comment. The evening ended in a shambles.

We played three performances before the scenery was mercifully shipped to Cain's warehouse. I don't know why. One performance was too many.

Performance Brings Rewards

I had made Broadway, even if my debut wasn't exactly auspicious. But another play followed, and then several others. Sweeter rewards finally came. They always will when we get right inside, and keep at it, projecting the best of ourselves, until we achieve what we have been striving for. There is no shortcut, as we have said, but the process of growth can be speeded up by intelligent and enlightened application and projection of ourselves.

People can only tell about us by what they see. In a play the producer, the playwright, the director, the designer and the actor never have a chance to explain what they had in mind or what they meant to do. They must do it. They must present their best and take the consequences. If they are not yet good enough or if they fail in performance through inadequate planning, training, rehearsal and teamwork, the play is a flop. The same thing is true in our lives.

Of course, in the theatre there are always a certain number of succès d'estime, in which everything is well done but the audience doesn't accept the production anyway. This is a calculated risk in the theatre and in life. It all depends upon what is important to you. Keep trying until you project the true image of what you are. When you are successful in doing that, you will have the reward of a life well-lived, and you will be indifferent to the plaudits of the multitude and the size of material rewards. You will have something greater than all of these things. You will have self-respect and self-fulfillment. You will have found the Kingdom within yourself and whatever you need to enjoy a rich, full life will come to you automatically.

A certain amount of trouble, suffering and failure are inevitable in life until we learn to rise above them. Jesus said, "In the world ye shall have tribulation: but be of good cheer; I have overcome the world." (John 16:33) He did this by projecting the inner image of His divinity into the affairs of the world. He proved that a high spiritual consciousness, noble ideals, and steadfast purpose have the power to change outer conditions. He made sure that what He presented to His world was the best that He had in Him. His constant awareness of Oneness with God was the producer of His drama, and as the playwright, the director, designer, and actor, He perfected His performance through constant rehearsal in prayer. He became a perfect actor of life by developing the constructive factors within Himself just as we are learning to do in this book. Jesus became the Perfect Man by constant awareness of the perfection of the Christ within Him, and by projecting it into His world. Our challenge in life is no less than this.

In the tryout stages of a play, the effect upon the audiences is carefully observed as the play is performed, and mistakes are assiduously corrected through constant rehearsal. Just as in life, we must continuously examine ourselves, taking honest inventory to determine what thoughts, attitudes and actions we must eliminate, and which ones we must strengthen in order to attain the desired results.

In the theatre, the director must keep his eye on the entire production, perfecting and coordinating the various elements until the desired total effect is achieved. He must sometimes be ruthless in cutting out unsuccessful elements, and replacing them with constructive ones. He must be willing to change things, no matter how hard it is to do. Again, the process is the same one that we must employ in life if we are to perfect ourselves. The negative thought, the destructive emotion, and the purposeless action must all be eliminated if we are to keep moving ahead. The great teachers of humanity have always practiced this principle. Jesus cursed the fig tree that did not bear fruit, and it died. This indicates that we must remove those ideas and attitudes that do not produce affirmative results in our world. Moses and the children of Israel wandered forty years in the wilderness on the largest "tryout tour" in history until they were ready to enter the Promised Land. The lesson here is that we must learn to understand and live by the Law—the commandments of inner and outer behavior —before we can get where we want to be—the Promised Land of peace of mind, health, happiness, freedom and accomplishment.

The Dynamic Power Within You

The children of Israel would never have made it without the leadership, guidance and discipline of Moses. The powerful spiritual dynamic of Christianity would never have become the great force that it is today if Jesus had not demonstrated its principles as a practical Way of Life and taught His disciples how to live by them. History is the record of man's travels along the pathway to perfection. It is the story of man's struggles with himself. It is the drama of the unfoldment of the human soul. Each of us must travel the path for himself. We all must learn the meaning of life and how to live it effectively. This is attained within our own minds and hearts. Trial and error, pain and suffering are one way. But there is another way— the High Road of understanding, faith and love. There is the way which recognizes that consciousness is the only reality—that the Law of cause and effect works from within outward—that we must purify and strengthen our inner lives before we can achieve anything lasting and worthwhile in our world. This is the way which we are dealing with in this book. It is the best way—the only true way. Let's learn how to follow it by taking definite steps to bring out the best in ourselves. Mastery of sound spiritual principles will accomplish this.

In the theatre, as in life, there are those who work in the outer only. Certain results can be achieved in this way, but the full potential is never reached unless inner development is achieved first. The good director and actor works first in consciousness—in developing understanding and feeling, just as we are learning to do through the use of sound mental and spiritual techniques. Action is meaningless unless it is intelligently directed toward a worthwhile goal or purpose. The good director must first have full understanding of and deep feeling for what the playwright is trying to say. The actor must have a complete identification with his character through understanding and love before he can effectively portray the role. In life, each of us is his own playwright, director, designer and actor. The purpose of life is to project a beautiful and worthwhile production upon the stage of human endeavor. As we work in this direction we help others, make the world a better place, and fulfill ourselves in the process. It is an exciting business. Let's know it and make it so.

The Refining Power of Repetition

The working process in the theatre, as in life, is one of rehearsal—going over the material until it emerges into proper form. The playwright goes over and over his play, often re-writing it many times. The director reads the play many times, analyzing, interpreting and planning until the master plan of the production is indelibly impressed upon his mind. The designer visualizes, sketches, mixes colors, and formulates the entire picture in his mind until he can actually see it. The actor identifies himself completely with the character he is to portray, learning to understand him by thinking and feeling as he does, until he is completely "inside" him. Then the actor projects every inner nuance through his own mind, emotions and body until the character emerges in appearance, voice, expression, gesture and movement. It must be sincere and complete in every respect. The actor becomes the character, just as in life we become the person we want to be by the same process. There is no shortcut, and no compromise is allowed. We must do a complete job, or the final result will not be satisfactory.

It is a matter of practice makes perfect. Remember, you are all of these people—playwright, director, designer and actor—at the same time. These are different aspects of the whole person. In the theatre, they must all work together under the producer to get the job done. Likewise, we must coordinate these different functions within ourselves in order to live effectively. Thought, feeling, imagination and action work together to carry out the will of the producer—our understanding of spiritual Truth—the Spirit of God indwelling each of us.

Once the play is ready for performance, run-through or performance rehearsals are continued until the play is finally presented before an audience for the first time. During early presentations the actors learn how to gauge their performances to the audience, and technical details of scenery, costumes and lights are perfected, changes are made, and final polishing is done. Finally, when the time comes for opening night in New York, every aspect of the production is as nearly perfect

as it can be made. If the play is a good one, if it has been well
rehearsed, and if the actors overcome the nervousness of the occasion
and give the performances they have learned to give, the play is a
success. If some of these "ifs" go wrong, the results are doubtful.

THE DRAMA OF LIFE

The theatre represents life. Just as theatrical achievement can only
result from observance and application of the laws of life, so in our
desire to live more effectively, we can learn from the theatre. Success
in either one depends basically upon the development of the basic
mental, emotional and spiritual attitudes with which we are dealing
in this book.

Living is a process of constant growth and improvement. The basic
principles must be applied constantly. The actor's job has only started
when he gives the opening night performance. From then on, for the
entire run of the play, he must recreate the character by skillfully
applying what he has learned to each performance. Certain aspects
are automatic, but the basis of the actor's art is his ability to bring life
and inspiration to his character and the play no matter how many
times it has been performed. He must create the illusion of the "first
time" at every performance. If you have ever seen a play early in its
run, and then again later, you will have observed that the performances
of some actors have become richer and fuller, while those of others
have become stale and flat. Freshness, imagination, ingenuity and
inspiration, within the framework of discipline, are necessary in the
theatre and in life. Conquest, control and application of ourselves
is a continuous process.

The learning process of rehearsals applies the tools of repetition,
frequency and intensity. The actor forms subjective patterns of action
and response which he uses subconsciously during performance. He
eventually becomes the thing which he has repeated during rehearsals.
His consciously planned thoughts and actions become habitual reactions which he uses without thinking. This principle can constantly
be observed in life. We all know how much easier it is to do a thing
after we have done it for awhile. We can all recall our early fumbling
and uncertain actions in learning how to typewrite, or drive a car.
As we learn a process consciously, it eventually conditions the subconscious to react automatically. The same principle that enables us

to do a thousand and one things without thinking about them can be utilized to condition our thinking, our feeling and our living along whatever lines we want them to go.

Just as a play is rehearsed until it is perfect, so we can rehearse our minds, our emotions and our actions until they become perfect. Just as in the theatre, life pays off on performance. "Him who has gets." We all have it. It is all a matter of what we are doing with it. Successful living takes discipline, application and vigilance.

Do you know how to get into the winner's circle? Do you know how to avoid the flops and make a hit with life's show? There is a way. It is a matter of consciously creating circumstances by establishing desirable patterns of thought, feeling and action in your deeper mind. The actor does it through rehearsal. We, who are all actors on the stage of life, can learn to do it through a process of life rehearsal which we call treatment. The various steps and suggested techniques are designed to help you "treat" your inner mind—to condition it to accept the idea of and produce the experiences of happiness, health, prosperity, success, freedom and harmonious adjustment.

RELAX AND ENJOY IT

Just before opening night of my first play as leading man in a stock company, I was furiously studying my lines right up to curtain time.

"I just can't seem to remember the words!" I moaned, just as untold numbers of actors had done before me.

"What's the trouble?" the grizzled character man who shared my dressing room inquired.

"They just won't stick," I fretted. "I don't see how I can ever get through the play. How have you managed all these years?"

"Very simple, son," he replied. "Here's my formula. It's never failed me: 'Wear what you have. Say what you know, and eleven o'clock always comes.'"

I've never forgotten this lesson. Before the season was over, I was able to attain nearly the same degree of relaxation during performance that this wonderful old character actor did. I have expanded his three steps into a guide to right action in living:

1. Be what you are.
2. Use what you know.

3. Give what you have.
4. Love as you would be loved.
5. "Know the truth, and the truth shall make you free." (John 8:32)

Condition your mind with these five steps and you will eliminate haste, tension, confusion, effort and worry—all enemies of smooth performance and right action. Just as "eleven o'clock," or the end of the performance arrives in every play—so in life we all arrive at our life's destination of achievement and unfoldment, if we just relax and do the best we can along the way. See through the outer confusion and problems of life to the quiet inner center of peace and perfection within you. Treat your mind to do this and you will be free of the negative attitudes and emotions which block right action.

My old actor friend taught me many tools of the acting profession which have later proved valuable to me as a practitioner and counselor. He used to watch me anxiously rehearsing my lines as I applied my make-up before a performance.

"What are you doing that for?" he asked one night. "You played the show last night. You got through it all right. Your lines will be there tonight when you need them. Relax—get quiet inside and stop worrying. Throw away the script! You can always ad lib if necessary but you won't need to; I'll always be there to bail you out."

Relax. Get quiet inside. Stop worrying. Throw away the script. Ad lib if you need to.

Words of wisdom wouldn't you say? We all know the advisability of relaxation, quietude and peace. Work toward them, then "throw away the script." If you have properly conditioned your mind you'll know what to do and say when the moment arrives. Jesus said, "It shall be given you in that same hour what ye shall speak." (Matt. 10:19)

Get the general structure of your life laid out, condition it into your mind through rehearsal—or treatment—and the details will take care of themselves. Put your reliance upon principle. You don't have to plan every moment and action. Establish the principle of right action deep within your subconscious and you can't go wrong. Review your life plan, clarifying your goals, desires, ideals, hopes, dreams and aspirations, then live each moment with joy, abandon, release and freedom.

Good actors are the most dedicated and disciplined people in the world. Nothing is too large or too small for them to undertake if it will help the play. The same thing holds true for each of us as an actor of life. Your life's performance is going to be exactly what you make it. It is up to you whether it's going to be a flop or a smash hit.

Effective treatment—or life rehearsal—is dependent upon:

1. *Definition.*   Form a plan and stick to it.
2. *Clarity.*   Be simple. Be sure you understand what you are doing.
3. *Frequency.*   Go over your objectives as often as possible until they become a living part of you.
4. *Repetition.*   Repeat your treatment until the response becomes automatic.
5. *Intensity.*   Mean what you say. Feel it. The subconscious responds most effectively to strong feeling.

The pattern of right action and true performance which emerges in your life will be dependent upon how faithfully and thoroughly you have formed the inner patterns through rehearsal—treatment. Here are the five basic requirements for achieving right results in your life:

1. Clarity of Visualization.
2. Strength of Feeling.
3. Power of Imagination.
4. Sincerity of Thanksgiving.
5. Completeness of Expression.

Treatment is clear thought about, and harmonious relationship with life. Treatment is the process whereby we strengthen our affirmative attitudes.

An affirmative person has the power of love working for him, because love is affirmative relationship to life. Learn to:

1. Get along with yourself.
2. Get along with others.
3. Get along with your world.
4. Get along with God.
5. Get along with life.

Put your best foot forward. Never let your guard down. Keep climbing. The show must go on. The universal principle of right action is always there to help you. Use it. Determine to:

1. Look your best.
2. Think your best.
3. Feel your best.

4. Speak your best.
5. Do your best.

Right action is just waiting to happen through you. Believe this and it always will. Be faithful, steady and consistent in the treatment work of conditioning your inner mind to accept ideas of order, harmony, balance and right action.

Move steadily ahead in life by following these suggestions:

1. See yourself the way you want to be.
2. Prepare yourself for this experience.
3. Stick to your goals.
4. Finish what you start.
5. Keep your plans to yourself.

You have the tools. Now go ahead and make your life a hit!

Daily Guide To Right Action

Nothing but good can take place in my life now or ever. There can be no wrong action. There is only right action. There are no mistakes. Everything happens for a reason. The law of cause and effect produces absolute justice in my life. I do not complain, whine, whimper or struggle. I get in step with life today. I get my bloated nothingness out of the way and let right action come through.

I never tell God what to do. I know He knows His business. I apply myself to learning mine. When I get myself straightened out inside, my life straightens out and I "fly right." I decide now to stop gumming up the works. I have the capacity of perfection and right action within me. I determine to live up to my full capacity in all that I do.

My thoughts and feelings blend together in a complete conviction of right action. Nothing can sway me from my purpose. I have a steady bead on the target and I move serenely ahead to completion and fulfillment. There is nothing I cannot be—nothing I cannot do—if I marry myself to the principle of right action and remain faithful to it.

There are no detours. All roads lead up the mountain. I find the right road for me and I follow it to the destination of peace and fulfillment. Right action takes place every step of the way throughout my life. I expect everything to work out in an orderly and efficient fashion. I believe in inner strength and solidarity. I am in harmony with the universal law of right action. Every experience of my life is an expression of right action. I give thanks for right action taking place in my life today and always. *And so it is.*

CHAPTER SIX

"BE THOU MADE WHOLE!"

Years ago in New York I let my problems and responsibilities completely exhaust me and I lost my zest and enthusiasm. There were days when I just couldn't get going. I started to complain about how much I had to do, and I dragged through my various activities with maximum resistance. Financial and physical problems developed which complicated the situation.

We were furnishing a new apartment and I was pressed into service to do some minor handy-man work. I resisted, but reluctantly went about my householder's chores. Suddenly, as I squatted down to fix something, there was a crack like a rifle shot as my left knee popped out of joint and I was unable to rise. After some assistance, the knee went back into place and I went on about my activities. But within a short time the same thing happened, and this time it remained locked. Nothing seemed to help. I forced myself to stand on it the next day when I gave a lecture, but this produced great strain and the condition got worse. The condition in the leg was not eased by my mental and emotional reaction. The accident had occurred at a particularly busy period and I reacted as if God had something against me personally. I limped around for nearly three months, when finally Mrs. Curtis said at breakfast one morning, "If you're not going to do anything about that knee, I am."

"I wish you would," I replied. "I'm getting sick of it." There is nothing more frustrating than a condition which fails to respond to treatment. When our previous treatment work had failed to produce results, I had increased the intensity of my efforts in this direction, and still getting no results, I had gone to a series of doctors who had not been able to help either. How could they? The problem was not in my leg; it was in my mind. The condition in my body was merely the projection of my inner attitudes of struggle, effort and resistance. At the same time I was forcing my legs to move forward, I was setting up innumerable psychological obstacles for them to overcome.

Our Inner Conflicts

This is an all too-common human situation. Our efforts to drive ahead are blocked by inner conflict, insecurity, indecision and fear. A strain developed. When we insist upon going two ways at once something has to give. In this case, it was my knee. In other cases, this inner conflict and resistance can produce any number of foot, joint, back and muscular difficulties. The human body cannot stand up indefinitely under the strain and overload to which we subject it. Physical difficulties are actually a blessing. They are the means by which our attention is called to the need for inner change. When this inner change is made, the condition is automatically healed. We need to understand the principle involved rather than resist it. We must learn to cooperate with the condition so that we can learn the lesson it is trying to teach us. There is always one.

Nothing "just happens" by itself. There is a cause for every effect. Physical illness, especially functional disorders, are a projection of something in the consciousness. The outer irregularity is nature's way of indicating the necessity for inner change.

All too often we stubbornly and blindly ignore these warnings, refusing to heed their message and learn their lessons. We seem to prefer to endure our pains and struggles.

I knew the principle, but I was failing to apply it in this situation with my knee. I was fighting the problem rather than learning how to solve it. Problems are outer; answers come from within. *Never try to solve a problem on the level of the problem;* problems cease to exist when we find the solution to them.

As I analyzed my difficulty, I saw clearly that my knee was a direct projection of resistance, pressure and wrong direction in my approach to my work. I needed a reorientation of consciousness. A sensible analysis of mental and emotional factors for the purpose of reaching understanding, followed by prayer treatment, is the only way this can be done. Either analysis or prayer are insufficient by themselves. They must be combined in scientific prayer therapy—prayer treatment based upon psychological and spiritual understanding.

I came to understand my problem clearly, and as I took time to understand the underlying cause, I knew the condition would be healed. Metaphysically, the leg represents the capacity to move forward, and the knee represents the capacity to turn freely in any direction. The physical expression corresponds to the mental and spiritual capacity. Spiritual mind treatment works on this level.

Mrs. Curtis and I treated together one morning, and as I hurried on to a rehearsal she promised to do some additional prayer work for me later in the day. She did, with remarkable results.

That afternoon during a radio rehearsal I suddenly felt a great surge of warmth and energy through my body and a deep sense of relaxation and well-being swept over me. All pain disappeared from my knee, my leg straightened out, the stiffness disappeared, and I walked without a limp for the first time in months. I was completely healed.

In reporting the healing to Mrs. Curtis later, we found that it occurred at the exact time that she had been experiencing an intense inner spiritual realization during her treatment for me. She had spent the day in quiet and relaxed study and meditation and had reached a high point of consciousness.

"It was as if I was on a different level entirely," described Mrs. Curtis. "A voice said, 'Are you afraid to go over?' 'Yes,' I said, 'but I want to.' Suddenly I passed into a larger dimension. Everything was peaceful, and beautiful and relaxed. I was in a realm of pure light and for the first time in my life I could see everything clearly. I understood more in that moment than I had understood in my whole life before. I knew I was myself, but I was more than myself. I seemed to be floating in space. I looked down and saw my body lying there, but I was free—the real me, was gloriously and completely free!

"After I became adjusted to my new state, I started to see the relationship between things. I could see why. Causes became clear. I was one with the earth, the sun, the moon, and the stars—the sky, and the sea, and I could see why they were as they were. I was one with God; neither time nor space had meaning—no measurement or dimension. I just knew that I was I, and that everything was wonderful and good."

Mrs. Curtis went on to explain that while she was in this state she was able to see inside of things, and that she perceived the nature of the condition in my knee. She saw what appeared to be an ugly swollen worm, twisted and inflamed, when suddenly she realized that she was really seeing an embolism that had developed in my knee. In her state of heightened consciousness, Mrs. Curtis looked through the diseased condition and dwelt upon the idea of freedom, wholeness and perfection. As she was able to see the knee perfect, the picture of the knotted blood vessel disappeared, and Mrs. Curtis had a complete realization of healing. I have already described the results which took place in my body at the same time. Mrs. Curtis returned to normal consciousness, and remained for several hours in a state of drowsy revery, savoring the beautiful experience.

The Legacy of Spiritual Mind Healing

This experience made a vital impression upon me when it occurred several years ago, and it has continued to influence me greatly. The experience had far greater significance than just the healing which I described, remarkable though that was, and continues to be. My knee was healed spiritually and a spiritual healing is always permanent. This type of healing is always accompanied by a change in the life of that individual. Many of the healing miracles of Jesus bear evidence to this. This experience and many others which are constantly taking place in my life and in the lives of those whom I am privileged to help have convinced me that the secret of happy, successful, effective living is one of learning how to cooperate with life instead of resisting it. This cooperation requires integration and coordination, the subjects of this chapter.

Use this approach while you are taking whatever outward steps may seem necessary at the time. Even if you are undergoing intensive medical therapy, assist the doctor with your own inner spiritual work. Everything works together in building the "whole man." As your inner realization grows, the change will come about, and eventually you will find no further need for outer means.

THE PRACTITIONER AND THE PATIENT

As I have been writing these pages I have been interrupted innumerable times by phone calls from people who need help. When we are in trouble or pain, all we actually need is to reach a realization that we have the strength and courage to overcome the difficulty. I endeavor, through love, understanding, and quiet words of explanation and encouragement, to focus the caller's mind upon strength, courage, and faith in the immediate availability of the Infinite Healing Presence. The fact that the person has called for help at all indicates receptivity and acceptance. With the removal of all personal resistance, we raise our consciousness to the realization that the Inner Power is working through natural means to correct the difficulty. Many people call each day for personal prayer treatment work, and hundreds more call our "Dial-a-Treatment" telephone where they hear a recorded prayer treatment. Many reports of healing demonstrations have come from this work, just as they do from my radio programs, which I always close with a prayer treatment.

The people who call a practitioner want to know that somewhere, someone is "knowing the truth" about them, focussing upon perfection and right action, no matter what the difficulty might be. It doesn't matter who is knowing this truth—you or your practitioner—the subjective Power of the Universe acts upon it just the same. The Law is no respecter of persons. It only knows how to create, and its natural action is to create good. That is why your constructive attitudes have the power to dissolve negative ones. That is why the practitioner's prayer treatment for you works as a healing action through you. It is almost as effective to have someone know good things about you as it is to know them about yourself. When you are receptive, you come to know subconsciously what the practitioner has realized about you in his prayer treatment. The healing power—the universal subjective mind—is common to all. It responds to subjective realization, and it doesn't matter who reaches the realization. This is the principle back of the practitioner-patient relationship. It is what Jesus was talking about when he said, "If two of you shall agree on earth as touching any thing that they shall ask, it shall be done for them of my Father which is in heaven." (Matt. 18:19)

When the mind changes, the conditions change. This can happen instantaneously, but since our minds are usually heavily conditioned with negative causation, it is more likely to come about after a period of time spent in re-conditioning the subconscious mind. It also depends upon the willingness of the person to cooperate by dissolving the destructive attitudes of mind and adopting constructive ones. We have to give in order to get. This is a basic law of life.

The first step is to believe in the principle. The second step is to come to a realization, either by oneself or with the help of a practitioner, that the real self within you is whole and perfect, and that there is a natural creative law which is constantly working to manifest and maintain this wholeness and perfection in your body and in your entire world of affairs. No matter what your problem or illness may be, if you can identify yourself spiritually, mentally, and emotionally with wholeness and perfection, form a conviction that the process of healing is working through you, and reach the realization that your desired good is already a fact in your experience, it will manifest by a natural law of right action. But the realization must be complete. We can demonstrate only in terms of our total acceptance and conviction.

REALIZATION: THE GOAL OF TREATMENT

The practitioner is always working toward the realization of wholeness in the patient. As has been pointed out, realization may come as the result of a long period of constructive prayer treatment and the sustaining of constructive states of mind, or it may come instantaneously. Realization comes when the deeper mind accepts what the surface mind has been working upon. Sometimes this brings immediate results which are often spectacular. At other times the realization is indicated by a deep sense of peace.

As I have said, I am always working with a number of individuals. Many complete healings are achieved as the result of the change which has come about in these people through our work. We never know when the complete results will be achieved, but good always results from the application of the principles of scientific prayer treatment. The realization reached in the subjective mind is felt in both the practitioner and the patient.

In my own experience, the realization is always accompanied by a deep sense of peace, and is a complete acceptance of good. I was tossing sleeplessly one night in the grip of some tough problems and decisions. I had thought, I had prayed, I had meditated, and I had discussed them and sought advice. Still there was no answer. Finally, as I lay there exhausted but still sleepless in the approaching dawn, a voice spoke out softly and clearly in the dark room, "There is a Superior Power." That was all, but it was enough. I lay comforted and still as peace engulfed me. I knew then that everything was all right. The realization had come, and I sank into a deep sleep. The feeling was still with me when I awoke, and that day everything took a turn for the better and my problems were all solved. They must have been. I no longer have them.

Now, I am not implying that your realization will be accompanied by lights, shivers or voices. I just want to point out that it is possible to so bring yourself into focus with constructive inner forces that you will reach a realization of peace, perfection and right action.

A young lady was suffering from intense pain following the extraction of a wisdom tooth. Neither aspirin nor prayer had brought any relief. Finally, she sat bolt upright and exclaimed desperately, "God is all of me. I am part of God. There is no toothache in God, so there can't be any toothache in me. It is gone. I feel fine. Thank you, God! Amen." The pain disappeared instantly and it almost scared her to death.

She accepted it, however, and was able to go to sleep with no further difficulty. What happened? Realization, of course. It came in spite of her extreme doubts about the ability of prayer treatment to help anything. Previously, prayer had brought no noticeable results. She assumed that she would have pain, and she would just have to stick it out. Finally, her intense pain, however, caused her to blurt out her own affirmation. This brought realization as the result of the previous spiritual work that had been done, by her deep desire for relief, and by her acceptance that pain was not necessary.

When we stop believing in something, it is no longer true for us. When we start believing something better, this becomes true for us. It is a simple law of mental causation. Try it and you will see. This book shows you the way. The belief must be a complete one of conviction and acceptance, however, leading to total realization. The results will reflect directly on our mastery of the principle. Do not become discouraged. Keep at it; and results will be achieved. The process is one of building a strong faith. Never measure your present potential nor your future possibilities in terms of present conditions nor past performance. There is no limit to what can be overcome and what can be achieved if we act in faith. Not just blind faith, but a practical, working faith which is scientifically built by disciplining the mind constructively.

THE HEALING PRAYER

The restoration of normal health in a patient is not brought about through suggestion, mental coercion, hypnotism, religious hysteria, nor the imposition of the personal will of the practitioner upon the patient. It is brought about when the practitioner reaches a realization of wholeness and perfection and it is experienced mutually at the subconscious level through the experience of shared prayer. It is not a case of so-called "faith healing." Realization is the result of systematic steps taken through explanation and prayer to dissolve the negative mental and emotional attitudes which are causing the problem because they were blocking the natural expression of the inner perfection. Once these disease-producing attitudes are removed, the healing is automatic.

As I have continued in this work through the years I have learned to meet each case in terms of what is required to reach and sustain the realization of wholeness and perfection. Sometimes the results are instantaneous. Sometimes the realization is reached instantaneously but results only appear after it has been sustained over a long period. In many other instances the negative conditioning and the resistance are so stubborn, both in the patient and the practitioner, that the realization is only attained after a long period of education and reconditioning. In some cases the actual specific change, or healing, never appears. But there is always an improvement in the over-all life of the patient when systematic and sustained scientific mental and spiritual prayer treatment is engaged in. The ability to follow through with expectancy and faith is the main problem. We spend years building up negative causation through unhealthy mental, emotional and physical habits, and through a way of life which brings on tension, anxiety and nervousness. Then, we become discouraged if the prayer is seemingly not answered. As we have said, people often say in essence, "I don't want to be good. I just want to stop hurting." We can achieve lasting and worthwhile results only by continual prayer treatment. The follow-through is essential for attaining the good life—just as it is with your golf swing. Desperate and spasmodic intentions and efforts are not enough. Paul said, "Pray without ceasing." (I Thess. 5:17)—Sustain constructive patterns of living on every level which will make you a whole person.

I have learned to meet the problems of an individual on the level he can most readily accept. I explain what can be expected if we learn the laws of life on every level and live by them. These laws are all affirmative in nature. Negative or positive results come about by the way we apply these laws. No limit must be put on principle. If we fail to receive the desired results, the error lies in ourselves, not in the principle. Shakespeare said,

> "The fault, dear Brutus, is not in our stars,
> But in ourselves that we are underlings."

As I have said, prayer—the scientific application of principles of right living on every level, spiritually, mentally, emotionally and physically—always works. Sometimes it needs to be accompanied by medical or psychiatric assistance. In some cases there is a need for a pill as well as a prayer—if the person believes in the power of the pill more than in the power of the prayer. Sometimes the prescription of a sensible program of diet, rest and exercise must preclude anything else. At times counseling is needed. In our work we rule out nothing that will help move the person closer to the realization of his true self. It all depends upon what the person can accept. All roads lead up the mountain of realization. Some just take longer, that's all. Problems, trouble, trial-and-error, and the experience of suffering all develop realization eventually. We say, "Eventually, why not now?" The means are available if we will only use them. No matter what means we choose to realize our true selves, our attainment must eventually include an inner development of spirit and soul (mind and emotions—consciousness) which will result in the manifestation of the "whole man." That is why the system of personal development in this book is basic and unassailable. It is a way of life. Health, happiness, prosperity, and all good things of life are natural attributes of the "whole man" and do not constitute ends in themselves. Reach a realization of this and it will become true for you. Let nothing interfere with your acting on this plan right now. Once awakened, we will never again be content to remain asleep.

"Faith without works is dead," Paul said. (James 2:20) "Be ye doers of the word." (James 1:22) "Arise, take up thy bed and walk," (Mark 2:9) Jesus commanded, and the lame man was made whole. The man was healed not only because of the power in the Master, but because of the power in himself—and he used it. He, himself, had to do something about it before results were attained. Jesus and all great spiritual leaders have taught a gospel of action. Life is action. We'll never get anywhere sitting around waiting for something to happen. We must couple our inner desires and conviction with intelligently directed thoughts.

"Lazarus, come forth!" (John 11:43) Jesus commanded, and the dead man came to life. Jesus infused life into Lazarus, but it was Lazarus who walked out of the tomb. This story is symbolic of each one of us. Jesus represents the spiritual power of life, which raises each one of us out of death into life when we use it. The story is important not so much because this miracle may have occurred centuries ago, but because of its personal application to our lives today. It is the living dead that we are concerned with—ourselves—who need to wake up and live. We can arise from the dead when we recognize and release the life forces within us and put them to work.

WHAT IS TREATMENT?

Treatment is a technique of prayer—not a formula. Your treatment, whether for yourself or someone else, will be an expression of your consciousness at that moment. Build the power of your inner consciousness by thinking about these various definitions of treatment:

—Treatment is

1. the process of consciously selecting what we want to experience and directing the inner mind to produce it for us.
2. conditioning the mind along constructive patterns.
3. the journey in mind from where we are to where we want to be.
4. the process of becoming attuned to the Universal Mind.
5. the method by which we overcome the limitation of self, condition and experience, and think with a larger awareness.
6. the process of unifying ourselves with our ideal.
7. constructive creative thinking about our better selves.
8. a building process. The tool is the mind. The material is thought.
9. talking to God in language which we both can understand.
10. ordering our minds so a larger pattern of good can come through.
11. the process of remembering and knowing that the river of life flows through us.
12. the process of remembering and knowing that we are one with Universal Mind.

—*Treatment is*

13. changing from separation to unification.
14. identifying ourselves with Good.
15. conditioning our mind to new concepts for the purpose of enlarging experience.
16. the process of transmuting negativity into constructive, creative action.
17. the process of getting by becoming. The more we are, the more we receive.
18. the process of identifying ourselves with what we want to experience.
19. assisting the evolutionary process.
20. specializing the law of growth at a particular point for a particular purpose.
21. preparation for experience.
22. the process of making deposits into our spiritual bank account.
23. the key to the door of the gateway which leads to the Infinite.
24. the inner process of selecting and accepting experience.
25. the process of re-conditioning the inner mind so it can be used as a constructive instrument to produce what we want.
26. the process whereby we create a larger channel through which good may flow.
27. clearing the sludge from our minds.
28. the process of detaching ourselves from false beliefs and accepting true ones.
29. mentally dissolving the unwanted so that the good and the true can come through.
30. drilling for spiritual water.
31. the process of identifying ourselves with Life and Love.
32. the process of moving from a "have not" to a "have" consciousness.
33. the process of picking ourselves up and putting ourselves back together.
34. tying up our loose ends.
35. concentrating our spiritual thought power at a specific point within ourselves.
36. praying with a definite point of demonstration in mind.
37. scientific, controlled prayer.
38. having clearly in mind what we want and keeping the mind steady upon it until the creative process responds and produces it.
39. turning our back on what we don't want to experience and turning our face toward that which we do.
40. selling ourselves on an idea.

—Treatment is

41. the marriage of thought and feeling. Everything we think and feel is a treatment.
42. the process of activating the spiritual power within us.
43. attuning the consciousness of the individual to the true nature of the indwelling spirit which is God.
44. the process of listening to our own thought and either strengthening or correcting it.
45. the process of taking our life into the higher areas of mind and coming to terms with it.
46. a procedure for making inner contact and setting up lines of inner communication.
47. pulling the life into focus.
48. educating ourselves spiritually.
49. aligning ourselves with That which knows only perfection.
50. giving orders to the responsive part of our mind.
51. taking up domain in the ideal.
52. relaxing our concern with the smaller self and projecting the concept of the larger being which we really are.
53. piling up evidence of good.
54. a method of eliminating time, space and difficulty.
55. clearing our minds of mental and emotional debris.
56. the process of converting our mental and emotional liabilities into assets.
57. a process of spiritual education.
58. consciously linking ourselves with the process of evolution.
59. consciously perceiving the nature of God.
60. looking at ourselves and God from a new angle.
61. rounding out our spiritual concepts within ourselves.
62. the process of becoming more ourselves.
63. reversing the mind from error to truth.
64. the vehicle which lifts us from the level of the senses to a higher state of consciousness.
65. moving mentally from the problem level to the solution level.
66. the process of consciously developing faith.
67. the process of repeating truths until we believe them.
68. conditioning the consciousness to the greatest possible fulfillment.
69. using the power of spirit to get things in proper order.
70. the process of mentally, emotionally and spiritually dwelling on the solution rather than the problem.
71. an aid to contacting and utilizing Divine Power.

—*Treatment is*

72. the tool which unifies the individual mind with the One Mind.
73. the process of getting ourselves out of the way so that the greatest good can take place in our experience.
74. the process of cleansing the mind and letting the natural creative action flow through.
75. turning toward the inner light which is God.
76. the process of bringing about an inner change within ourselves.
77. the process of bringing ourselves into a state of conscious Oneness with God.
78. getting clearly in mind what we want, and accepting it mentally.
79. conditioning the mind along constructive channels.
80. cooperation with the Law of Increase.
81. the process of building an awareness of the presence of God.
82. the technique of going through the experience in mind and emotional response before we have the experience.
83. "laying up treasures in heaven."
84. specializing the Law of Growth.
85. the process of transcending ourselves.
86. bringing the conscious and the subconscious into focus.
87. ridding ourselves of impurity of thought, fear, doubt, suspicion, anxiety.
88. the process of formulating clear ideas and of turning them over to the subconscious to produce for you.
89. the means whereby we overcome the limitation of self, the limitation of condition, the limitation of circumstance, and live in the awareness of Truth.
90. the process of impressing thought forms upon the subconscious.
91. a way of changing.
92. a way of life.
93. a process of self therapy which combines psychological, spiritual and physical aspects of being to achieve a unity of the "whole man."
94. forgiving—"giving for."
95. knowledged prayer. (Prayer is the means by which we relate ourselves to the Infinite.)
96. the journey into inner space.
97. the establishment of agreement between the outer and the inner.
98. focus upon the wholeness and perfection of the situation.
99. flowing with the river of Life.
100. selling ourselves on a spiritual idea.

HOW TO GIVE A TREATMENT

It doesn't matter how much you read about treatment, you have to actually give one if you want it to work.

Follow these steps each day, morning and evening, and you will change your life:

1. Relax your mind and body. Become completely still. Free your mind.
2. Recognize the reality of the One Power. All things have One First Cause. Know It. Love It. Praise It. Worship It.
3. Identify yourself as an individual expression of the One Power. What is true of it is true of you. Accept this Power as the motivating force of your life.
4. Give thanks for everything. See this world as a wonderful place and your life as a wonderful experience.
5. Cleanse your mind of all fear and negation by affirming faith and all constructive states of mind. (See Chapter 2, p. 18.)
6. Deal with each problem or condition by dissolving the false belief which caused it. Get to the specific cause for each problem. Reverse your thought and align it with Truth.
7. Strengthen your contact with the Source of Inner Perfection. See and feel Divine Energy flowing into every part of your body and experience. Visualize wholeness. You are naturally healthy. Know it.
8. Place your treatment in the Creative Law, give thanks that it is already done, release it and let it happen.

A COMPLETE TREATMENT

Here are the way these steps unfold when you give an actual treatment:

I   "Quietly now, I relax and let the free full flow of life surge through my entire being. As I become perfectly still, I know that the power within me is good. As I cooperate with it, it is capable of producing all good things in my world. My mind is free and fertile as I experience the renewing relaxation of inner peace. I am ready for constructive experience.

II   "There is One Life, One Power, One Reality. 'The Lord Is One.' There is an Infinite Intelligence—One First Cause back of all things. This One is unconditioned, unlimited, uninterruptible and inexhaustible. God is the All-Good. I praise God from whom all blessings flow. I give thanks for this omniscient, omnipresent, omnipotent and omniactive Beingness which is the Source of all things.

III   "I am one with the One Power. There is no place where God leaves off and I begin. 'I and my Father are one.' (John 10:30) I am a spiritual being, made in the image and likeness of God. My soul is one with the Reality which is Good. My mind is one with the Infinite Intelligence. My heart beats in rhythm with the creative Law. My body is the form and use to which I put the physical elements of the cosmos. I am integrated and unified with all that is.

IV "I give thanks for the wonder and beauty which is everywhere. I give thanks for life and the privilege of living it. I am grateful for my divine heritage. I thrill to the experience of being a human being. This world is a wonderful place and I give thanks for its riches which are mine to use. I give thanks for the people with whom I share the joy of living. I give thanks for all experience. I give thanks for everything.

V " 'The Lord is my light and my salvation; whom shall I fear? The Lord is the strength of my life; of whom shall I be afraid?' (Psalm 27:1) I align myself with the creative action of the Infinite Law. I eliminate all unworthy thoughts and feelings, and I fill myself with constructive ideas and intentions. I dissolve all negation of every kind. I cleanse my mind of all confusion and blockage. I am an open channel through which right action takes place. I have confidence, conviction and faith that this is so.

VI "All problems disappear from my experience as I eliminate the emotional conflicts which caused them. Where the problem seems to be, God is already there. I have no problems; they are illusions—nothing trying to be something. I refuse to recognize or accept them. Problems are merely phases of experience. It is through experience that I grow. I give thanks for these opportunities to become the person I really am. I am free from all problems. I embody all the answers and solutions which lead to perfect order and right action and I express them now.

NOTE: Step VI is the body of your treatment. The first five steps are preparatory and the last two are the summary, conclusion and release. The specific scientific spiritual mind therapy is done in Step VI. Give major time and attention to this step. Analyze the nature of the symptom, and specify the cause and dissolve it. Study the table of correspondences in Chapter 2 to help you find the basis of physical ailments. Causes of other human problems are categorized in later chapters in the book. Be specific in your treatment; work upon each problem. Isolate each one and deal with it. Be definite in dissolving every mental or emotional conflict which could cause it. Keep at it until you reach a sense of peace and freedom and a conviction and realization of order and right action. In some cases, treatment work

must be done over a period of time so that your affirmative consciousness on this particular point overcomes the original negation and
disease. Keep at it. Continue your treatment work until you get results.
You are working with a principle. It cannot fail. It always works.
Sustain your faith and continue your work. Negative conditions always
disappear in the face of steady, consistent, constructive mental, emotional and spiritual treatment.

Every condition has a cause, whether you know it or not. In case
you cannot isolate the cause back of a particular difficulty, work to
dissolve it by affirming: "Anything unlike the nature of God is dissolved from my consciousness. As the cause is removed, the condition
disappears and I am whole, healthy and free." Expand this idea, and
also treat to know that the cause will be revealed to you. Treat regularly to know what you need to know and it will come to you. Then
deal with the information by dissolving it through continued treatment.

In this Step VI, the body of your treatment, you will deal with
several problems. Be specific about each one and do definite work on
each one in turn before going on to the concluding steps of your
over-all treatment. Here is specific Step VI work to deal with a cold:

"All confusion is dissolved from my consciousness. I am free from all
emotional upset and disturbance. The toxins of worry and temper are
cleansed from my consciousness and from my body. I cleanse myself of
all negation. There is no tension. There is only release. There is no fric-
tion. There is only ease, order and right action. There is no hostility or
hurt. There is only love and healing peace. As I change the chemistry of
my thought and feeling, a health-giving stream of spiritual light flows
into my body, cleansing and healing it completely. I am open, free and
pure on every level. I am completely healed now. And so it is."

Do you see how it is done? Deal with each problem individually
in this manner before going on to Step VII. You will deal with different problems as they arise. Do not try to deal with every problem you
have each time you give a treatment. Deal with what you need to
without pressure or effort. You can always come back to it another
time if necessary. But you will be amazed at how rapidly and completely your problems will disappear when you use regular spiritual
mind treatment not only as a therapy but as a way of life.

In addition to dealing with ailments and problems under Step VI,
you will want to allot adequate time to dealing with your desires,
goals, plans and objectives. Devote the major portion of Step VI to

this building work even though bothersome problems bid for your attention. Remember, you have the capacity to choose what you want to think about. Treatment is the process of consciously thinking about what you want to think about. Our problems only possess the power which we give them through our mental and emotional assent. In treatment we free ourselves from the tyranny of problems by focussing the mind upon the healing freedom of solutions and fulfilled objectives. Consistent mental and spiritual treatment work upon important thoughts, ideas and aims will move you steadily along toward accomplishment, and, at the same time, help to heal you of your problems and ailments. There is no limit to the good which comes from consistent constructive spiritual mind treatment. Just do it and you'll see.

Now we complete the final two steps of our basic treatment:

VII "Now that all seeming problems and desires have been dealt with, I am attuned to the constructive action which produces all good in and through me. Divine Energy is flowing into every part of my consciousness, my body, and my experience. I am free. I am whole. I see myself the way I really am. I am whole and perfect. I see and feel the healing action of the creative law through all things and in all places. Right action is taking place. I am made whole.

VIII "I give thanks that all of these things are done. I place my treatment in the Law of Creative Action. I accept it as an already accomplished fact in my experience. My mind is completely free from any further concern. I act as though these things are true because I know they really are. There is no further concern. I release this treatment completely and I let it happen. I give thanks that it is done. And so it is."

This is the structure for a basic treatment, which will take you about thirty minutes to give when you fully develop Step VI. This should be done night and morning in this form or some other which may develop as you progress in understanding, skill and facility. The actual words used, of course, will depend upon you. They must flow freely from your own consciousness. Treatment is a highly personal matter—the expression of your inner spiritual consciousness—so you must develop these techniques as you practice them regularly. My purpose in this book, and in my earlier book *Your Thoughts Can Change Your Life*, is to give the philosophy, techniques and structure to inspire you to adventure into this way of life yourself. It is not the only way, but it is a good way. Try it. It works.

Daily Guide To Integration and Coordination

I am a whole person. All difficulties are cleared away and I am in tune with the life force which flows through me. I am an integrated unit of expression. I am more than the sum total of all of my parts. I am a son of God, complete and perfect in every detail. This is my idea of myself and I do everything I can to make it come true.

The spirit within me blends everything into a unified whole. My mind, my emotions, my body and my experiences all work together to make me a complete being. I look through details as I form a clear and total picture of my whole self. There is no conflict between my will and my imagination. They work together as perfect team mates. I am an integrated point of power which penetrates and dissolves all error. I can do all things through the inner life which strengthens me. I am a well-knit unit of thought, feeling, spiritual awareness, material experience and physical action.

All parts work together to form the perfect whole. I flow with the tide. I take advantage of the great stream of creative action which is moving through me. I integrate, I cooperate, I coordinate with life. My life is my expression of the One Life. I coordinate myself with all that is good, true, noble and beautiful. I work easily and well because the life within me does the job through me. I bring everything into focus with the One Perfect Idea. I live to express the glory of God. I coordinate everything with this purpose.

Freely, peacefully and quietly I release all concern as I let go and let Life live itself through me. I do my very best to be what I am supposed to be and do what I am supposed to do. I am a completely integrated and coordinated person now. *And so it is.*

CHAPTER SEVEN

GOD HAS HAD HIS ARM AROUND YOU

FOR A LONG TIME

In *Hollywood* a few years ago there was an aspiring young actress whom we will call Jane Smith. She had been studying for a number of years and possessed an exceptional talent, and showed great promise. She had played minor parts in a number of motion pictures. She was a beautiful girl and had a pleasing personality but behind the beauty and the warmth was a great sadness and an almost brooding loneliness and preoccupation. She came to me for consultation one day and told me her story.

She was an unwed mother. The boy involved was weak and didn't want to assume his responsibility, so she had had to go through pregnancy, the baby's birth and the subsequent adoption procedures without any kind of emotional or family support. This had done two things; it had made her bitter but it had also built into her a great strength which she had now channeled into her career, and it was beginning to show results. However, back of it all was a great longing for the baby that she had given up. Even though she had renounced her rights to him, she wanted to see her child again just to know if he was all right. That is what she thought. After considerable discussion, however, we came to the conclusion that actually her motive wasn't to find out about her child as much as it was to gratify a longing within herself. We raised the question: "Is this fair?" Because any interference with the child at this point, six or seven years later, after he had become adjusted to his new home, would only serve to distract him and would disturb her further because she could have no lasting gratification about it. And, at the same time, it would greatly upset the foster parents. She saw this, and decided not to do anything about it, and I didn't see anything of Jane Smith for some time. Several months later, she came back and requested help on the same basic problem.

Things were not going well with Jane Smith; it was difficult to recognize her as the same girl. The outlines of her once beautiful face and body were still there, but only the shadow remained. It was as if the life had gone elsewhere. The sadness and air of brooding loneliness and preoccupation were intensified, and altogether Jane Smith exuded an atmosphere of being the unhappiest and most unhealthy person in the world. This comes very close to describing exactly what she was.

She reviewed the happenings of the months since I had seen her last. As we said, she had determined not to endeavor to see her child, but— and here is the focal point of our whole story—she had not given up the intense desire to do so. Her mother-love and longing gnawed at her day and night, waging incessant warfare with the better judgment of her rational mind. At one time she even went so far as to fly to Canada where the child lived with his foster parents, determined to see him no matter what the consequence. Anything to quiet the yearning inside her and find peace! However, her strong reasoning power and innate sense of fair-play gained the upper hand before she followed through with her plan, and she returned to Hollywood on the next plane without even leaving the airport.

However, the spectre of unrequited mother-love was still there, and Jane found herself on an emotional toboggan which was carrying her downhill with frightening speed. She was wretched in every way. Her career was at a standstill; she was content merely to exist. She no longer tried out for parts in pictures, but was content to take extra jobs which paid her only enough to exist. Until recently—when the doctor had stopped even this activity, saying, and quite rightly, that her state of health would not permit it. The diagnosis included: malnutrition, bleeding ulcers, anemia, complete loss of appetite, a deep cough— to mention only some of the ravages of the flesh which were obvious to even the most casual observer.

However, even though she was aware of the gravity of the various diagnoses, Jane had accepted no treatment of any kind. It was almost as if she was cooperating with the forces of destruction. As it turned out later this was exactly what was happening with her. She was cooperating with a death wish as a way to put an end to her intense emotional suffering, but the will-to-live, present in everyone of us, had brought her to my office seeking help.

Jane Smith was literally killing herself by letting an unresolved emotional conflict get out of hand. She was ridden with guilt and remorse for the actions which had led to illegitimate motherhood. Then she felt guilty and unworthy because she had given up her child. She felt bitterness and resentment toward the man who was too weak to marry her and accept his responsibility. With the passing of time Jane developed a persecution complex, which convinced her emotionally that her child had been unjustly taken from her by the adopting parents. It is all pretty straight-line once we start to unravel the situation, isn't it?

Now, in our Science of Mind practice we are not concerned with judging moral issues. We believe that a pretty safe position is the one the Great Teacher took when He said, "He that is without sin among you, let him first cast a stone at her." (John 8:7) That this young woman was wrong there is no doubt, but from the story I have told you we have seen that she was suffering horribly for her mistakes.

Remember the physical conditions which resulted—malnutrition, ulcers, profuse bleeding, anemia, and bronchial congestion and coughing. The life was running out of and being snuffed out of Jane Smith. The conditions named were only the physical evidence of the destructive mental and emotional states within this young mother. The ulcer was produced to carry out the assignment which the mind was giving. She had an intense but frustrated desire to be known as a mother, and developed an unbalanced condition in the reproductive system, which manifested as an irregular menstrual cycle. She was on the verge of weeping constantly, choked up with bitterness, remorse and resentment until this feeling reproduced itself physically in the respiratory system. As for the bleeding—blood represents life—and since her main purpose in life was being thwarted, Jane Smith was letting the life run out of her, so the body had responded by bleeding. This death-like pall of defeat and dejection carried into all phases of her life and was destroying the normal expressions of work and relationships with other people. Jobs had ceased, and she had cut off all friends, including the entire list of eligible men who had been seeking Jane's affection, one of whom had proposed several times.

As the explanation was made as to the relationship between her destructive unresolved inner emotional conflict, and the dire conditions in her life, the color started to flow back into Jane Smith's face, and she literally came back to life. She saw that she must dissolve all of the conditions at the point of cause. Her life, her career, her entire well-being were at stake. She made the decision to release the past completely. She had previously retained a detective agency to make a report on her son, and she knew that he was in wonderful hands so there was no longer any concern about him on this score.

With the help of Science of Mind prayer treatment, Jane was able to reach an inner acceptance of that which was for the best interests of everyone concerned. She forgave herself and others and so was freed from the killing burdens of guilt and resentment. In the larger awareness which prayer gives us Jane regained her intense love of life, and with it came the energy, the ambition, and the channels through which to express it.

This case chronicles the instantaneous healing power of treatment. Following her first session with the practitioner, the young lady ate a full meal and had a good night's sleep for the first time in several months. In the weeks that followed, all physical conditions were healed completely, and all other aspects of her life became ordered also. She renewed her interest in her career and today is well established as a television and motion picture actress.

As for her personal life, her great capacity for love and motherhood flowed into constructive channels as soon as her inner problem was resolved. Today Jane Smith is happily married to a fine man of solid background and position, who has provided the completing factor in a relationship which for both of these people is a forward step in their attainment of happiness and adjustment to life.

Jane Smith was healed of actual physical conditions and got her life in order through a change of consciousness. This change was brought about through treatment, or scientific prayer—prayer specifically designed to accomplish specific and definite results. Whether you are working for yourself or for someone else, the principle is exactly the same: the conscious mind is cleared, and definite thought patterns are impressed upon the subconscious, which works in cooperation with the universal creative power in bringing them into form. In Jane Smith's case, we replaced the feelings of sorrow, grief, guilt, frustration and loss with new attitudes of release, acceptance, forgiveness, expression and fulfillment. These new attitudes produced a new set of results. *This is true healing: exchanging separation for wholeness at the mental and emotional levels.* New causes produce new effects.

This book is about men and women who have built new lives by reconditioning their minds to accept affirmative ideas. That is what treatment is—reconditioning the mind to accept affirmative ideas. Chapter 6 was devoted to defining treatment and developing a master plan for general daily correction and conditioning of your subconscious. This is an extension of the system of personal help presented in *Your Thoughts Can Change Your Life*. That book and this have one simple and definite objective: *to develop a system whereby we can help ourselves through conscious conditioning of the mind and emotions.* The body of each book is taken up with specific techniques and how to apply them. There is no limit to the spiritual, mental and emotional tools available for us to use. Let's push forward in our quest of *how* to use them.

Your Thoughts Can Change Your Life was built around twelve basic mental and emotional attitudes essential to complete integration:

1. Relaxation	7. Identification
2. Expectation	8. Conviction
3. Recognition	9. Realization
4. Unification	10. Projection
5. Dedication	11. Action
6. Intention	12. Cooperation

From these twelve steps on the ladder of accomplishment was evolved the Circle of Completion and several other techniques of treatment, including: Visualization, Seven Aspects of Spirit, The Use of Light, Meditation, Contemplation, Alignment, Plus-Minus, Denials and Affirmations, Forgiveness, The Golden Bridge, Retrospection, Self-Emptying and God-Filling, The Triangle Technique, The Motion Picture Projection, The Spiritual Helicopter, The Power of Silence and others.

These are all essential tools in learning how to solve your problems through spiritual power. As I have said, this book is an extension and expansion of *Your Thoughts Can Change Your Life*, so they should be used as companions in your journey toward personal growth and perfected experience. Everyone agrees that spiritual power is the only power. Everyone asks, "How do I use it?" Everyone agrees that "more things are wrought through prayer than this world dreams of." Everyone asks, "How do I pray?" Everyone agrees that there is an answer to every problem. Everyone asks, "How do I find those answers?"

These two books deal with these questions of "How?" A forthcoming book will show how the ancient teachings of the Bible provide modern techniques for doing the same thing. But right now, let's explore the following additional treatment techniques, discover what they are, and learn how to use them:

I. CHARACTER VISUALIZATION

In Your Thoughts Can Change Your Life and in this book, I am presenting workable techniques. They are the fruit of many years of trying to do something about myself, and then in helping others.

One of the most common problems is dealing with the pressured situations of work and life in general. We often act in ways which are far removed from the Higher Self.

We need a definite technique to help us get back on the beam. Jesus said, "In the world ye shall have tribulation: but be of good cheer; I have overcome the world." (John 16:33)

A few years ago I found that I was letting my heavy daily responsibilities and work load get the better of me. I became irritable and short-tempered, and behaved in a manner most unbecoming to one in my position. Now, in this teaching, we don't say that we don't have problems. We do, however, insist that there is a way to deal with every problem, whatever it may be, and that we have a responsibility to do so. We learn through experience, and experience is the process of learning how to solve problems. The unforgivable sin is repeating the same mistake until it forms a pattern. When Charles Schwab first went to work for Andrew Carnegie, the old Scot counseled, "Make any mistake you want to, but don't make the same mistake twice." Life offers us the same leeway: Make your mistakes but don't continue to make them. Life deals harshly with those who refuse to change.

I decided that I'd better do some changing, so I got still inside and opened my mind for instruction and guidance. The question in my mind was, "How do I express my best self at all times under all situations?" Then I waited for the answer. It came in the form of three visitors, each one presenting a different aspect of myself.

The Seer

First came the visualization of the mountain which I told of in *Your Thoughts Can Change Your Life*. I climbed it, and found at its summit an ancient and venerable man with a peaceful, kindly visage and long-flowing white hair and beard. I sat at his feet, told him my troubles, and was filled with ineffable peace and contentment as he comforted me and assured me that all was well. As he faded from my inner vision his voice sounded a caressing blessing and his smile was a benediction of grace. Only then did I realize that I had been in the presence of my Master—the Ancient One who lives in the higher levels of consciousness of every one of us. The Seer, the Teacher, the Higher Self, the Christ within—the individualization of God which has always existed and will always exist. The Unchanging One—complete and perfect—That which you really are.

The Seer, of course, is a Master symbol, a projection from the inner realms of Spirit—pure Truth, but nevertheless available as tangible fact. This is the Guardian Angel who hovers over you. You are this Great Being, projected into form and experience. He is responsible for you, but you are responsible to Him; because He is powerless to appear in and through you unless you maintain yourself in receptivity and awareness for His coming. You may see Him, you may hear Him—listen and He will speak to you:

"Speak to Him thou for He hears, and
    Spirit with Spirit can meet—
Closer is He than breathing, and nearer
    than hands and feet."

Tennyson, "The Higher Pantheism" (1869)

At other times you may just be aware of His presence. However it may happen, just know that He is there, whether you are consciously aware of Him or not. He is the Source of your inspiration. He is the Power which accomplishes all things in and through you. He is the Lord. Love Him and serve Him.

In times of stress or crises, let go of your little self and let this Great Self take over. It will heal you, refresh you and straighten you out. Visualize this bright and shining Personage, and let It's Presence transform and heal you. Visit with Him regularly. He'll never turn you away.

You at Your Best

I sat in silent reverie, gloriously free in the memory and feeling of this transcendent experience. Into this atmosphere my second visitor arrived. I recognized him immediately. He looked as I would like to look—as I try to be, but never quite achieve. Crisp, fresh, well-groomed and efficient was he, but kind, gentle and unhurried even in the midst of tremendous activity. He was seated at a large desk. Telephones were ringing, people were coming in and out of the office, he was writing, dictating, broadcasting, making plans and giving orders; in fact, all of the things I do during the course of a busy day. My friend, however, did everything perfectly, while many of my efforts fall woefully short. My visitor never lost his temper nor raised his voice. He was a model of proper behavior. I admired him. I loved him. I decided to emulate him. I made him my model.

This visitor, of course, was another aspect of myself—the worldly human in proper balanced relationship to himself and to his environment, well-integrated and perfectly expressing the True Self through a variety of experience. This vision allowed me to see how I should be —how *I could be if I applied myself.* This "best self" could not have appeared unless it was really there all of the time, any more than the Seer could. These Master Patterns are deeply buried in the subconscious and work as cause when we cooperate with them. We become consciously aware of them through techniques of treatment and meditation, and sustaining the constructive attitudes we are talking about in this book.

It is easier for me to visualize myself the way I want to be and to behave the way I want to behave when I keep the perfect model before me, and it will be easier for you. We will still fall far short of perfection, but we will be moving in the right direction when we try to express the potential of perfection within us, symbolized by these two friends. The Seer is God in you. The second visitor—the better self— is God's idea of you in expression. When you become aware of the strength of this inner potential, you project a new cause; outer conditions, circumstances and experiences change accordingly. We are always projecting a perfect picture of ourselves the way we are at that particular moment. Be sure that you keep yourself the way you *really* are. *Keep always within you and before you the image of that which* you want to be. These three "characters" will do the job for you. Here is the third one:

The Pixie

This character didn't arrive during the meditation where I met the other two. He came along later, at a time when I most needed him.

One day as I was toiling wearily at my desk, bogged down in a mass of details, and taking myself very, very seriously, I paused and leaned back in my chair pondering the situation and wishing I were somewhere else—anywhere. Did you ever have the feeling? I guess we all have.

The question is, what to do about it. As I sat there longing for my particular slow boat to China, I became aware of something on my shoulder and tickling my ear. I turned my head slightly and saw a most remarkable personage—an elfin creature of tiny stature, with a beaming face and a tinkling laugh. He was a kind of a boy, but when his eye caught mine for an instant, I glimpsed a depth which carried me straight into eternity, but just for an instant. There was more immediate business at hand!

"Hey! Chase me!" my visitor commanded as he danced merrily up and down my shoulder and executed a perfect slide down the arm of my chair. "Come on, sobersides. Chase me!"

"What—who are—where—" I mumbled, completely amazed and baffled, but captivated by this fey creature.

"Chase me, you dolt! Come on get going! Anybody would think you were chained to that desk. The way you're carrying on you might as well be—and believe me, you will be unless you learn how to chase me." And he jumped up on my desk, grabbed a pile of manuscript and scattered it all over the room as he flew through the air with the greatest of ease and started swinging joyously from the drapes. His whoops of laughter filled the room, and serious as I had been, I couldn't help but join in the fun.

I started to chase him, just as he commanded. First my laughter joined his. Then I followed him around the room, trying to emulate his ridiculous capers as he danced and cavorted. Together we turned my stately office into a three-ring circus—and a shambles. At one point I stooped to retrieve some pages of my precious manuscript, but the elf came dashing from nowhere and executed a perfect place kick into the waste basket.

"Hey you, that's a chapter for my book!" I remonstrated.

"Leave it there," he commanded, with unusual authority for one so tiny and gay. "Take my word for it. That's where it belongs. Who wants to read anything that came out of you the way you were this afternoon? You were so dull and serious that they'd fall asleep out of sheer boredom before they had read half a page."

"Well—" I groped uncertainly. I tended to agree with him. I had lost my spark, and writing had become a real effort. I stopped to ponder my sad fate, and forgot all about my fantastic visitor. But he was still there.

"Hey, rain-in-the-face! Don't you laugh anymore? Look at your forehead. Do you really want all of those wrinkles? And the chickens could roost on that lower lip of yours!" He practically collapsed in a paroxysm of laughter, but I was in no mood for his tomfoolery. I was an important man! I had big things to do. I had to save the world!

I moved ponderously to one of the bookcases which line my study and searched intently for a volume. As I pored over it, it suddenly was knocked from my hands and fell to the floor. As I stooped to pick it up you-know-who tweeked my nose and said, "Let it lie! What do you want to read that dusty old junk for? Chase me for awhile, and then write a better one! Come on—chase me!"

Suddenly I got the point. Chasing my pixie became the most important thing I had to do. I took off my coat, loosened my tie, removed my shoes, and really relaxed. I opened the windows wide, took some deep breathing exercises, stretched, did some push-ups, stood on my head against the wall for a few minutes, turned on some music and executed a dance step or two, switched to the ball game for a few minutes, and finally lay down flat on the floor and laughed until the tears ran down my cheeks.

"That's it. That's the way to chase me!" There was my Lilliputian friend standing on my chest and beaming with satisfaction. "Keep it up! Maybe you'll amount to something yet. So long slow-poke! Don't take any wooden nickels. See you later, alligator!" And he was gone, with the ring of his laughter still in my ears, as I fell into a deep sleep.

When I awakened I lay there thinking about the little man who had come to brighten my afternoon. Who was he? Where had he come from? What did he want? Funny fellow. Reminded me of someone I once knew. Who was it? Then all of a sudden I knew. It was I, of course. Who else?

And it is you. How long since you have laughed? How about letting your pixie take over for awhile? It's quite an experience, and most rewarding.

Did I really see the pixie or was it a dream? Who cares? I don't. Do you? All I know is that the pixie is an important part of myself, just as the Seer and the well-integrated and efficient man who were my first two visitors. Each of them is there all of the time, just waiting to help. Neither one is more important than the other. They are different aspects of our natures. Develop each one of them. Take time to know them. They are archetypes—inner invisible forms, waiting to be projected into your world. They represent the trinity of spirit, mind and body. They represent wisdom, knowledge and joy. They are potentiality, initiative and action.

You are quite a person, did you know that? Shakespeare said,

> "All the world's a stage,
> And all the men and women merely players . . .
> And one man in his time plays many parts,
> His acts being seven ages."

(*As You Like It*, Act II, Scene 7)

Start with the three characters with whom we have just visited. Play each part to the hilt. Visualize and develop them. You will be a balanced, happy and well integrated individual when you do.

You see, these aspects of our natures have been provided for us as part of our standard equipment. Jesus said, "The Father knows what things you have need of before you ask." Live your life fully. Develop your capacities and keep an expectant, positive and joyous attitude. Never despair. As an early teacher of mine once said, "Remember, God has had His arm around you for a long time and He isn't going to take it away now." Use these techniques as working tools to help you constantly remember this truth.

II. COOL, CLEAR, WATER

Learn to visualize in treatment; see what you want to see instead of seeing the imperfect condition which exists. Your troubled and worried mind could be compared to a stagnant pool in which the water has backed up and stopped circulating. In your treatment visualize cool, clear water flowing in and purifying the polluted pool. Taste the freshness and sweetness of the water. Let the healing flow cleanse and heal you internally and externally, and let it wash clean any troubled situation which may confront you. Clean water symbolizes the spiritual action of your own mind.

III. WARM INTERNAL AND EXTERNAL BATH

"Your conversions don't last," someone criticized Billy Sunday, the sensational evangelist.

"Neither does a bath," he retorted, "but it doesn't hurt you to take one once in awhile."

A treatment can be thought of as a warm internal and external bath. Wash yourself clean inside and out. Mentally dissolve all of the tarnished thoughts, feelings and attitudes that are sullying your consciousness. Remove all blockages and obstructions. Flush the congestion and confusion out of your system. Whip up a good suds and lather away the dirt and tarnish which obscures the real you. Take a bath of pure spirit and all your sins (mistakes) will be washed away.

IV. REVERSING THOUGHT

Treatment is a matter of turning your thought from negative to positive—from destructive to constructive. This often entails a complete reversal of the creative flow within you as you re-channel the healing energy.

Sometimes we feel like a snowball rolling downhill, accelerating and accumulating at each turn. The negative consciousness gets bigger and bigger and we are headed toward sure destruction at the bottom of the hill. Now—move in, slow down the destructive pace and stop the snowball. Then roll it, push it, or carry it back up to the top of the hill. Visualize this and it will help you reverse your thoughts.

Or, imagine that you are a skier. You sailed down the run all right, but now you seem unable to get back up the slope. Note that there is a ski-lift running to the top. Reach up, grab hold and let this constant running power carry you along to the hill-top. Treatment is a matter of getting ahold of yourself and using the power within you for constructive purposes.

V. MENTAL SURGERY

This can be one of your most effective methods of visual treatment. Remember, treatment entails using the conscious mind to strengthen your specific subconscious convictions or pictures of good.

In this method, your conscious mind is the surgeon, complete with scalpel, scissors and sutures. You are operating on your inner consciousness to remove all the thoughts, attitudes, feelings, convictions, prejudices, hurts, and other falsities which do not belong there. Be definite and specific. Make actual incisions. Cut out the infected area. Get rid of the malignant growths of fear, hate, inferiority and guilt once and for all. Cut out the offending and dead tissue.

This is a drastic but most effective way of eliminating the inner causes which are producing your difficulties. Just as in physical surgery, you, the surgeon, do the cutting. God, the Great Physician, does the healing.

VI. CUTTING HEADS OFF THE SNAKES

Years ago, as a beginning student of the Science of Mind, I went to Dr. Ervin Seale, Minister of the Church of the Truth in New York City with a load of problems that would choke a cow. He counseled with me and treated for me over a period of months, but my problems continued, even though I was able to bear up under them with amazing strength.

"Why do these situations hang on?" I asked Dr. Seale after one particularly edifying session of treatment. "Why can't I get rid of them?"

"You are," he replied.

"Not so you could notice it," I retorted. "I've got problems everywhere."

"Those are just the snakes continuing to wiggle after their heads are cut off," Dr. Seale explained. "They'll die off as soon as you realize that and stop paying attention to them."

And, of course, he was right. The heads represent the causes, while the bodies of the snakes represent the outer symptoms. Get rid of the causes (negative mental and emotional attitudes) and the effects die out automatically.

Treatment is often a matter of going down into the snake pit of your own subconscious and performing this task of decapitation. Nobody likes snakes; nobody likes problems. But don't be afraid of them. Many ferocious looking snakes are really completely harmless. We frighten ourselves by looking at them. They can't hurt you, and actually do a lot of good in helping to maintain balance in nature. The same with problems. They are really helpful in the process of growth, but when they have served their purpose it is time to get rid of them. Jump into the snake pit, snip off their heads, and go on about your business with no concern about the fact that they may continue to wiggle around for awhile. Nothing can live without a head—even you and I. Let's use ours.

VII. PULLING WEEDS

The minds of some people are a vast unweeded garden that is going to seed. Overgrown with unproductive weeds and clogged with underbrush, they are in need of a thorough trimming. Learn to weed your mental and emotional garden. Actually pull out the weeds which are using up your creative soil. It is necessary to do a complete job of it or they will grow again. It isn't enough just to cut off the tops, you must pull out every bit of the roots too.

Visualize a great big pig-weed. Sometimes their roots go to a depth of several feet and have a number of branches. This is just the same as the weeds of prejudice, doubt, fear, guilt, suspicion and all the rest which take root in our subconscious minds. It isn't enough just to get rid of the thoughts and actions (the bush), we must get rid of the subconscious feelings and reactions (the roots).

So keep digging and get rid of everything which doesn't belong there. Pull out the stubborn roots. If they break off, go after the pieces. If you can't dislodge the roots, use the weed-killer of treatment and prayer, developing wisdom, understanding and awareness until they are all gone, just as you would pour a chemical weed killer on some unwanted vegetation.

A surface job is not enough either in weeding your garden or your consciousness. Did you ever try to get rid of a patch of crab-grass or devil-grass? The main growth is a network of roots beneath the surface. Unless they are killed individually, the grass will grow again. The same with your mind and the weeds that grow in it. Every live root produces some kind of plant. Every thought and feeling is a cause which produces some kind of an effect.

VIII. PLANTING YOUR GARDEN

Everything grows in good soil. The whole point is to have the kind of garden we want by selecting the proper seeds, planting them and then doing a good job of cultivation, watering and fertilizing.

Now let us imagine that having pulled the weeds and cleaned out the underbrush of our consciousness, we have turned over the soil, and properly mulched it and prepared it for seeding. Having carefully selected the seeds or seedlings (thoughts, ideas, feelings, goals, desires, objectives), prepare the rows and firmly press the seeds into the ground. Cover them over, work out the proper program of fertilizing and watering, keep up with the required weeding and cultivation, and let them grow. Nature does the job. We merely select and cooperate. We trust nature as it brings the seeds to plant and then to harvest. Trust it to do the same with the garden of your life.

If you want the seeds to grow in your garden, you must leave them alone after they are planted so that they may take root and grow. The same thing is true with your thought and idea seeds. Carefully select them and plant them deep in the creative soil of your subconscious through desire, intention, visualization and imagination. Warm them, moisten them, and help them with your praise, expectancy, blessing and thanksgiving. But then forget about them and let them grow. Just keep the weeds down and the soil in good shape and your seed will grow. A seed knows more about how to be a plant than you do. An idea knows exactly how to become a tangible fact. Cooperate with your ideas, and let them grow. Survey the garden of your consciousness and know that "the fields are white already unto the harvest."

IX. FOCUSING

Focus your attention upon the idea which you wish to bring to completion. Concentrate your energies and your activities upon your objective. There is nothing so powerful as singleness of purpose. "Concentrate" means "to bring to the center."

You can start a fire with an ordinary reading glass by focusing the sun's rays upon a specific point. You can do the same thing with your mind. Focus your thoughts and feelings together upon a single objective and they will have the impact of a rifle bullet scoring a bull's eye. However, if your thinking is loose and disorganized it will be like spent shot falling harmlessly around the target instead of hitting it.

The power of focusing is illustrated by the various adjustments on the nozzle of the hose with which you water your lawn. The fine spray gently covers a wide area, but if you want force, you turn on the single stream. It is all a matter of focus.

Try an experiment. Take a single sheet of paper and stand it on end. It is not strong enough to support anything. Roll it up and it will support many times its own weight. Focus.

Gather your thoughts and feeling together and visualize the power flowing into the area that needs to be healed, into the idea that you want to demonstrate, or into the situation that needs to be changed. You must get results when you focus your powers upon a single objective.

X. RINGS OF PROTECTION

Visualize yourself in the center of a number of concentric rings which you have drawn around yourself as a kind of spiritual armor. You may visualize any number of rings, but we will start with ten: Life, Love, Truth, Faith, Joy, Wisdom, Peace, Unity, Guidance and Protection. These emanate from your consciousness and are expressions of your positive spiritual nature. You express yourself through these good qualities. They form you as an individual and maintain you in balanced expression. These rings of spiritual armor form an impenetrable screen through which no evil may pass, but through which all good things may filter through to you. Keep these ten qualities and all other positive attitudes in good repair and "surely goodness and mercy shall follow you all the days of your life." (Psalm 23)

The person who is filled with faith, strength, and a sense of divine protection will emerge unscathed from the fiercest battle. But the one who is filled with apprehension, dread and fear will probably be destroyed—from the negative forces within himself. Nothing can hurt us if we refuse it the power to do so. "Perfect love casteth out fear." (I John 4:18)

Daily Guide to Guidance and Protection

I am divinely guided and protected today. Nothing can hurt me or cause me to deviate from my true course. I know who I am, why I am here and where I am going. My life has purpose and meaning. I am here to live, and I determine to express myself fully and magnificently.

I am free from all fear; I have a strong and vital faith. My faith makes me whole. There is nothing I cannot do—nothing I cannot be—when I set a true course and follow it. I set this course today. I follow the Star of the East as it leads me over the desert places of life to the place where understanding and wisdom are born in the manger of my own consciousness. I bow down and worship with childlike simplicity and purity the perfect life which God has given me. I bring gifts of love, dedication and service to the Christ child—the Higher Self within me.

"Yea, though I walk through the valley of the shadow of death, I will fear no evil: for thou art with me; thy rod and thy staff they comfort me." (Psalm 23) I am never alone. The Presence and the Power within me know what things I have need of before I ask. The Infinite Intelligence needs me through which to express. Nature wants me to be a success. God wants me to reach my destination safely. Everyone is on my side. Everything is in my favor. I attune my mind and heart to accept this truth.

"If God be with me, who therefore can be against me?" I put on my spiritual armor and go forth into life. Divine Mind tells me where to go and what to do, and takes care of me every step of the way. I am free in my inner conviction that I am divinely guided and protected now and always. *And so it is.*

CHAPTER EIGHT

YOUR MAGNIFICENT POTENTIAL

Does treatment work? Does it actually get results? Does it really help? Can I do it myself?

These are legitimate questions. I have given examples of the results obtained by people I have treated. The following quotations are the statements from people who have learned to use scientific prayer treatment as a means of dealing with their own problems:

TREATMENTS FOR HEALTH

"The first treatment I used when first coming into Science of Mind was for my eyes. It took me over a year to come to the realization that I had no need for glasses. I had worn glasses for twenty-five years. I took my last driver's license without them, which I had been unable to do before. I know it was my treatments that did it. I still thank God for this realization." v.g.

"Three years ago I had to undergo a minor operation and I started treating myself as soon as I knew of it. I came through this operation without a bit of pain and no sickness whatever. Why I tell of this certain treatment is because I had the same kind of operation in 1940 and suffered with terrific pain and was sick in bed for two weeks unable to eat anything. This time I was home in two days doing my work, with no sign that I had had this operation and feeling like a million. I treated myself just before going into the operating room and my realization of perfection was immediate." v.g.

"One evening, while cooking, I inadvertently placed my open hand on the sizzling griddle as I stooped to look into the oven. Normally my hand would have been severely burned and blistered. Recognizing that there could be no inharmony within the "Body of God," and that my hand was some part of this Body, I accepted that the harmonious, peaceful action of God as Intelligent Life was operating within the hand; that its substance, being perfect, was unharmed; that Spirit knows no pain therefore there could be no pain in my hand.

"Instantly the shock and pain vanished. There were no blisters. And the only evidence was a shiny seared look which lasted a few days." D.W.

"While on a hike in the mountains a friend slipped, injuring her ankle and leg. On account of the rapidity of the swelling it couldn't be determined as to whether the leg was broken, bones dislocated or simply a severe sprain. I felt that a doctor should be consulted, but the husband had gone so completely to pieces it was unthinkable that he should drive over the mountain roads then, and it was several days before they did make the trip.

"I did everything possible to ease and care for this friend from the physical approach, while at the same time I kept up treatment work for both of them. I specifically worked with the idea that the perfect pattern had in no manner been harmed. I worked to know that the Perfect Healing Power of Spirit was now active, restoring, renewing and adjusting every bone, every ligament, tendon, muscle, etc., in accordance to that protoype.

"Then the day before we returned to town, my friend moved on the bed and her ankle gave a loud pop. After this she was easier and some of the swelling went down.

"Later, the X-Ray showed that the tibia had been split lengthwise by the heel bone pushing up and wedging into it. The fibia also was broken. Yet now, at the time of the X-Ray, the heel bone had gone back into place allowing the tibia to spring back together. The break in the fibia also was perfectly lined up. The leg did not have to be set. A cast was put on and although the doctor expected that it would have to be worn at least two months, he removed it at the end of six weeks. The lighter cast which replaced the first heavy one also was taken off sooner than expected. The doctor remarked about her rapid progress as that form of break takes the longest to be healed." D.W.

"When I first began this work I treated myself, by the realization method, to rid myself of what everyone had termed "hay fever," or in my case, "rose fever." I simply knew, by the Grace of God, that any of God's creations as beautiful as a rose, could not cause me distress if I did not accept it. I have never had hay fever since." L.Y.

"I have treated away several colds and headaches for myself, and, in just the last two or three weeks, I have treated for cuts that would ordinarily take weeks to heal, which have healed in two or three days." L.Y.

"I am thankful for the faith in healing which I have come to feel, because of the healings of three of my grandchildren as the result of Science of Mind treatment.

"Penny, now almost fifteen and radiant with health was only five when she was undergoing medical treatment and being prepared in Children's Hopital for a heart operation. I treated for her and the rheumatic fever disappeared. There was no heart murmur.

"Kim at the age of sixteen months was stricken with encephalo-myelitis. On the twelfth day, still in a coma, she was brought home from Children's Hospital to die or to be hopelessly mentally retarded according to the doctor's verdict. Kim is nine now—with eyes that beam and indicate anything but a retarded mind. The doctors them-selves call this a miracle.

"Then there is Jan—she was only a few months old when one eve-ning even I thought she was dying. Standing over her bed I saw a miracle take place. When the doctor called in the morning to see if she had survived the night—she was up in her high chair as though nothing had ever happened.

"My sister's present good health can be attributed to the Science of Mind. Seven years ago she was a cancer patient. All tests have been negative for over six years, and I know they always will be." M.K.

TREATMENTS FOR BUSINESS

"I used treatment one time in my work as a real estate salesman. For some unknown reason the buyer and seller of a piece of property had a personality clash while going over the property. I could feel trouble was in the air so I just sat down and while they were arguing and walking over the property, I began to visualize them on friendly terms and in complete mutual agreement and then I affirmed, 'Mr. Jones and Mr. Smith are in complete harmony of agreement. They are both using the same source of knowledge and they understand each other perfectly.' It worked like magic and they were laughing when they approached me; then they parted in a friendly mood.

"On another occasion I was debating which stock to buy. I had several to choose from, but I knew I could not afford to make a mistake. I went to work on myself for guidance and a clear intuitive urge to buy a certain stock came over me. I did not hesitate; I called immediately and bought the greatest number of shares I could afford. We did not make a mistake.

"Another time a client requested a certain type of property he would like to buy. We had no property listed such as he described. I decided to drive around the area. Perhaps I would be likely to find the property he described. While driving slowly, I began to treat that there is a place for Mr. Wilson somewhere near to meet his requirements. I went to work asking farmers in the area, and the second stop did the job. Mr. Wilson found the ranch property that far surpassed his expectations and I made the sale." N.D.M.

TREATMENTS FOR RIGHT ACTION

"One Sunday night I gave a treatment for perfect activity for the next day. I treated in the morning in the same spirit, as it was a crucial day for me. The result was interesting in that nothing would work as I had hoped; everything blew up in my face. Nothing was right. However, as weeks went by the results turned out to be for the best after all, and I was judging from appearance again, and not in 'righteous judgment.' " J.F.

"I believe I have been quite successful in treating myself to come to a point of peace and contentment with my present living conditions; although I am not satisfied by any manner of means, and I know that when the time is right, or when I am right for it, the position I want will be waiting for me." L.Y.

"I have used treatment for general health and well-being. Through treatment I have been able to overcome fears and to come to a better understanding of how Truth works. My general health has improved and my outlook on life is up 100 per cent." A.M.

"Through treatment for prosperity and success I have received many wonderful blessings. My financial affairs have been worked out very successfully." A.M.

"The treatment to change conversation from negative to positive is a treatment that I have used any number of times and in almost every instance that I have used it, it has worked. The most startling time I did this, at least to me, was once when I was in a group of women and the conversation had turned to the Negro. There was one woman in the group that really got started on the subject and was becoming quite strong in her language in regard to Negroes. I had not taken part in the conversation or said one word, but silently I started to treat her for love. It seemed that I came to a realization almost immediately and she became quiet, turned and looked directly at me and said, "It was wrong of me to say these things and I suppose I will be punished for them." I didn't say a word and she turned and walked out of the room. What startled me most is that she is one of those persons who would rather die than admit she was wrong." V.G.

You can achieve similar results when you develop faith in the Power that heals, and learn to attune your mind to it. This book provides the basis for doing exactly that. Chapter 6 developed the background and approach of treatment. Chapter 7 developed ten special techniques of treatment. In this chapter we add several more. All of these methods, plus the ones in *Your Thoughts Can Change Your Life* give you a fine set of tools to use in handling your problems.

The following ten techniques complete the first ten listed in Chapter 7:

XI	The Golden Cone	XVI	Impressing a Pattern on the Deeper Mind
XII	The Matrix		
XIII	Superimpose and Dissolve	XVII	Your Spiritual Bank Account
XIV	Selection and Release	XVIII	Walking on Water
XV	Spiritual Solvent	XIX	Radiating Light
		XX	Practicing the Presence

We are now ready for Number XI:

XI. THE GOLDEN CONE

Visualize a cone of light emanating from an overhead light like this:

Bring your problems and troubles, one by one, into the pool of light and let the light dissolve them and transmute their energy into constructive channels. All problems disappear when brought into the light of spiritual understanding. Sit quietly under the Golden Cone and let its light shine upon you. Carry it with you and fit it over any problem or blockage that may confront you. The most difficult of situations will respond when placed in the light of the Golden Cone.

XII. THE MATRIX

There is a perfect pattern of all things in the One Mind. Since your mind is an individualization of the One Mind, these perfect patterns are also in your mind, and will demonstrate perfect results in your experience as long as you work in accord with them and refrain from interference or deviation.

For instance, there is a spiritual pattern of the perfect body. If your body is ill, it needs to be re-aligned with the matrix, or perfect inner pattern. Visualize the imperfection and distortion disappearing as you re-establish the perfect pattern. You may do this with any part of your body, or with any situation or circumstance which may arise. Perfect order, harmony and balance exist at the center of the universe. This perfection is normal for you. Know this and make your experience conform to it. Nothing short of this is good enough. "As above, so below." "In my Father's house are many mansions," all of them perfect and whole.

XIII. SUPERIMPOSE AND DISSOLVE

Motion pictures have developed many techniques to help tell a story. Frequently a picture will be superimposed over another to show what someone is thinking, or how things should be or could be, to indicate simultaneous action, or for some other reason.

Learn a lesson from the movies. If the picture you are projecting is not to your liking, mentally superimpose a new picture upon it. See the situation or the condition as it should be, and let this new image become a reality. As the desirable picture grows, the undesirable one will fade from the screen of your experience.

Other motion picture techniques are the "dissolve" and the "lap-dissolve." You will be looking at the screen, and the picture will fade out; the screen will go black for an instant to indicate the passage of time or the end of a sequence. This can be an effective mental exercise when you dislike the picture on your screen of life. Dissolve it, and let things remain dormant momentarily as you prepare yourself for a new picture.

In the "lap-dissolve" the old picture fades out at the same instant the new one emerges. For a moment, both pictures are showing on the screen, one superimposed upon the other. When using this technique of visual treatment, you are literally dissolving the picture of things the way they are while focusing the picture of things the way they should be. When the new picture fills the screen, the old picture fades away. It works. Try it. (Also, see "Motion Picture Projection," *Your Thoughts Can Change Your Life*, page 165.)

XIV. SELECTION AND RELEASE

Select what you want to see, hear, respond to, react to, or believe, and ignore those stimuli which could only harm or confuse you. Your job as a spiritual being is to keep your consciousness high and clear. Do not let it get dragged down into the mud and smog of mass thinking and worldly experience. "Judge not according to the appearance, but judge righteous judgment." (John 7:24)

Straight thinking is the key. This depends upon being able to discern between truth and error—between fact and reality. We are interested in truth and reality. For example, a person's body may be broken and diseased. This is a fact, but it is not the truth. The real person within the body is whole and perfect. This is the concept which your mind and imagination must accept and bring to reality. We choose our own experience by what we believe.

Sit, relax, and quietly examine yourself and your world of possessions and experience in the light of truth. Whenever you encounter what is not good or true, deny and reject it by saying, "This is not I." Be merciless and thorough in the weeding-out process. Get rid of the junk. It cannot be a part of your life if you refuse to accept it. Affirm, "This is not I"—until you arrive at the irreducible reality, the real you. Continue this scientific inner spiritual treatment until your thought and inner vision can perceive those areas where you can say, "This *is* I." Submit wholly to this conviction, and let it come to fulfillment in your experience.

Devote more time to the selection and affirmation of the truth about yourself than you did to the denial and rejection of false beliefs. Visualize, imagine and affirm that you are the healthy, happy, successful, vital and free person that you desire so earnestly to be. Build more stately mansions in your soul. All this is a matter of selectivity and release. Shakespeare said, "Assume a virtue, if you have it not." (*Hamlet*, Act III, Scene 4) William James said, "Act as though you were and you will be." All you have to do is to really believe something and it will come true. This is the principle of release.

XV. SPIRITUAL SOLVENT

Imagine that you are filling a pool or a bathtub with a marvelous fluid that can instantly dissolve the undesirable things, and cleanse and purify the treasures worth keeping. Call this liquid the spiritual solvent. Take a bath or swim in it and you will find your problems, pressures and fatigues washed away. Nothing except good can remain, for only the good can flourish. Immerse yourself regularly in the spiritual solvent and you will always emerge fresh and new.

You can throw your problems or troubles into the solvent and let them dissolve. Reject your cares and worries; throw them in, as you would clothes in a washtub. The spiritual solvent can handle greasy overalls or delicate lace with equal ease. Use the spiritual solvent, and be cleansed within and without.

After you have dissolved the unwanted attitudes and situations, you can use the spiritual solvent to brighten and freshen your thoughts, desires, goals and ambitions as well. Submerge them into the shimmering pool of spirit and they will be strengthened. Let them be electroplated with the action of spirit. Spirit contains everything necessary to bring your objectives into manifestation. Let them be coated with the garments of form by regular immersions in the pool of spirit.

XVI. IMPRESSING A PATTERN ON THE DEEPER MIND

Visualize the most perfect picture of yourself, and hold it firmly in mind until it is impressed upon the photographic plates of your deeper mind. Once this picture of perfection is stamped upon the subconscious, the creative power goes into operation to reproduce it in actual experience. Think of some of the deep impressions you had in early childhood and see how they have appeared in your experience.

People who live together over a long period begin to look alike. One woman I know was so closely identified with her mother that she not only looked like her, but acquired her mother's mannerisms and ailments. She contracted asthma just as her mother did. Long after she reached maturity, warts like her mother's appeared on her hand. People acquire the characteristics of their environment, working conditions and experience simply because the creative mind is amenable to suggestion. Automatically, the mind photographs that which it sees or visualizes. This is subconscious identification.

Use this phenomenon to your advantage, and choose the pattern of your experiences. Form pictures of goals already achieved, money at hand or on deposit, a beautiful home, a fine car, a better job—yourself as a better person. Visualization is an important step in demonstration for it activates the creative process. You must then cooperate by building conviction, sustaining consciousness, and cooperating with properly directed work and action. But, select what you want first and impress its pattern deeply upon your inner consciousness. (See "The Ladder of Accomplishment," *Your Thoughts Can Change Your Life*.)

XVII. YOUR SPIRITUAL BANK ACCOUNT

"Lay not up for yourselves treasures upon earth, where moth and rust doth corrupt, and where thieves break through and steal:

"But lay up for yourselves treasures in heaven, where neither moth nor rust doth corrupt, and where thieves do not break through nor steal:

"For where your treasure is, there will your heart be also," Jesus instructed. (Matt. 6:19-21)

Open an account in the universal creative bank of spirit. Everything good that you think, feel, say or do will be deposited to your credit. Every constructive thought, attitude and action is an asset. What is negative, worried or destructive is a withdrawal. Maintain a balance in your spiritual bank account by making regular deposits of constructive good. To the degree that you establish credit, you have all the resources of the Universe behind you in any project you undertake, because the Infinite always backs up its depositors with a never-ending supply and a constant flow of spiritual energy and power. All you must do is to maintain the balance through treatment, prayer, meditation, and sustained affirmative attitudes.

Store up pleasant experiences and impressions in your memory. Drink deeply of the beauties of Nature. Impress the beauty of the sea, the forests, the fields, and the mountains upon your inner mind as a reserve account to be drawn upon whenever it is needed for creative effort, corrective purposes or other constructive activities.

Our gross worth is infinite. "All that I have is thine." (Luke 15:31) Our net worth is determined by subtracting negative attitudes, wrong actions, prolonged mistakes, bad habits, and limited conditioning from this abundant supply. All of these destructive factors squander our wealth by needless dissipation.

Let us take account of ourselves, and review the statement of our spiritual finances. We all have more assets than we might imagine. No matter how diminished your bank balance, you can increase it by rapidly starting to use your resources constructively. When you live and work by spiritual principles, you not only utilize the spiritual energy of the universe wisely, but automatically redeposit it into your account. What a glorious system! Spiritual finance is amazing. You're richer than you think.

XVIII. WALKING ON WATER

One day, surrounded by a pack of troubles, I meditated upon the wholeness and perfection of the Inner Power. A deep sense of peace enveloped me and I revelled in the quietude and strength which filled my entire being. I actually became One with a power greater than myself and minor concerns were forgotten. I was being led "beside the still waters"; I was lying "down in green pastures." (Psalm 23)

I visualized myself walking beside a large body of water, rough and turbulent. As I recoiled from the angry tossing of the waves and was ready to run for shelter, my attention was drawn to the distant glow of a steady golden light. As I watched it in rapt fascination, rays of light extended in every direction. One beam reached me on the shore.

"Come to me," commanded a strong, vibrant voice from across the water. "Don't be afraid. Come!"

I was irresistibly drawn toward the light, and walked out over the waves on the beam that was extended to me. I was steady and strong as long as I kept my focus on the light. But whenever I let it waver and reacted to the wind and the waves below me, I became afraid and started to sink. The power of the light pulled me up, however, and I reached the golden island which the light had formed in the midst of my sea of troubles. From this firm base I gathered the strength to do whatever I needed.

This vision, of course, is symbolic and obviously parallels the Scriptural account of Peter walking on the water. My mystical experience was undoubtedly subconsciously suggested by this story. Whatever the explanation, it had a profound effect upon me, and can be of great value to you if you use "walking on the water" as a technique for overcoming troubles and difficulties.

The light, of course, is spiritual understanding. The voice which commands and bolsters your faith is that of your Higher Self. The beam of light upon which you walk to the island of spiritual realization is your faith, and will carry you over the turbulent waters of life as long as you believe.

Many people are engulfed in the sea of their problems and troubles. This need not be so. Practice walking over the turbulent waters of mind and emotion. You can do it.

XIX. RADIATING LIGHT

"Ye are the light of the world. A city that is set on a hill cannot be hid.

"Neither do men light a candle, and put it under a bushel, but on a candlestick; and it giveth light unto all that are in the house.

"Let your light so shine before men, that they may see your good works, and glorify your Father which is in heaven." (Matt. 5:14-16)

"The light of the body is the eye: if therefore thine eye be single, thy whole body shall be full of light." (Matt. 6:22)

"It is better to light one candle than to curse the darkness," says an ancient proverb.

As a boy on my father's ranch near Cheney, Washington, it was my job to ride out and bring in the cattle when I returned from school late in the afternoon. It would often be dark by the time I located them in the distant hills. As the darkness fell, the cold came quickly, and the eerie howl of coyotes would echo across the fields. It was a lonesome and frightening experience, and I often wished I had been born anything but a farmer's son.

But once I "rounded up the dogies" and headed home, everything would become all right. I would catch a glimpse of the light from the coal-oil lamp which my mother always placed in the kitchen window as soon as it became dark. From then on, all I needed to do was "come in on the beam." The light made all the difference.

Light is the visible evidence of energy—of spirit. We are this light in form and expression. Our intelligence determines the use of the light. Our mentality is competent to use and disperse it. Ideas and thoughts are the momentary pause of light as it circulates through our consciousness. A smile is our reaction to a momentary glimpse of light.

The light is within you. Let it shine forth. Visualize yourself as a point of light within the Great Light of the One Mind. Let the light of your thoughts, hopes, dreams, aspirations and inspirations radiate from you, lighting the way for all people on the path of life. Actually see the beams as they pierce the darkness. Send them out. Let the light shine.

Picture yourself as a great beacon. Your light is revolving, sweeping up the darkness as it goes. Your light can be seen for great distances, and does great good as it restores everything within its scope to order. Or, picture yourself as a bright light from which emanate expanding circles of light. Everything within these circles is healed and blessed. All problems are solved. All situations are righted. Let your light radiate without ceasing. Where there is light there can be no darkness.

XX. PRACTICING THE PRESENCE

The infinite presence of good—God—is all around us, flowing through us, healing, cleansing, and creating. Developing the conscious awareness of the Presence is one of the oldest spiritual disciplines known to man, and still one of the best. It is actually just a matter of enjoying the feeling of being one with God; revelling in the freedom and "peace that passeth all understanding." (See *Your Thoughts Can Change Your Life*, page 59).

Sit quietly in a relaxed manner, close your eyes, empty your mind of all conscious activity, and remain in a state of quiet meditation. Soon you will feel that you are part of Something much greater than you are. It is all of you; you are part of It. It loves you better than you love yourself. There is no place where this Great Presence leaves off and you begin. There is no separation between your life and the One Life which is the origin and source of all things. Blend with It; walk hand in hand with It; talk with It; love It; stay ever in Its Presence.

You will never be lost or afraid as long as you practice the Presence of God. Wherever you go, whatever you do, know that you are being guided and directed by the One Mind. The entire universe is present in every cell of substance, the infinite is expressed in every segment of space, and there is eternity in every hour.

"Whither shall I go from thy spirit? or whither shall I flee from thy presence? If I ascend up into heaven, thou are there: if I make my bed in hell, behold thou art there." (Psalm: 139:7, 8)

There is no place where God is not. "Yea, though I walk through the valley of the shadow of death, I will fear no evil: for thou art with me; thy rod and thy staff they comfort me." (Psalm 23:4)

This sustained feeling of faith, confidence and oneness is brought out in the following little piece which is one of my most popular radio talks:

"Talk It Over with the Boss"

"I had a talk with the Boss today. He was there waiting for me as if he had been expecting the interview all along. In fact, once I had spoken, he let me know that the principal part of his job consisted in being there whenever I wanted him. He told me further that he is always waiting to hear what I have to say, and that he would always answer me and give me what I want and believe. He also told me that if I couldn't arrange to speak with him personally, I could always send him a thought letter, and he would give his attention to it. However, he pointed out that with him, as with all business executives, personal contact was better, and action would be quicker and surer if we took time to talk things over.

"Today's talk wasn't the first one I have had with the Boss. We have been having executive meetings and just plain 'bull sessions' for some time now. As a matter of fact, once I got to know him, I found that these talks with the Boss every morning and evening were becoming the high points of my day. I never missed a meeting if I could help it, and the few times I couldn't make connections, I always tried to keep in constant touch with the Boss by sending those thought letters as he suggested. In this way, I have been able to maintain constant contact with him, and it is always a big help to me in carrying on the business of the firm.

"This schedule of morning and evening meetings, with a flow of correspondence in between, has produced such excellent results and my promotions have been so rapid that lately I have been dropping in for a chat with the Boss at almost any hour of the day or night. His door is always open and he seems glad to see me, always. Beginning with our first meeting, something tremendous has resulted from each session, and I have always felt that I was a better, more valuable member of the firm as a result.

"As I am writing this letter to the Boss and a large number of co-workers in the firm, I am sitting in the peaceful quiet of my study. The Boss is here with me, looking over my shoulder and up from the paper as the thoughts flow across it. We had a talk about this correspondence just a few minutes ago, and he said he was in favor of the idea. In fact, the Boss said he was personally interested in the project—had been for some time—and that he would see to it that it was handled and composed properly.

"Funny thing—after all this time of working closely with the Boss, I'm not at all sure I can describe him to you. But, at the same time, I must present him to you, because I want you to get to know him as I do. There are unlimited openings and opportunities with the firm, and I know that soon we will all be working together. I believe the best way I can describe the Boss is to tell you that you will know him when you see him. He is not a man, but he functions as man, and he is like all men. You've never seen anyone run a business the way he does. He seems to be everywhere at once. I'm proud to be associated with him.

"If you are contemplating a change, I know you will find a step in this direction the wisest you've ever taken. The best thing about working for the Boss is that you can become associated with the firm wherever you are. You don't have to make extensive plans or preparations; the Boss will handle all details for you. All you have to do is send him a thought letter and tell him you are ready. He'll let you know that he is interested, and will suggest that you have a talk with him. Don't worry about where or when. He'll take care of that, too. Just be sure you do talk to him, and tell him everything that's on your mind and in your heart.

"There are a number of us working here in the same office with the Boss. Most of us are doing the same work, but there's no conflict or interference, and everything we do seems to complement what the other fellow is doing. All of us have increasing numbers of occasions to talk with the Boss, and even though we all seem to talk to him at once, there is no confusion. We all have perfect confidence that he is hearing us and acting upon the words we speak to him. The Boss plays no favorites, yet we are all favored.

"There are more and more of the executive meetings and 'bull sessions' every day, and this method of operation has paid off in increased production. We are all constantly in touch with the Boss and with each other by thought, but when the chips are down—when there are decisions to be made and work to be done—we always talk it over with the Old Man directly.

"Now I've said it. We don't usually call him the 'Old Man' in public or when we are talking to him in person, but one day in the office he heard us calling him that when we didn't think he was listening. He didn't seem to mind! So since we are all working together now, I know it is all right to let you in on the secret. You understand that the 'Old Man' is just our every day nickname for the Boss. I don't really know how he prefers to be addressed. Sometimes we don't call him by name at all—we just talk to him or with him.

"We talk to the Boss aloud or silently, in offices or in churches, in airplanes or in subway trains, from mountaintops or from depths of coal mines, from the expanse of the prairies and deserts or from a raft in mid-ocean, in the ordered silence of our homes or amidst the cacophonous turmoil of a busy street. No matter where we are, we always speak from within and the Boss—the 'Father which seeth in secret'—always rewards us openly."

Meditation and contemplation will help you practice the Presence. Learn to develop and release your Magnificent Potential through their use:

Meditation

There are many techniques of meditation, all equally effective, depending upon who is meditating. Whole books have been written upon the subject, but it is up to you to find your own method. There is no right or wrong way. Meditation is simply the process of attuning your mind to the One Mind; of becoming aware of the larger scope of things; of occuping the mind with spiritual Truths; of discovering the inner meaning of all phenomena; of identifying oneself with the Real; of forgetting oneself in the greater glory which is God.

How you go about doing these things is up to you, but it is essential that you do them through some technique of meditation. Your growth as an individual and your state of well-being depend upon it. Some of my favorite techniques of meditation are given in my earlier book *Your Thoughts Can Change Your Life*. After studying this book thoroughly you will find this diagram useful as a guide for your meditation:

Contemplation

This term is often used to describe a highly concentrated form of meditation, but we will use it here to mean "seeing true"—using your power of spiritual perception to see things the way they really are rather than the way they seem to be. Learn the difference between a fact and the Truth. Jesus said, "Judge not according to the appearance, but judge righteous judgment." (John 7:24) Things are not always what they seem to be.

Look at every object, every person, and every situation with the intention of seeing the good that is there. Observe and learn from what you see. Let things tell you about themselves. Let problems and circumstances impart their lessons to you. Let every thing tell you its secret.

Ralph Waldo Emerson said, "Prayer is the contemplation of the facts of life from the highest point of view." Attune yourself to the inner Oneness through treatment, meditation and prayer, and then just look around you, letting your attention focus where it will. Pause awhile and you will be amazed by what you see.

AN ADVENTURE IN TOTAL EXPERIENCE

We become the thing we contemplate. In this chapter we are interested in unifying with the One Source of all things. When this is accomplished, we can easily specialize it to produce specific results. But until we recognize and unify with the One Source, we will have to struggle and produce only limited results. The secret of secrets—the key to the kingdom, the pearl of great price—is the ability to unify oneself with the One Complete Power. This Power is greater than the sum total of all existing things. It is the Universal Intelligence. It is yours to use, if you are interested, and if you are willing to undergo the necessary discipline to make it apply to yourself. This book shows the way.

Meditation and contemplation are unifying processes by which we unite with the One. Meditation is complete attention to any idea. We are interested here in the One Idea. Contemplation is a form of meditation whereby we observe and absorb the full meaning of specific objects which suggest deep underlying causes and meanings.

For example, as I write these words, I am in the desert, looking out of the window of my cabin westward toward Palm Springs, California, where Mount San Jacinto ordinarily towers majestically. Today, however, this inspiring peak is obscured by clouds which are emptying their precious cargo into the parched desert for the first rain in this area for many months. I am always inspired by mountains, and this one has been a source of inspiration on many trips to the desert over the years. Many dreams have been born out of the contemplation of its lofty slopes. It has lifted me above the mundane and trivial into a sense of Oneness with the Universal. Today is no exception. Even though the mountain itself is not visible, I know it is there. Even though the sky is obscured by heavy dark clouds, I know it is there. Even though the sun is blacked out this morning, I know it is there. And now, as I write this, there is a break-through. A bright blue eye winks at me as a patch of sky is glimpsed through a break in the clouds. At the same time, I see the very summit of the mountain, capped with the glory of the season's first snow, as the scudding clouds re-form themselves. And to make the picture complete, a shaft of sunlight breaks through, giving a cathedral effect through the clouds as it emblazons the face of the mountain. All this is happening as the rain continues to fall, the wind blows and the desert is thirstily drinking up the bounty from heaven. The air is washed clean, and the fresh smell of falling rain and drinking earth combine to complete the picture of total experience. I rush out into the midst of all this glory to revel in the total experience, and drink in the magnificence of God with every part of my being. I am one with air, water, light and earth. The elements are mixed in me and all of my senses—seeing, hearing, smelling, touching and tasting—are unified by my inner spiritual perceptions and responses, and I am one with God. I have sensed again the complete unification which I came to find. Nature has again refilled me and I am pregnant with ideas and creative joy as my pencil fairly flies over the paper and sheets of paper mount on the pile which will form this chapter.

I have just had a glimpse of total experience—just a glimpse, but enough to remind me that I am One with all the magnificence of Life. I am re-connected with the Source. I will never feel separated and lonely again, and neither will you as you open the portals of your higher awareness to total experience and integrate and coordinate your total being.

This book will change your life, just as its ideas have saved, rebuilt, and given meaning to mine. We can grow through pain, problems and perplexed experience. This is one way to God—the one that most of humanity follows. But there is a better way—the way of developing inner perfection and power through unfoldment and growth. May this book help you on your way.

Daily Guide to Unfoldment and Growth

I am unfolding and growing toward my true potential. I know that I am a son of God, and it does not yet appear what I shall be. I find myself within the great Self which is God. I am a human being, and I am becoming aware that I am a spiritual being. I am a creature of unlimited possibility. I am aware of my divine potentiality.

There is no limit to my capacity for knowing the Truth. I am capable of perceiving Reality. I can see the Light. I can hear the inner voice. I can experience God. The kingdom of Heaven is my native home. I am a spiritual being, in material form, going through human experiences, learning the necessary lessons for the purification and growth of my soul, and evolving toward the attainment of my Sonship. I place no limit on principle. I strive to be "perfect, even as my Father which is in heaven is perfect." (Matt. 5:48)

Nothing can hold me back. I am on my way. I have a long way to go, but I know that I will get there. Look how far I have come! I assist the natural process of evolution by endeavoring to travel the vertical path of enlightenment. I spiritually assist the evolutionary process of growth. I am a co-creator with God. I consciously create circumstances. I am never dormant. The spirit within me is vital and strong. My true self is ever moving toward complete expression and fulfillment. I grow until I attain full stature. I unfold into infinity.

I am aware of my destiny. I am never afraid. I move serenely into the future with deep faith and certain conviction that complete good is already at hand and I am experiencing it. I am completely identified with my Magnificent Potential. *And so it is.*

CHAPTER NINE

"I NEVER MET A MAN I DIDN'T LIKE"

Haying time was over, and we were celebrating the filling of our new barn. How big and red it was! And how comfortable it was for the sixteen big work horses that occupied the stalls. Everyone was proud and happy as the neighbors went home and we went to bed after the "barn-warming" party.

Sometime during the night we were awakened by the flashing of light and the crackle of flames. Running to the window with my father, I saw the entire roof of our new barn ablaze. With an anguished cry, my father ran toward the barn where the horses were neighing in fear as the flames enveloped them. Without hesitating, my father plunged into the inferno to release his beloved livestock. My mother and I, terrified, called after him but he was not to be deterred. He managed to release the ten horses on one side of the barn. As he staggered out after them, the flaming hayloft collapsed where he had been a second before, and the remainder of the horses were burned. It was as if we were in there with them. Those horses were members of our family. We loved them, and their dying neighs were terrifying.

But there was no time to spend grieving. The flames were threatening the farmhouse and the rest of the buildings. Action was needed. I ran nearly half a mile across the fields to my uncle's farm to get a garden hose to help fight the flames, and carried it back at a dead run. Everyone was doing his part. The rest of the farm was saved, but our hearts were heavy and our minds and bodies weary and spent as the dawn came up on the smoldering ashes.

The next day as we started to pick up the pieces, it was without the help of my father whose feet were so deeply burned he couldn't walk. And he hadn't even noticed the pain the night before! My job was to return the garden hose to my uncle's farm. To my amazement, I couldn't even lift it, yet the night before I had carried it nearly a half mile as fast as I could run!

Now what was it that strengthened us the night before? It was love which sent my father into the burning barn at the risk of his life, oblivious to the painful burns on his feet. It was love—complete, integrating, unifying and strengthening. Love was manifest on every level —instinctive, intuitive and active. Love is the one complete power. Love is life in action.

Love is more than just a word, even more than an attitude. Love is a way of life; an approach to living. Its first line of expression is on the personal level. Will Rogers stated his attitude toward life when he said, "I never met a man I didn't like."

How many of us can say the same? Why was Will Rogers able to love everybody when most of us have trouble in even getting along with ourselves? Perhaps that's the key: *To love others we must first love ourselves. To get along with others we must first get along with ourselves.*

THE HEALING POWER OF A GOOD DISPOSITION

Many of us have bad dispositions and unpleasant character traits which make it impossible for anyone to like us, ourselves included. Actually, a bad disposition results from personal dissatisfaction. When a person is at war with himself he is not going to get along very well with others. Nothing is more neglected nor more important than our dispositions. Your disposition is indicative of your attitude toward life; your disposition is your habitual adjustment to yourself and your surroundings.

There is no excuse for a bad disposition. It is simply a matter of bad manners. Many people with unpleasant dispositions hasten to justify themselves by saying, "I can't help it; that's just the way I am." They expect to be excused for the meanness and hurt which they inflict on others. But such expectations are most unfair. A typhoid carrier could actually be less of a health hazard to others than a person with a bad disposition. The cause of nearly every ailment or negative condition in the human experience can be traced to a faulty disposition.

Disposition problems are the result of breaking the law of love. The only way to get over a bad disposition is to develop a good one. It is impossible to become mature in mind and spirit without a good disposition. Every truly great person has a good disposition. If, by chance, you can think of one notable exception, ask yourself, "Would I trade places with him?" Of course not. A person may become famous—or infamous—but he can never rise above his own lowest level until he learns to conquer and control his own disposition. How is yours?

TWENTY TERRIBLE TYPES

Are you one of these easily recognizable types whom people avoid like the plague—and can you blame them? Here are twenty terrible types to start with:

1. The sour-puss	11. The party-pooper
2. The crank	12. The blow-hard
3. The hot-head	13. The sulker
4. The kill-joy	14. The itch
5. The wet-blanket	15. The door-slammer
6. The bulldozer	16. The bully
7. The scatter-brain	17. The cry-baby
8. The pill	18. The complainer
9. The "Scrooge"	19. The critic
10. The fuddy-duddy	20. The wheedler

Easy to recognize aren't they? "There's one in every office." Examine yourself carefully. If any of these shoes fit you, waste no time in throwing them out and getting something that is more becoming. It isn't hard to change if you really want to. Admit your faults and go to work on them. Bad traits of disposition are symptoms of inner conflict, unrest, and a desire to punish one's self. Find out what is "bugging" you, correct it, forgive yourself, form a new inner image, and you will project a more favorable outer picture. Your disposition is evidence of your own idea of yourself. No one can do a thing about it except you.

In reviewing a long-forgotten Broadway play, one critic evaluated my performance as follows: "To do a creditable job with the character he portrays, all Donald Curtis needs to do is to be born over again as nearly unlike himself as possible." This is often the minimum requirement in changing our dispositions—to be born over. Spiritually, mentally, and emotionally, that is. We are allowed to continue to operate in the same body. But here is a wonderful bonus to this business of dis-

position building: Your *health improves as your disposition improves.*
"A merry heart doeth good like a medicine: a broken spirit drieth the
bones." (Pr. 17:22) Don't worry about the body ailment. Let's get to
work on the disposition.

Where do we start? Where we are, of course. Go over the list of the
"Twenty Terrible Types" and decide which kind of "personality
halitosis" you have. Maybe your best friend won't tell you, but sooner
or later everyone else will, by staying away from you in crowds. If we
want to be happy, healthy and successful, we have no choice but to
change. A *pleasant disposition attracts; an unpleasant one repels.* Just
change characters. Go down the list and cast yourself as just the opposite of each of these types. Visualize yourself as pleasant, charming,
kind, gentle and well-mannered and then "act as though you were and
you will be."

Your disposition can be improved once you recognize your faults,
dissolve them, and develop their opposite. Self-improvement can be
realized through the technique of forgiving—"giving-for."

"These six things doth the Lord hate: yea, seven are an abomination
unto him:

1. A proud look
2. A lying tongue
3. Hands that shed innocent blood
4. A heart that deviseth wicked imaginations
5. Feet that be swift in running to mischief
6. A false witness that speaketh lies
7. He that soweth discord among brethren."

(Proverbs 6:16-19)

Disposition problems are not new, it seems. Let's get rid of ours.
Consider again Chapter 2 where we changed the thirty negative attitudes to affirmative ones by forgiving, "giving-for" the old negative
attitude a new constructive one. Use the same principle in changing
your disposition.

CHANGE YOUR DISPOSITION BY FORGIVING

If you have a bad disposition you will find it necessary to "give-for"
the undesirable traits in the first column, the desirable and pleasing
qualities in the second column:

Disposition Liabilities	"Give-For"	Disposition Assets
1. Irritation	⟶	Pleasantness
2. Complaining	⟶	Accepting
3. Criticizing	⟶	Approving
4. Grouchiness	⟶	Good Humor
5. Bad Manners	⟶	Good Manners
6. Thoughtlessness	⟶	Thoughtfulness
7. Edginess	⟶	Steadiness
8. Selfishness	⟶	Selflessness
9. Whining	⟶	Singing
10. Gruffness	⟶	Tenderness
11. Negative	⟶	Positive
12. Demanding	⟶	Understanding
13. Gloomy	⟶	Sunny
14. Cold	⟶	Warm
15. Distant	⟶	Intimate
16. Unchanging	⟶	Flexible
17. Undignified	⟶	Dignity
18. Uninterested	⟶	Interested
19. Cruel	⟶	Kind
20. Suspicious	⟶	Trusting
21. Cowardly	⟶	Brave
22. Mean	⟶	Exemplary
23. Explosive	⟶	Calm
24. Irascible	⟶	Dependable
25. Quarrelsome	⟶	Peace-loving
26. Unpredictable	⟶	Consistent
27. Stingy	⟶	Generous
28. Martyrdom	⟶	Realistic
29. Self-righteous	⟶	Understanding
30. Bullying	⟶	Friendly
31. Bellicose	⟶	Calm
32. Vicious	⟶	Gentle
33. Destructive	⟶	Constructive
34. Unhappy	⟶	Happy
35. Unfair	⟶	Fair
36. Unreasonable	⟶	Reasonable
37. Angry	⟶	Forgiving
38. Sarcasm	⟶	Praise
39. Superiority	⟶	Modesty
40. Stubbornness	⟶	Givingness

Disposition Liabilities	"Give-For"	Disposition Assets
41. Uncooperative	————————→	Cooperative
42. Cranky	————————→	Serenity
43. Touchy	————————→	Tranquility
44. Immaturity	————————→	Maturity
45. Self-Hatred	————————→	Self-Approval
46. Disagreeableness	————————→	Agreeableness
47. Envious	————————→	Generous
48. Jealous	————————→	Loving
49. Possessive	————————→	Confident
50. Boastful	————————→	Quiet

When you have finished your personality and disposition inventory and have dissolved all the undesirable traits in the first column by "giving-for" them their opposites in the second column, you will be well on your way toward being the kind of person you really want to be.

Overcome Your Irritations

In this sample treatment we give "Pleasantness" for "Irritation." The same technique can be successfully applied to every point on the list.

"All irritation is dissolved from my thoughts, my feelings, and my behavior as I immerse myself in the soothing pleasantness of love. I forgive myself for all unpleasant attitudes and actions. I give for them new and fresh viewpoints and deeds. I am spiritually, mentally and emotionally reborn. I am a new person. I am understanding and patient. I love all people and they love me. I am never annoyed or demanding. I am forgiven for my faults, weaknesses and past infractions as I give for them a new viewpoint and a new determination to do unto others as I would have others do unto me. I am a pleasant person. Other people feel better when they are near me. I bring peace to every situation. I am never annoyed. I endeavor to understand and to share my understanding with others. I give thanks that I am forever free from irritation. I give thanks that I am a kind, pleasant and loving person now. And so it is."

Now, select other points of concern to you, and in your own word pattern strive to develop your good disposition. Five "disposition destroyers" cause more unhappiness than all the rest put together. Get rid of them and you won't have much trouble with the rest. They are:

1. Irritation	3. Negativity
2. Selfishness	4. Suspicion
5. Cruelty	

We have said that a good disposition has an actual healing effect upon the organs of the body. Refer again to the table of correspondences in Chapter 2 where we worked out the psychological causes underlying different diseases and how to deal with them in treatment. Review this list carefully and you will be amazed how many physical ailments are caused by bad traits of disposition within the individual which he can change if he wants to. Once we understand that the cause of all of our experience is rooted in our inner thoughts, feelings and attitudes, it is easy to see, for instance, that skin trouble could be caused by inner irritability, gall bladder trouble by bitterness, tuberculosis by selfishness, arthritis by stubbornness and hostility, neuritis by anger and resentment, heart trouble by cruelty and jealousy, and so on. The list is endless. We heal ourselves by healing our dispositions.

This is primarily a matter of working toward emotional maturity. A good part of the spiritual mind therapy which we are talking about in this book is geared toward helping us achieve this maturity. We just need to grow up. A mature body, unfortunately, often houses a most immature personality. As long as we sulk, have moods, and lose our tempers, we have some work to do on ourselves. If we slam doors, bawl out drivers at traffic intersections, if we cry, whine, complain, criticize or gossip, we are emotionally immature and need to do something about it. If we are childish, petty or vindictive, then the subject of this chapter is of vital concern.

Smiles Pay Dividends

We have seen how a bad disposition makes us sick. It logically follows that a good one heals us and keeps us well. If "a broken spirit drieth the bones," we must also remember that "a merry heart doeth good like a medicine." (Pr. 17:22) A smile is universally welcome, for it:

1. Cheers the heart	4. Promotes health
2. Keeps us in good humor	5. Beautifies your face
3. Preserves peace in the soul	6. Induces kindly thoughts
7. Inspires kindly deeds	

We are grateful to the anonymous compiler of this list. Most of us have long been familiar with it. The question is: "Are we doing what is necessary to bring about all of these desirable things?" The answer is simple: Smile. Just smile. "Laugh, and the world laughs with you; weep, and you weep alone." *

An agreeable disposition is evidence of love. Love is the one great healing power. Learn to love and you will learn to live. Love and you will be loved. Love has many pleasant faces. Love produces health, happiness, abundance and fufillment. Love is the greatest thing in the world. You can't just talk about it; you have to feel it; you have to express it.

When Love Takes Over

One lady I know talked a great deal about love, but had some difficulty practicing it consistently, just like the rest of us. This lady was domineering. She was easy to get along with as long as she had her way. She had definite ideas about how our church should be run, and she and I soon had a clash of wills. The results and reverberations didn't do credit to either one of us. The lady went to a practitioner with her tale of woe and spilled her venom all over the place, telling the practitioner what a horrible person the minister was and how he should be given his walking papers. (Every minister will readily recognize the type.)

However, the practitioner would have none of this, and simply and very wisely treated the situation for love.

"But what good will that do?" expostulated the dowager. "Love is wonderful, but something has to be done about this, I tell you. Why, that man is impossible. Why, do you know—?"

"Yes, I know," replied the practitioner. "I am married to him." It was my wife who was the practitioner. "Now, let's have that treatment for love."

The hostility abated and the good woman was somewhat mollified as she went on her way.

The next morning, however, she called Mrs. Curtis in rage and hysterics.

"What are you doing to me?" she screamed. "Are you practicing

* Ella Wheeler Wilcox, "Solitude."

black magic on me? You should see my body! I'm broken out from head to foot with angry red welts. I demand to know what you have done to me."

"I haven't done anything," Mrs. Curtis replied quietly, "except to treat you, Dr. Curtis and the whole situation for love."

"Well, stop it! Stop it right now! If this is what love does, I don't want any part of it. Stop your treatment right now. I'll handle this matter myself!" And she hung up.

Meantime, in my shower that morning I became aware of a breaking out on the inside of my right arm. There was a burning, itching sensation and it was quite painful. I was more than a little miffed when I mentioned it at breakfast and Mrs. Curtis only smiled.

Nothing happened for a few days. I heard nothing more from my tormentor. It was just as well, because I was too busy trying to keep from scratching the burning rash which was spreading over my body.

Finally, Mrs. Curtis told me the whole story about the visit from the lady, the treatment, and the subsequent telephone call. We both laughed loud and long at what love had done. The explanation is very simple. Love was introduced into a situation where there was hostility, hurt, resentment and misunderstanding which the combatants were not ready to relinquish. This automatically produced a conflict. This didn't bother the love, however, because love is the greatest force in the world. It went ahead and did its work. The skin problems which the lady and I experienced were the result of the chemicalization which took place. This always happens when two incompatible elements are brought together, and is well known in the field of chemistry. It is also well known in the field of spiritual mind healing and treatment. Chemicalization is often one of the steps in the healing process, during which purification and cleansing is taking place. It takes place on every level—the mental, the emotional and the physical.

This is usually accomplished without anyone being aware of it when everyone cooperates with the treatment and does not resist it by hanging on to personal animosities or other selfish or negative attitudes. In this instance, the lady and I were both hanging on to our hurt feelings, and unwilling to relinquish them, we were subconsciously resisting the treatment with results similar to bringing salts and acids together in the chemistry laboratory. When I became consciously aware of what was happening, I got busy with my own treatment work and joined Mrs. Curtis in treating the entire situation for love. As I developed kindly feelings toward the lady, and reached an awareness of love and forgiveness, my skin cleared up, and the incident was forgotten.

No effort was made to contact the lady, but in a few days she came into my office and volunteered her services to help around the church in any capacity where I might need her. I accepted and assigned her to an important job which she faithfully discharged for several years, without one further word about our initial disagreement. Her skin condition? It cleared up just as mine did. Love conquered all. It always will.

True love can only be expressed when we are complete within ourselves and constantly express this completeness. Love is an affirmative attitude toward life. Love is the desire of Life to express itself. Love is God in action. Love is the expression of ourselves at our highest and best. Love is dedication to purpose. Emerson said, "Love is the soul flowing through us."

In his magnificent treatise on Chapter 13 of I Corinthians called, *The Greatest Thing in the World*, Henry Drummond lists nine attributes of love:

1. Patience	5. Courtesy
2. Kindness	6. Unselfishness
3. Generosity	7. Good Temper
4. Humility	8. Guilelessness
	9. Sincerity

We can readily see that "Love is the fulfilling of the Law," (Romans 13:10) and that since, "God is love," (I John 4:8) the cause of all problems is lack of love. Therefore, the answer (the healing) of all situations is to treat (fill) ourselves with love so that the natural action of life may flow through us. In the larger sense, that's what this book is all about. (See Chapter 8, pages 112-113 of *Your Thoughts Can Change Your Life*, for a helpful technique of developing love as the basic step in demonstrating desired good in your world.)

Love is expressed in *seven* major areas. Each one is of vital importance, and absolutely essential to balanced, happy living.

1. *Love God.* St. Augustine opined that the only guide necessary for the good life was to "Love God and do as you please." If we truly love God—the All-Good—we can never do anything unworthy. Our identification with the One is sufficient to keep us attuned to noble

purpose and ideals. God is the Source of our supply of all things: "a very present help in trouble." (Psalm 46:1) Many people profess love for God, but want to hang onto their petty selfishness and hostility at the same time. This won't work, and only produces problems, troubles and illness. God demands more than lip service. Love of God must be constantly demonstrated in all that we do. All that we say, think, feel and do gives evidence of our capacity to love. Let's determine to love God and go on from there.

2. *Love Life.* "I love life, and I love to live," proclaims the famous song.* Love of life releases the energy of the spheres through our entire being. Life is energy—Spirit—Life! The will to live is our strongest drive. When this weakens, we die. Life is for living. Jesus said, "I am come that they might have life, and that they might have it more abundantly." (John 10:10) You have heard it said, "Only two things are inevitable: death and taxes." But, this is not so. The only thing inevitable is life. We must live. If we resist the flow of life we break under the strain. If we flow with it, we are swept along to victory. Life is a continuous, never-ending process. "In my Father's house are many mansions." (John 14:2) "There are . . . celestial bodies, and bodies terrestrial." (I Cor. 15:40) We live forever. The sooner we start living—really living—the better.

3. *Love Nature.* Nature is external evidence of the glory which is God. "O Lord our Lord, how excellent is thy name in all the earth! Who hast set thy glory above the heavens . . . When I consider thy heavens, the work of thy fingers, the moon and the stars, which thou hast ordained; what is man, that thou are mindful of him . . . ?" (Psalm 8:1, 3, 4)

As phenomenal as is a human being, we are dwarfed by the magnificence of Nature. The panoply of the heavens sing out the glory which is God. The entire physical universe is the body of God. This magnificent greensward, the Earth, is our share of it. It is ours to be lived in and enjoyed. The earth, the air, the sea, the hills and valleys, the deserts and mountains, the trees, the flowers, and the beautiful creatures of the multitudinous kingdoms—all of these are Nature's. How could one not love such wonder?

4. *Love Yourself.* If you love God, life, and Nature, you must love yourself. Your first expression of love must be toward yourself. If you

* "I Love Life," Irwin M. Cassel and Mana-Zucca, John Church Co., Philadelphia, MCMXXIII.

hate yourself, you will hate everything else. You are man—made in the image and likeness of God—possessed of divine attributes; a creature of infinite potential. Man is God's highest creation. The Psalm continues: "Thou hast made him a little lower than the angels, and hast crowned him with glory and honour. Thou madest him to have dominion over the works of thy hands; thou hast put all things under his feet." (Psalm 8:5, 6)

Shakespeare, too, was caught up in the contemplation of the wonder of his own species: "What a piece of work is a man! How noble in reason! How infinite in faculty! In form and moving how express and admirable! In action how like an angel! In apprehension how like a god! The beauty of the world! The paragon of animals!" (*Hamlet*, Act II, Sc. 2)

It is you who is being described. Love yourself. The real *Self* which you have been entrusted with—to express, to develop, to glorify. Love what you really are, and you will have taken the first step toward fulfilling your destiny.

5. *Love People.* All the reasons for loving yourself as an expression of God automatically apply to others. We are *all* expressions of the Divine Fact. We are all members of the same family. We are brothers because we have the same Father, no matter how divergent our worldly paths may be. The Christ—the Higher Self—is within each one of us. To reject or dislike people is to reject God and deny the whole principle of love. We may not like what a person does, but we must love him. We must identify with him, learn to understand and help him. Through the love we share with others, we find ourselves. When we shut off love, we shut off that much of life. Interest, encouragement, sharing, helpfulness, concern, sympathy—all of these are means by which we express love for other people. We find ourselves in others; in every living human being. "There is One Mind common to all individual men." (Emerson)

6. *Love Your World.* Your world is what you make it. It is an extension and a reflection of your own consciousness. Your world is neither good nor bad. It just is. The world really has no power to move you or affect you in any way. It seems to, but when we see it in its proper perspective in the scheme of things, we recognize it as effect only, and not cause. Jesus said, "In the world ye shall have tribulation: but be of good cheer; I have overcome the world." (John 16:33)

Enjoy the world and participate in its actions. Luxuriate in its comforts. Use the things of worldly experience wisely, for actions and objects have their place in the Great Plan. Conveniences can make life easier. Possessions and money can enrich us if we use them wisely, and possess them instead of letting them possess us. Love the world in its proper relationship. Do not reject it; accept it, but remember that you make your world what it is, and you have dominion over it and everything in it. Never relinquish this birthright. Remain always in charge of your experiences. Keep every aspect of your life in its proper place, and view it in its proper perspective. The world *is* your oyster. You are sitting on top of it. If you don't like the world the way it is, go out and make a better one—one that you and everyone else can love. That will keep you so busy that you won't have time to sit around and cry about what a mess this one is in. There may be a reason. Let's reverse the action and build our world on love.

7. *Love Your Work.* If you don't like what you are doing, change it. No matter what adjustment is involved or how much inconvenience or temporary loss of income is incurred, change jobs lest you die in one you don't like. Life is too short to squander in unrewarding work. It is through work that we express the creative urge within us. It is through work that we perfect ourselves. It is through work that we give form to the creative energy which flows through us. It is through work that we live. Work is therapy. Let love flow through your work. Let your work express the love that you feel for God, life, nature, yourself, people and your world. Be proud of your work. Exult in it. Pour yourself into it. Hold nothing back. Be your own boss! Let your work be your monument. Don't worry about how it is received or what reward it will bring. Do what you like best. Do it to the best of your ability, "as to the Lord and not to men," (Eph. 6:7) and you will be fulfilling the action of love in your life. "Be about your Father's business," (Luke 2:49) and you will be a living, creating action of love in the great scheme of things.

HOW TO BE POPULAR

Everyone wants to be loved. The more love you give the more you receive. Love is a way of life and must be expressed in everything we do. The loving person is inevitably a popular person. If you would be popular, here is a formula for success:

1. Smile.

2. Look at people with interest.

3. Get people to talk about themselves.

4. Express enjoyment over being with them.

5. Say kind things and pay compliments.

6. Forget yourself and think of the other person.

HOW TO OVERCOME LONELINESS

The person who knows how to express love will never be lonely. Try doing these five things:

1. Look around you and get interested in your world.

2. Learn to like people.

3. Decide to live your life fully.

4. Choose your goals and stick to them.

5. Give something of yourself every day.

Daily Guide to Love

I express love in everything I think, feel, say and do. I am the complete expression of love. I love the greatness and goodness which is God. I am warmed by the currents of Divine Love which flow through me and form my soul in patterns of love.

I love life and I love to live it. I thrill to the surge of spiritual energy which enlivens my entire being. I tingle in the embrace of the Infinite. I am cleansed by the love which lifts me to new heights of awareness and realization. I learn to love the real Self within me. I forgive myself for shortcomings and mistakes. As I get rid of those characteristics which I do not like, I begin to love myself. God created me, and the Creator continues to love that which is created. I love what God loves. God loves me. Therefore, I love myself, and I love all other people, because we are all created in love and united in love.

I see only good in others. I love the good which is expressed in every living human being. I know that everyone is doing his best at his own level of development. I give him credit, help him where and when I can, and continue to love him all the while. I obey the commandment, "Love one another." (John 15:12) I have never met a man I didn't like. I love people.

I love the world in which I live. I love the power which I have been given to change it, mold it and make it after my will. I love the great law of cause and effect which makes my world a product of my consciousness. I love the idea that I am responsible for what I do in and with my world.

I love my work through which I express the glory of God. I love the free full flow of life as it moves through me in purposeful expression. I love the creative process. I love the opportunity to assist it through expressing love in everything I do. I love. *And so it is.*

CHAPTER TEN

YOU ARE A WONDERFUL PERSON

"*You're fired! Stop by the cashier's window on the way out. You're check is ready for you.*"

There was no mistaking the words. Jack turned and walked numbly from the manager's office, and slumped against the outer door, desperately trying to fight down his feeling of nausea.

"So it's finally come," he muttered to himself. "They've finally caught up with me. Well, pilot, this is where you jump. This is the end of the line. Now what, you ruptured duck?"

Stopping just long enough to pick up his check, Jack pulled himself together and walked briskly out the door and with a sardonic mock-salute, turned his back on the place where he had been employed for over twenty years.

"Good riddance to bad rubbish!" he spat. "Never could stand the place anyway." He started to whistle as he cocked his hat and gave a fair imitation of a jaunty walk as he turned into Joe's Bar.

"Just one before I go home," he assured himself. "I deserve it. I haven't had a vacation for a long time." It was just five o'clock.

Jack's wife found him there sometime after midnight and took him home, considerably the worse for wear.

"I can't say I'm used to it, or that I like it, but there is certainly nothing new in the experience," she spoke grimly in my office the next afternoon. "But this time there's one big difference. I've been used to Jack coming home without any money from his pay check because he had drunk it all up. I could always say, next week will be different, and get by somehow, but now there's not going to be any next week—not for pay checks anyway. We're at the end of the rope, Dr. Curtis. We owe everyone in town, and Jack won't be able to get a job. Everyone knows about him. Dr. Curtis, what are we going to do?"

Jack's attractive but trouble-worn wife sobbed uncontrollably for a few minutes but quieted down and listened intently as I started to talk to her. It was not a new experience for me. With only minor variations, I have heard the story and experienced the scene hundreds of times during the years.

Jack Could Have Succeeded

Jack should have been sitting on top of the world. Handsome, brilliant and talented, he had been voted the one "most likely to succeed" by his college graduating class just before World War II. He had a good job waiting for him in one of the big companies in his home town, and he and his boyhood sweetheart were married the day he graduated.

Things went smoothly for a while, but when war was declared Jack enlisted in the Naval Air Corps. He was a natural, and became one of the hottest pilots in the service. His wife followed him where she could, and he got home for an occasional leave. But it was hard for Jack to slow down. He had started to drink, and the leaves became an extended binge. But nobody really noticed it. It was war-time. Everyone was doing it.

They did notice it, however, in the years that followed the war. Everyone tried to get back to normal, but Jack had liked the excitement of flying and combat. Neither the wife nor the job he left behind him seemed to hold the same bright promise that they once had. After a few years of excessive drinking, his work became haphazard. He became dull in mind and sloppy in appearance, and despite the birth of his two children, he was indifferent at home. On several occasions, he was arrested for drunkenness, and was often absent from work with a Monday morning "cold."

Jack resisted all efforts to get him to Alcoholics Anonymous, nor would he seek help any place else.

"I'm not an alcoholic," he proclaimed. "Sure I drink, but so what? Isn't a fellow entitled to a little fun? I work hard and I need to relax. But drinking doesn't mean anything to me. I could stop just like that if I wanted to."

But he never seemed to want to. Disappointments, failures and setbacks came along and Jack's only remedy was to get drunk. He aged rapidly, and became flabby and paunchy. His company was patient for years, but finally had to let him go. Only his wife stuck with him.

She had heard my radio broadcasts and had read some of my books and had come to me seeking guidance.

A Wonderful Rebirth

I saw her and Jack frequently during the months that followed. Jack was ready for help. He admitted his alcoholism. He said he had wanted to stop drinking for a long time, but when he found he couldn't, it frightened him so much that he drank even more.

Nearly everyone now recognizes that alcoholism is a disease, not just a moral defection, and needs to be treated accordingly. Jack asked for help. We went to work.

First of all, I put him in touch with a member of Alcoholics Anonymous, many of whom are students of the Science of Mind and attend my church. He went on their "program" with the famous "Twelve Steps," and attended meetings regularly.

Jack then consulted a doctor of internal medicine and endocrinology, who corrected glandular deficiencies, balanced the blood chemistry, and prescribed a program of diet and body re-building as part of the over-all program of his rehabilitation.

Finally, Jack became a serious student of the Science of Mind, not as a religion primarily but as the means of helping himself come back to life, as so many others are doing. Jack came to see me regularly for consultation and treatment sessions. He came to understand himself for the first time, and to realize that the good things of life don't come out of a bottle. He never had another drink, and recently celebrated several years of sobriety.

SELF, COOPERATION AND HEALING

Who was responsible for Jack's recovery? He was, through cooperation with the Power within him, and with the assistance of the rest of us. I certainly claim no personal credit. I was simply there when he needed me, as were the members of A.A., the physicians, the teachers, the psychologists, psychiatrists, and the many others who are dedicated to helping humanity.

You will note that Jack's recovery program included three major approaches, the Science of Mind, Alcoholics Anonymous, and the medical doctor. It might also have included a psychologist, but in this case Jack received his psychological and spiritual therapy through Pastoral Counseling.

My point is that there is only one therapy—the therapy of the "whole man." You are really your own doctor; the rest of us help. You make yourself sick by resisting the natural forces of life; you become well when you cooperate with them.

The treatment techniques described in this book are for the purpose of helping you flow with the natural forces of life to achieve healing, fulfillment, and the solution of difficulties. No approach knows all the answers, but the Infinite Healing Presence within you does know them. All sincere practitioners of the healing arts will utilize any helpful healing force. There is no longer any feeling of separation between science and religion. Religion can be scientific, as we endeavor to be in the Science of Mind. We believe that religion must move out of the realm of creed, form and ceremony into a practical and scientific guide to purposeful living. Medicine has its religious aspects, because every sincere physician knows that he only prescribes or treats, whereas God heals.

There is an increasing tendency for those of us in the various fields to work together on a single patient. Man is made up of spirit, mind, body and experience. Doesn't it make sense that a specialist should work on his specialty, and that the specialists should all work together? If you are building a house the electrician doesn't put in the plumbing, but he and the plumber each know where the other's pipes and conduits are going. The carpenter and the plasterer don't interfere with each other's work, but they certainly work together.

It has been gratifying to me to work on a number of cases with physicians, psychologists, psychiatrists, and, in some cases, attorneys. Sometimes we all spend several sessions together with a patient, working together to help him. No one person, field, specialty or teaching knows all the answers. God, the Infinite Intelligence, does the healing. The rest of us are just members of the staff.

After his first few months of sobriety, Jack was re-hired by his old firm, and has progressed steadily, fulfilling the promise of "the man most likely to succeed" whom the company originally hired nearly twenty-five years ago. And he wasn't the only one who reached some realizations about himself. His wife did some soul searching too, and in her own words told me, "Dr. Curtis, through coming to understand Jack and his problem, I see that I was as much to blame for it as he. I thank God every day for you and the Science of Mind, who have helped me become a better wife and a better person."

How had Jack lost his way in the first place? This case history is valuable only if we can learn through Jack's experience. As we have seen throughout this book, our problems and difficulties are the result of our negative mental and emotional states. Fear and hostility are behind negativity; faith and love are the constructive forces. Jack's drinking was the symptom of deep-seated emotional problems. The same cause-and-effect relationship exists with all human symptom-problem experiences.

In Chapter 2 we presented a table which charted fifty physical ailments, their causes, and suggested treatment. Here is a similar chart to help you deal with some of the most common human problems:

Problem	Probable Psychological Cause	Treatment
1. Accidents	Suppressed emotions, Violence, Aggressiveness	Freedom, Peace, Serenity
2. Age	Fear of the unknown, Limitation, Race thought	Faith, Growth, Curiosity
3. Aimlessness	Lack of purpose, Inferiority, Self-rejection	Focus, Interest, Purpose
4. Alcoholism	Fear, Lack of love, Inferiority	Faith, Love, Confidence
5. Bed-wetting	Insecurity, Anxiety, Frustration	Confidence, Peace, Expression
6. Bondage	Fear, Limitation, Rejection	Faith, Freedom, Truth
7. Boredom	Death wish, Selfishness, Spiritual blindness	Interest, Love, Awareness
8. Business problems	Fear, Haste, Carelessness, Insufficient knowledge	Faith, Attention, Wisdom
9. Car sickness	Fear, Instability, Bondage	Confidence, Balance, Freedom
10. Cheating	Insecurity, Lack of love, Self rejection	Confidence, Love, Acceptance of self
11. Compulsive eating	Emotional turbulence, Self-rejection, Lack of love	Peace, Love, Self-acceptance
12. Conflict	Mixed emotions, Fear, Resistance	Peace, Faith, Cooperation

	Problem	Probable Psychological Cause	Treatment
13.	Confusion	Fear, Lack of organization, Ignorance	Faith, Purpose
14.	Conversation difficulties	Selfishness, Lack of interest, Inferiority	Interest, Love, Confidence
15.	Crime	Hatred, Lack of love, Fear	Love, Peace, Understanding
16.	Depression	Overload, Selfishness, Fear	Life, Interest in others, Joy
17.	Diet (to correct)	Carelessness, Ignorance, Self-rejection	Self-Acceptance, Stewardship, Purity
18.	Difficulty	Struggle, Antagonism, Resistance	Order, Cooperation, Release
19.	Disappointment	Weakness, Fear, Faulty values	Strength, Faith, Sense of values
20.	Discouragement	Fear, Negative expectancy, Overload	Expectancy, Enthusiasm, Joy
21.	Disharmony	Emotional conflict, Hostility, Fear	Love, Peace, Faith
22.	Disillusionment	False values, Need for love, Lack of spiritual understanding	Truth, Love, Understanding
23.	Divorce	Hostility, Selfishness, Separation	Love, Understanding, Union
24.	Domestic Help	Lack of concern for others, Irritation, Thoughtlessness	Kindness, Understanding, Consideration
25.	Drowsiness	Self-centeredness, Lack of interest in Life, Boredom	Participation, Interest, Enthusiasm
26.	Drug Addiction	Lack of love, Fear, Self-rejection	Love, Faith, Self-acceptance
27.	Dying	Fear, Lack of spiritual understanding, Superstition	Faith, Wholeness, Awareness
28.	Etiquette	Lack of concern for others, Lack of self-respect, Carelessness	Love, Self-respect, Order
29.	Exercise (neglect of)	Lack of organization, Self-rejection, Lack of interest	Order, Self-respect, Interest
30.	Failure	Fear, Limitation, Self-rejection	Faith, Confidence, Correct Self-evaluation
31.	Fame (adjusting to)	Egotism, False values, Lack of spiritual understanding	Understanding, Balance, Truth

	Problem	Probable Psychological Cause	Treatment
32.	Fatigue	Resistance, Boredom, Overload	Ease, Enthusiasm, Co-operation
33.	Fires	Hostility, Anger, Resentment	Love, Harmony, Forgiveness
34.	Frustration	Lack of purpose, Lack of interest, Lack of participation	Purpose, Expression, Fulfillment
35.	Getting along with people (difficulty in)	Hostility, Self-loathing, Selfishness, Boorishness	Love, Understanding, Forgiveness
36.	Gossip	Maliciousness, Self-hatred, Hostility	Love, Kindness, Purity, Truth
37.	Grief	Lack of spiritual understanding, Ignorance, Self-pity	Understanding, Enlightenment, Interest in life
38.	Hate	Ignorance, Fear, Superstition	Understanding, Faith, Forgiveness
39.	Housekeeping problems	Disorder, Lack of love, Lack of interest	Purpose, Interest, Love
40.	Hurry	Anxiety, Lack of organization, Fear	Faith, Confidence, Order
41.	Hurt	Hatred, Guilt, Rejection	Love, Forgiveness, Understanding
42.	Ignorance	Imperceptiveness, Stubbornness, Laziness	Understanding, Truth, Awareness
43.	Immaturity	Lack of love, "Smother love," Selfishness, Evasion of responsibility	Love, Interest in others, Confidence
44.	Indecision	Lack of confidence, Lack of purpose, Lack of interest	Faith, Direction, Understanding
45.	Insecurity	Lack of love, Fear, Lack of organization	Love, Faith, Purpose
46.	Insomnia	Tension, Guilt, Fear	Relaxation, Ease, Order, Faith
47.	Investments (bad)	Greed, Selfishness, Poor judgment	Generosity, Sense of values, Understanding
48.	Juvenile delinquency	Lack of love, Evasion of parental responsibility, Lack of understanding	Love, Understanding, Maturity, Guidance

Problem	Probable Psychological Cause	Treatment
49. Lack of love	Interested only in self, Hurt, Fear, Hostility	Faith, Kindness, Interest, Love
50. Legal difficulties	Hostility, Self-punishment, False values	Love, Order, Harmony, Understanding, Truth
51. Leisure time (what to do with it)	Disorganization, No sense of values, Lack of interest in life	Organization, Sense of values, Interest, Joy
52. Living Quarters (difficulty in finding)	Insecurity, Negativity, Rejection	Faith, Expectancy, Acceptance
53. Loneliness	Self-centeredness, Lack of love, Lack of interest in others	Love, Participation, Circulation
54. Loss	Fear, Greed, Insecurity	Faith, Generosity, Security
55. Lying	Fear, False values, Dishonesty	Faith, True values, Honesty
56. Manners (bad)	Hostility, Selfishness, Ignorance, Carelessness	Love, Interest, Understanding
57. Marriage (unable to find mate)	Hostility, Insecurity, Lack of love, Self-rejection	Love, Selflessness, Self-improvement
58. Marital problems	Selfishness, Lack of love, Immaturity, Lack of consideration	Love, Understanding, Kindness, Consideration
59. Martyrdom	"Poor little old me," Selfishness, Rejection, Lack of love	Faith, Self-confidence, Love, Understanding
60. Melancholia	Fear, Negativity, Overload, Joylessness	Joy, Gaiety, Ease, Beauty, Freedom
61. Menstrual problems	Resistance, Rejection, Fear, Race belief	Ease, Peace, Understanding
62. Misfit	Self-rejection, Lack of love, Lack of self-understanding	Right place, Wholeness, Order
63. Money problems	Fear, Limitation, Greed	Faith, Security, Desire to be of service
64. Morbidity	Death wish, Lack of interest in life, Depressing thoughts and feelings	Life, Enthusiasm, Love, Action

Problem	Probable Psychological Cause	Treatment
65. Nervousness	Fear, Anxiety, Tension, Insecurity	Peace, Faith, Quiet, Wholeness
66. Nightmares	Guilt, Fear, Tension, Pressure	Relaxation, Peace, Ease, Order
67. Obscurity (lack of recognition)	Lack of love, Self-rejection, Inferiority	Confidence, Purpose, Faith
68. Obsession	Superstition, False values, Accumulated negativity, Fear	Truth, Wholeness, Faith
69. Parental problems	Immaturity, Insecurity, False values, Diffidence	Understanding, Faith, Truth, Maturity
70. Persecution	Guilt, Self-rejection, Hostility	Forgiveness, Love, Wholeness
71. Poverty	Rejection, Limitation, Separation	Wholeness, Union, Acceptance
72. Power (how to handle)	Insecurity, Fear, Uncertainty	Dominion, Faith, Right action, Love
73. Pregnancy and birth (difficult)	Fear, Life-rejection, Race belief, Ignorance	Faith, Life, Wholeness, Normalcy
74. Property and ownership problems	Insecurity, False Values, Limitation	Faith, Stewardship, Right action
75. Quarrels	Hostility, Anger, Misunderstanding	Love, Quietude, Understanding
76. Retirement problems	Withdrawal, Lack of interest, Limitation, Stagnation	Interest, Circulation, Freedom, Action
77. Sales (difficulty in making)	Fear, Lack of confidence, Negative expectancy	Faith, Confidence, Expectancy
78. Sex problems	Lack of love, Insecurity, Life rejection, False values	Love, Confidence, Strength, Life
79. Smoking	Hostility, False values, Lack of love, Insecurity	Love, Truth, Ease, Balance
80. Social problems	Greed, Hate, Selfishness	Love, Understanding, Kindness
81. Spiritual problems	Superstition, Guilt, Fear, Ignorance	Truth, Guidance, Love, Awareness
82. Stealing	False values, Insecurity, Lack of love, Greed	Faith, Love, Confidence, Truth
83. Success (how to handle)	Fear, Limitation, Insecurity	Order, Balance, Right Action

Problem	Probable Psychological Cause	Treatment
84. Suicide	Depression, Life-rejection, Lack of love	Life, Faith, Love, Joy
85. Telephonitis	Insecurity, Lack of organization, "Butterfly mind"	Order, Purpose, Definition
86. Tenants (problems with)	Lack of love, Lack of interest, Hostility, Greed	Kindness, Love, Helpfulness, Interest
87. Theft (loss through)	Fear, Insecurity, Selfishness, Dishonesty	Faith, Confidence, Sense of values
88. Time (not enough)	Unrest, Confusion, Insecurity	Order, Planning, Security
89. Travel difficulties	Fear, Disorganization, Confusion, Self-centeredness	Confidence, Joy, Order, Interest
90. Trouble	Hostility, Animosity, Selfishness, False values	Love, Understanding, Empathy
91. Too busy	Lack of planning and organization, Escape, Imbalance	Order, Right Action, True Expression
92. Unemployment	Fear, Rejection, Inferiority, Insecurity	Faith, Right Place, Expectancy
93. Unhappiness	Negativity, Fear, Self-Rejection, Resistance	Joy, Freedom, Love, Faith, Pleasantness
94. Unpopularity	Fear, Rejection, Inferiority, Hostility	Love, Faith, Pleasantness
95. War	Greed, Selfishness, Hatred, Aggression	Love, Generosity, Understanding, Peace
96. Worry	Fear, Lack of Confidence, False values, Inferiority	Faith, Strength, Purpose, Guidance
97. Wrong place	Lack of direction, Confusion, Not knowing what you want	Direction, Right place, Peace, Conviction
98. 99. 100. Ad Infinitum } Your Particular Personal Problems	"The Four Demons": * Fear, Hostility, Inferiority, Guilt	Faith, Love, Confidence, Forgiveness

* See *Prayer Can Change Your Life*, William R. Parker and Elaine St. Johns, Prentice-Hall, 1957.

Again, as with the earlier chart in Chapter 2, this table is meant as a guide to help you be specific in treating these various human problems. While it is impossible to be mathematically exact in the matter of psychological causation, these suggestions will help you pinpoint your inner problem. Remember, as we use the term "psychological cause," we refer to the entire inner life of the individual—the emotional, mental and spiritual factors.

CONQUER YOUR PROBLEM BY
ELIMINATING ITS CAUSE

Everyone has his share of the problems listed in the left-hand column of the previous list. These are invariably caused by some combination of the negative states of consciousness listed in the middle column. Dissolve these through specific denial and cleansing, and then affirm and build the constructive attitudes in the right-hand column. Conditioning your consciousness along these lines will not only eliminate the specific problem, but will improve your entire life. When you use these tools to assist you in this business of living, people will say, "You are like a different person." And for a very good reason; you will be.

If you have a problem, correct the cause, and the problem will disappear. If you have no specific problem, concentrate on the affirmative attitudes in the right-hand "treatment" column. Developing these constructive points is bound to help you. In correcting conditions, always concentrate the major part of your treatment on the solution. Your change-over from negative to positive is the process of healing.

You will note that "fear" is listed as the underlying cause of the majority of the problems. Fear is the essence of negativity, just as love and faith are the supreme expression of constructivity. In attuning your consciousness to God through affirmative prayer treatment, the process is to dissolve fear and affirm love and faith.

Always be as specific as possible in your treatment. Dissolve the specific fear which you may have. The human mind has the capacity to build all kinds of phantoms—most of them in the "fear" family: fear of life, death, illness, failure, success, sex, self, others, thinking, speaking, of being alone—fear of anything or everything. Fear festers and destroys. Rid yourself of it and develop:

1. Faith in yourself.   3. Faith in other people.
2. Faith in life.   4. Faith in God.

Here are two sample treatments to serve as a guide:

Treatment to Heal Alcoholism

There is One Life—one Infinite Intelligence which is the First Cause back of all things. This Presence and Power is the essence of my being. Whatever is true of this One is true of me. It is whole and perfect, and so am I. God is free from all fear and negativity and so am I. God is love and so am I. The "real self" of me is made "in the image and likeness of God."

I strive to be my "real self" at all times. Whatever is true of God is true of me. I think well of God; I think well of myself. I am an important part of a magnificent wholeness which knows no trouble, which has no problems, which knows only how to be whole. I accept my wholeness now. Nothing can keep me from being my true Self except my false self. I get rid of this false self right now. I am finished with it once and for all. There is no place for anything but the good, the true, and the beautiful in my life.

I have unwavering faith in the goodness and justice of life. No one is against me; no thing opposes me. I am not afraid. I am strong and confident at all times. All inferiority is dissolved. I can do whatever I need to do at the exact moment it needs to be done. I have faith in myself. I have faith in other people. I trust them. I love them, and I know they love me. I experience full and complete love now and always.

I forgive myself and others for past mistakes or wrongs. There is no more hurt, disappointment or disillusionment. I have no time to feel sorry for myself. I have too much to do. God needs me, other people need me, and I need myself. I eliminate everything that is false from my life and I build all things which are true. I am finished with false ideas, false appetites and false habits. I am clean and pure in body, mind and soul. I am one with God. I am pure. I am whole. I am free. I am my true Self now. And so it is.

A treatment such as this one, given with frequency, intensity and expectancy, has the power to change your consciousness and correct any condition or problem. Formulate these ideas in your own words. When we form new mental, emotional and spiritual habits, the old physical and action habits disappear. There is no need for alcohol when you can drink of the pure and wholesome ideas which come to you during regular prayer treatment.

There is no need to fight drinking, smoking, or any other bad habit or problem. If you try to fight it you will always lose. So don't fight. Approach your particular problem in a different way—through peace, love, faith and awareness. You will be a different person when you fill yourself with different ideas. Identify yourself with good—with God—Life, whole and sweet. God never was drunk, never smoked a cigarette, never had a belly-ache—never worried, hurried, or fell down. Why do we? Because we forget who we are. Remember that you are a wonderful person and you will be remembering the Truth.

Treatment to Stop Accidents

"For it is only the finite that has wrought and suffered; the Infinite lies stretched in smiling repose." (Emerson, "Spiritual Laws") I immerse myself in the consciouness of peace today. I flow with Life. There is no resistance or blockage in my thought, feeling or action. Peace and love dissolve all obstructions. I cooperate with the creative action of Life.

I get along with other people because I first get along with myself. I am fighting no battles. I am at peace. All hostility is dissolved. I express only love. All fear is gone. I have deep and abiding faith. I don't believe in conflict. I believe in cooperation, ease, order and freedom. I cooperate with life, and life cooperates with me. I enjoy the easy and ordered flow of life in action. I am free from the fetters of fear and superstition. I am uncluttered in all departments. I am ordered, balanced and free.

I am not antagonistic. I am cooperative. I cooperate with life, with other people, and with myself. I flow with the main stream of purposeful, creative action. I stop hitting my head against stone walls. I stop fighting windmills. I no longer try to hold back the wind or stop the waves. I know that God grants me "the serenity to accept the things I cannot change, the courage to change the things I can and the wisdom to tell the difference." *

Deep peace is flowing around and through me, freeing me from all conflict, congestion and confusion. I travel serenely through life. I no longer bump into things. I follow true inner direction. I do not stumble and fall down. I walk uprightly with my God. I am divinely guided and protected. I am safe in the everlasting arms. I move confidently and

* Prayer by Reinhold Niebuhr, adopted officially by Alcoholics Anonymous.

serenely through life. I give thanks for peace, safety and protection. I give thanks for life—joyous, abundant and eternal. And so it is.

YOUR SPIRITUAL REALITIES

The miracle of being a human being is magnificently apparent when we study the structure and meaning of our own bodies. Truly, we are "fearfully and wonderfully made," and as Walt Whitman said, "there is more to a man than that which lies between his hat and his bootstraps." Plato taught that there are perfect patterns for all things in the Infinite Mind. This certainly applies to the human body. Every part of it has a spiritual significance and correspondence. As Paul said, "There are . . . celestial bodies, and bodies terrestrial." (I Corinthians 15:40) Our physical bodies are but the outer form of bodies of much subtler essence. Let's look at the spiritual meaning of our various parts.

The following table will help you understand how to treat an indisposition in any part of your body by affirming, strengthening and stimulating the spiritual correspondence of that particular part.

Spiritual Correspondences of the Human Body

Head

Head	Awareness
Mind	Reason
Nerves	Communication
Brain	Thought
Face	Recognition
Eyes	Perception
Ears	Understanding, Balance, Faith
Nose	Direction
Teeth	Analysis
Mouth	Praise and Thanksgiving
Tongue	Appreciation
Skin	Protection, Individuality
Voice	Communication
Throat	Expression
Breathing	Life
Neck	Flexibility
Hair on Head	Vitality, Strength

Body

Back	Support
Body	Manifestation
Chest	Potential
Hand	Attention, Grasp
Fingers	Persistence
Fingernails	Examination
Thumb	Comparison
Wrist	Freedom
Arm	Action
Elbow	Movement
Shoulder	Power
Leg	Forward Movement
Knee	Variety
Ankle	Ease
Foot	Understanding
Heel	Conviction
Toes	Concentration
Toenails	Detail

Organs and Functions

Lungs	Inspiration
Liver	Assimilation
Heart	Love
Abdomen	Soul
Kidneys	Purity
Generating Organs	Life
Bladder	Retention
Stomach	Receptivity
Bones	Permanency
Womb	Creativity
Bowels	Elimination
Backbone	Righteousness and Inspiration
Blood	Life and Joy
Veins and Arteries	Circulation
Muscles	Power
Touch	Selection
Glands	Distribution, Order, Maintenance
Solar Plexus	Feeling
Joints	Unity

BLESSING YOUR BODY

Use this list regularly and systematically to stimulate the flow of life through every part of your body. Go through your entire being with affirmative statements like this:

"Blessed be my head, which represents my capacity to know God."
"Blessed be my mind with which I think of the wonder of God."
"Blessed be my eyes through which I perceive the beauty of God."
"Blessed be my ears with which I hear and understand the word of God."
"Blessed be my mouth with which I praise and sing the glory of God."

And so on through the list, assisting the healing and recreative process. If you have illness or disease in any of these areas, this table will help to show you the cause, and through expanded understanding, will help you reverse your thought so as to accept your own wholeness and integration.

Truly, you are a wonderful person. Know it, accept it, and live by this premise.

Daily Guide to Faith and Confidence

I am part of something which is greater than I. I believe it. I know it. I accept it. This awareness gives me faith in God and confidence in myself. I am never alone. I am safe and secure in the knowledge that all good things are constantly taking place within, around, and through me. I am strengthened and supported by the spiritual structure of the universe. I am an integral part of the Great Plan. I am an individual expression of God.

I go forward into my world with courage and assurance. Why should I falter? I have the use of superlative equipment. My mind is my use of the One Mind. My blood stream is my share of the teeming, pulsating action of the One Life. My heart beats in harmony with the One Love which is the creative action of God warming the entire Universe. The wisdom and understanding of Infinite Intelligence are mine to use. I use them diligently and well. My consciousness is infiltrated with them. I am guided and directed by them. I am an instrument which expresses the greatness of the One.

Whatever I do is the expression of God working through me. Whatever I know is my awareness of that which has always been known. There is no limitation upon me. There is nothing I cannot do, nowhere I cannot go, nothing I cannot be—if I believe I can, and if I am willing to grow into and cooperate with the wonder which dwells in my heart.

I move serenely forward into larger experience today. I eagerly anticipate all impending events with enthusiasm and expectation of good. I have confidence that everything is working out for the best interests of everyone concerned. I have faith that this is so. *And so it is.*

CHAPTER ELEVEN

HOW TO BE A WINNER

Carl had always wanted to go to school. From the very beginning,
when many youngsters are rebelling against this threat to their freedom, this young man was eagerly looking forward to the great new
world of knowledge which school would unlock for him. Actually,
it wasn't much of a school, back there in the central Nebraska farming
country before the turn of the century—one room in which were
housed numerous pupils of the eight grades, all under the supervision
of one teacher, but it represented growth and learning. It was the
typical country schoolhouse which has been the cradle of learning for
so many Americans and it was the open sesame to all that was new and
wonderful.

Carl was late entering school his first year—he was needed at home
to help with the last of the harvest, and to haul the golden corn into
the great cribs on his father's farm. Then there was the fall plowing,
the repair of fences, the butchering for the winter, and the many other
tasks which go with farming. Even though only six years old, Carl was
the oldest boy in the family. Since he was large for his age, he was
pressed into the back-breaking work side by side with his father and
uncles, holding up his end as a man. The strain settled itself permanently in the young body as a stoop of the shoulders, which Carl still
carries today, more than sixty-five years later.

Finally, in that Nebraska autumn in the early 1890's, the snows
came and the six-year-old Carl was released to go to school, but only
after he completed his early morning chores. He could then begin the
three-mile trek across the field to the country schoolhouse. It was
clearly understood that he would return in time to help his father
with the evening feeding and milking which often took until way
after dark. Many times the eager youngster fell asleep at the supper

table with his head in his plate, completely exhausted, and unable to open the wonderful books which he had planned to read by the light of the coal-oil lamp.

Carl was trying hard to catch up with his class. In addition to his tardy entrance, he was further handicapped by being large for his age. The teacher expected him to be farther along than he was, and taunted him unmercifully. Then, too, his rural speech—a mixture of ungrammatical American and German "platt-deutsch" was hardly up to minimum requirements. So, in addition to learning "readin', writin', and 'rithmetic," he had to learn how to speak correctly.

However, no obstacle was too great for this little man to overcome. His desire for learning and self-improvement was intense, and by midwinter he had caught up with his class, and was making real progress with his studies. He had a quick ear, and he listened intently to the voice of his teacher. Soon he was able to eliminate the slovenly, guttural pronunciations and regional idioms from his speech. He was gradually learning the relationship between the words he heard, and the letters on the pages of the McGuffey first-grade reader. By Christmas time of that year, the teacher was encouraged by the improvement—even though it could hardly be called reading. The great pride of written expression was developing in Carl, and he stubbornly grasped the stub of the pencil in his grimy and work-thickened fist, as he laboriously learned to spell out the letters of his name.

At home, Carl was given help by his older sister, Anna, and the two of them then shared their treasure store of knowledge with the younger brothers and sisters, who were stair-stepped down to the cradle. During the long winter evenings after supper, the entire family would often sit huddled around the iron stove for warmth, while Carl and Anna struggled to read the stories from the primers and readers which they had brought home from school. Often these were cut short in their most interesting part by Papa, who announced that all must go to bed so that they would be able to get up early for tomorrow's chores.

The bleak winter months sped by, and Carl grew—in all ways. Naturally serious and intense, his features settled into a permanent half-frown, as he pored incessantly over his beginner's books, and his already tall frame became stooped with the combination of weariness and effort. However, he was happy because the person inside the body was learning and growing, and the young mind was absorbing knowledge like a sponge.

Then came the spring. It was no time for a farmer's son to be lolly-gagging in a school room! There was work to be done on the farm—plowing, planting, fixing fences, and a thousand and one other tasks—so Carl was taken out of school, and put into the fields where he worked from sunrise to sunset.

Carl struggled to get an education for many years with this serious handicap of part-time attendance each year. He could only go when he wasn't needed on the farm, so his education took a back seat. Although he could read and write, spelling was and continued to be his weak point. At the age of seventeen, Carl had still not finished the eighth grade. Yet, he was determined to see it through. He arrived at the country school that autumn, late in November, and took his place in the row of desks along with those who were several years his junior, including several of his own brothers. He was over six feet tall, and had been taking a man's place for a number of years, but the thing he wanted more than anything else—education—eluded him. Finally he dropped out of school, and remained on the farm; bitter and resentful toward his father because he felt he had deprived him of his opportunity to get ahead. Along with his resentment, however, there continued to burn deep within him a desire to do better than "just be a farmer." He was a capable farmer, but thoroughly unhappy. He actually blamed the farm, along with his father, for depriving him of his chance for an education.

On reaching the age of twenty-one, he left the farm to seek his fortune in the city. There he was like a fish out of water. Since he knew nothing but farming, he failed at several jobs, and missed out on examinations for several others because he couldn't spell. Finally, disillusioned and discouraged, except for his love of a pretty schoolteacher who appeared in his life, he returned to the farm to work for his father. His bitterness and self pity continued, but he took his inner anguish out in hard work. Gradually, he started to get ahead. There was something inside that wouldn't let him fail. A power was there working for him as soon as he would cooperate and let it take hold.

Bit by bit, he started leasing land and planting crops of his own at the same time he was working for others. The pretty schoolteacher had become a farmer's wife by this time, abandoning the classroom for the wheat field. Side by side they worked to build a life together, and rear their family. There was little time for anything but work, but now and then Mrs. Carl would get out her class exercises and teach her husband many of the things he had missed by not being able to attend school. As his interest was once more channeled into learning, he dropped his bitterness, irritation, and hard-driving ambition. He worked out a sound plan for himself and his family, and started to study scientific farming, and made many contributions which are still in use today. He was later invited to lecture at colleges and universities on scientific farming. With these various outlets for expression, the real person emerged from Carl, and his entire life and being bloomed and prospered. He became the owner of one of the largest and best-managed farms in that part of the country, and today is known throughout the state as a champion of the farmer. He has held political office, and has been given honorary recognitions personally by two presidents of the United States, as well as serving in appointive capacities under several administrations.

Carl isn't a great man, but he is real; he is solid. And by overcoming weaknesses within himself he has become a valuable and serviceable citizen.

This is a true story. I know, because Carl is my father, Spokane County Commissioner Carl W. Rudolf, of Cheney, Washington, now in his seventies, vital, healthy and productive, and with that air of authority which comes when a person intends to do something and does it.

BELIEVE IN YOURSELF COMPLETELY

My father's story illustrates what can be done by a person who believes in himself and moves steadily ahead toward his goal. Prepare yourself physically, mentally, emotionally and spiritually to make yourself a productive unit of achievement. Utilize your magnificent potential to bring about specific results in your life. Know what you want and follow through until it is achieved.

When we have a strong and specific desire, tremendous power is generated within us. If we know what we want, if we develop a strong and directed desire for it, and if we follow through to completion, we will always achieve our objective. This makes life a glorious adventure. Life is full of joy and meaning if we just apply ourselves and make an effort to find out what it is all about. Keep your interest, enthusiasm and determination high and the way will be filled with meaning and fulfillment. But for some the way seems tortuous and meaningless, and may even lead to conclusions such as that of Shakespeare's Macbeth when he despairs:

> "Tomorrow, and tomorrow, and tomorrow,
> Creeps in this petty pace from day to day,
> To the last syllable of recorded time;
> And all our yesterdays have lighted fools
> The way to dusty death. Out, out, brief candle!
> Life's but a walking shadow, a poor player
> That struts and frets his hour upon the stage
> And then is heard no more: it is a tale
> Told by an idiot, full of sound and fury,
> Signifying nothing." (*Macbeth*, Act V, Sc. 3)

Fortunately for the human race, such conclusions are greatly in the minority. In our own way, most of us are much more likely to identify ourselves with George Bernard Shaw's thrilling statement of dedication:

> "I am convinced that my life belongs to the whole community; and as long as I live, it is my privilege to do for it whatever I can, for the harder I work the more I live. I rejoice in life for its own sake. Life is no brief candle for me. It is a sort of splendid torch which I got hold of for a moment, and I want to make it burn as brightly as possible before turning it over to future generations."

Is it any wonder that George Bernard Shaw was a creative giant? The world, smarting under his barks and sallies, often ridiculed and quarreled with him, but we have all been permanently enriched by the sweep of his genius. He used satire, wit and criticism in his many plays, essays and constant gratuitous comments upon the state of the world and man in general, to serve the community, and the world in which he lived. His dedication to life is revealed in the brief statement above. This is the creed by which he lived. It did not deter him when success was slow in coming. He had a driving inner dedication and he served it joyously. It did not hurt him when the world rejected his suggestions. He did what he set out to do, in his own way, undoubtedly believing with Shakespeare:

> This above all: to thine own self be true
> And it must follow, as the night the day,
> Thou canst not then be false to any man. (*Hamlet*)

Of course, Shaw's way is not your way or mine, nor does our talent express what his did. The point is that he dedicated his life to expressing what was in him. This could well be our dedication in life: *To express what is in us.* The law of life will fit this expression into its proper category. Our job is to *do.* Life, nature and time will determine what is to be done with what we do. If we mean what we do, its meaning will become clear as a part of the great scheme of things.

MAKE THE MOST OF YOURSELF

1. Be honest with yourself about yourself.
2. Find out what you can do better than anything else.
3. Find out how you can adapt this ability to the needs of mankind.
4. Devote your life to developing and performing this activity in the service of others.
5. Don't worry about yourself. Use reasonable common sense and you'll come out all right.

It has been said:

"He has achieved success who has lived well, laughed often and loved much; who has gained the respect of intelligent men and the love of little children; who has fitted his niche and accomplished his task; who has left the world better than he found it, whether it be an improved poppy, a perfect poem, or a rescued soul; who has never lacked appreciation of earth's beauty or failed to express it; who has looked for the best in others and given the best he had; whose life was an inspiration; whose memory is a benediction." (Bessie Anderson [Mrs. Arthur J. Stanley] prize-winning definition of "Success" in a contest conducted by Brown Book Magazine, 1904)

The successful person is the good person. The meaning and purpose of life is revealed only to those who learn how to:

1. Cultivate the virtues.
2. Moderate conduct.
3. Venerate God.

These entail the development of understanding. This book endeavors to present specific techniques which will help us understand:

1. The nature of God
   and the Universe.
2. Life itself.
3. The World.
4. Ourselves.
5. Others.

It is what we are that counts. If we would discover the purpose of life we must work toward becoming the kind of person to whom the great rewards of life may come. Don't be afraid to dream—to extend your consciousness. "Man's reach exceeds his grasp." (Glenn Clark)

HOW TO MAKE YOUR DREAMS COME TRUE

1. Be aware of God.
2. Be realistic with yourself.
3. Be married to your dream.
4. Be faithful to it.
5. Be patient.

"THE LITTLE ENGINE THAT COULD"

Since 1911, American literature and folklore have been enriched by the regular appearance of that little fable, *The Little Engine That Could*, author anonymous.

You remember:

"Once upon a time a happy little train was on its way to deliver a load of toys and goodies to the boys and girls on the other side of the mountain. However, her engine became tired and could go no further. One of the toys, a little clown, started looking for help. The first possibility to appear was Shiny New Engine, but he scornfully refused to pull the trainload of toys over the mountain. Big Strong Engine came by on another track, but he also refused, and so did Old Rusty Engine when he appeared. Finally, along came Little Blue Engine, and she accepted the job. 'I think I can, I think I can, I think I can,' she said, as she started up the mountain with the trainload of toys. She continued this chant until the train reached the top of the mountain. Then, as they started down the other side to their happy destination she puffed steadily, 'I thought I could, I thought I could, I thought I could.'"

Several generations have now been influenced by the positive impact of these statements of "The Little Engine." Their scientific lesson has never been more clearly demonstrated than by the history of "The Little Engine" itself, and its author, Mrs. Frances M. Ford of Philadelphia, who was not recognized as the author until after her one hundredth birthday. Coincident with that anniversary several years ago, Grosset and Dunlap published a new edition of the original story with Mrs. Ford credited as the author for the first time. And thereby hangs a tale.

"I had something to say, so I said it," Mrs. Ford told me as I interviewed her in Philadelphia in 1953. "I didn't dream that there was ever going to be so much excitement about it. I wasn't thinking about writing something big and important when I thought up the story of *The Little Engine*. I just wanted to say what I believed, and this was a way to do it.

"I never was a professional writer," Mrs. Ford continued. "I was just writing to fulfill a need. My job in 1911 was with a Mr. Morris who operated a business called the After School Club and was selling encyclopedias for children. As a sales promotion device, Mr. Morris offered a bonus plan whereby parents could write in about problems concerning their children, and an answer would be dispatched to the child, approaching the situation from his point of view. My job was to write these letters.

"As Uncle Nat, I wrote hundreds of letters to children all over the country. At first I used to write the letters under my own name, but the children seemed reluctant to accept advice written by a woman. Uncle Nat was much more successful in getting his point across, so I sacrificed my identity to his.

"I don't know how many of these I wrote during the several years I was with the After School Club. Hundreds I guess. If a child wouldn't eat his cereal, wouldn't behave, or wouldn't study his lessons, sooner or later he was bound to hear from Uncle Nat. I recall that *The Little Engine* was originally written to a child who became easily discouraged. Later, the same letter seemed to fit other cases, so *The Little Engine* was sent to many children. It always seemed to do the job.

"In fact, since the recent stories about me and my *Little Engine* have been published in newspapers and magazines, I have received over two hundred letters from people in every state in the Union, telling me how they had been brought up on *The Little Engine* and how its simple little lesson had come to the surface to help them in times of trouble and stress. Several people have told how they owed their lives to remembering it, because it encouraged them to put forth that extra effort which meant the difference between success and failure. One letter is from a veteran who gives *The Little Engine* credit for pulling him through a terrible battle in the South Pacific during World War II.

"It is very gratifying to know that I could be the means for helping so many people," Mrs. Ford continued, "but there is nothing to make such a fuss about now. I just wanted to teach the children some common sense, that's all. Some of them seem to have gotten it. I'm glad.

"And don't think *The Engine* hasn't stood by me through thick and thin too," her eyes flashed. "Life hasn't all been 'down the mountain' for me either. I had as much climbing to do as any of them, and I've almost come to a stop lots of times. But something within me has always put me over the top. And, you know, now that I look back on the tough times and the problems, I believe I always learned the most from them. *The Little Engine* is just one of the lessons, but I have a lot more in here," she bubbled as she pointed to her heart, and then laughed.

Mrs. Ford's senses and faculties were sharp and keen, and her insight and sense of humor made her a sheer delight to talk to. I came away refreshed and inspired by the contact with this delightful person who was "one hundred years young." Her understanding of the meaning of life, her insight and good will, were all expressed in *The Little Engine*.

Victor Hugo said that there is nothing so powerful as an idea whose time has come. *The Little Engine* continues to be a great idea, and a significant force for good. Glance again at the brief version given earlier, or better still, get a full copy of the story and interpret it metaphysically. It is all there:

The train loaded with toys may well express man, with his natural gifts and his potential of ideas and creative expression, filled with the abundance of all good things and moving easily along in life. On the other side of the mountain is the destination of true happiness to be attained through service and sharing. However, to reach this destination, he must first move up the mountain, which represents spiritual realization as well as material obstacle. Problems can only be solved through spiritual means.

"I think I can, I think I can, I think I can," is our song of identification as the Idea grows in us. We take hold of the problem, and our faith and conviction give us a momentum of intelligent action which carries us over all obstacles. That which we think we can is what we are doing. Every part of our being rejoices in our full and abundant creative activity. We smile and bless and give thanks for the action of Good through us. Recognition, complete acceptance, and thanksgiving warm us as we make our demonstration, "I thought I could, I thought I could, I thought I could."

The greatness of *The Little Engine That Could* lies in the simple fact that it has been doing its work of conditioning the minds of boys and girls for a number of years now, without anyone needing to, or probably even thinking of giving it a deeper meaning. It just works. As Mrs. Ford said, "It's just good common sense, that's all."

"The Little Engines" are constantly at work inside each and every one of us. They are our original creative ideas. Our recognition and use of them weaves into the fibre of our consciousness the positive spiritual qualities of faith, love, unity, confidence, and resourcefulness. Mrs. Ford and *The Little Engine That Could* have made a practical contribution to their time because they have aided in the influencing and conditioning of man's mind toward the affirmative.

What do you want your life to say? What do you stand for? What is your guiding star? Choose your goal with purity of motive and honesty and purity of intention and let nothing deter you. The world needs men and women who can tackle the thing that cannot be done—and do it. You can do it—whatever it is, if you think you can, if you prepare yourself, and if you stick to it.

HOW TO ACCOMPLISH YOUR PURPOSE

1. Take inventory of yourself. Catalogue your abilities. Count your blessings.
2. Decide upon your objective and know that you can achieve it.
3. Dissolve all doubts and strengthen your conviction that God is working through you.
4. Go ahead and do what you have to do. Act confidently.
5. Give thanks that it is already done.

EFFECTIVE LIVING

"To live, to learn, to serve" could well be taken as a motto for effective living. The real reason for living is to discover our purpose for living and to express it the best way we can. We can attain peace of mind and achieve the resulting success when we listen to the still small voice within and do what it tells us to do. Every successful man who ever lived has lived by this precept. Poets, prophets and teachers have proclaimed its importance. Thoreau said:

> "If one advances confidently in the direction of his dreams, and endeavors to live the life which he has imagined, he will meet with a success unexpected in common hours. . . .
>
> "If a man does not keep pace with his companions, perhaps it is because he hears a different drummer. Let him step to the music which he hears, however measured or far away."
>
> Henry David Thoreau, Walden; XVII,
> "Spring"; and XVIII, "Conclusion."

To Socrates' dictum, "Man, know thyself," we must add the direction, "Be your best at all times." When we do this even our mistakes will have a kind of majesty about them. We can become ourselves only when we know ourselves. Introspection, examination and meditation are our daily tools for attaining the larger life. The techniques of treatment in this book and in Your Thoughts Can Change Your Life are designed for this purpose. Study to understand them and then use them faithfully. They are the keys to the kingdom.

Many people in this world are completely dedicated to helping others. The legion of those who serve is constantly growing. These angels on earth, these servants of the Great One, are the unselfish souls who find their reward in serving an ideal. They are the real salt of the earth. These join with the countless numbers of others throughout the world who form a vast invisible army dedicated to helping others. Upon them rests the hope of humanity. Their dedication is the salvation of the world.

There is one particular angel worthy of mention. Her name is Mary Louise Zollars. She is one of the many volunteer workers who transcribed the tape recordings, the lectures and class notes and typed the material for this book, and help me regularly getting material in shape for our other publications, scripts for radio broadcasts, correspondence courses and lessons for our membership, and many other purposes. No task is too large, too small or too tedious for this team of workers. They serve cheerfully and their work is of the highest calibre. Mary Louise differs from them only in one respect: *she does her typing with her toes.* Now a woman of early maturity, Mary Louise was born a spastic. She has long since settled the matter of her dedication, and has overcome almost unbelievable difficulties in her determination to lead an active and useful life. She is a delightful person, always in the best of spirits, and has hosts of friends. She asks nothing except the opportunity to give of herself, which she does unstintingly. She believes with Michelangelo that "trifles make perfection, and perfection is no trifle." I have never found a mistake in any of her work. She once retyped an entire script before I could stop her because she discovered a minor error. Those of us who are privileged to know this remarkable lady are constantly inspired by her. Milton said, "They also serve who only stand and wait," but Mary Louise has preferred to be more active.

Another remarkable person who reminds many of us of the immortal remark, "I cried because I had no shoes, until I met a man who had no feet," is Floyd Corbin, the well-known teacher, psychologist and author who "sees without physical eyes." * A dedicated student of the Science of Mind since he lost his sight in an accident several years ago, Floyd has dedicated his life to helping others with his lectures, books, phonograph records and psychological counseling. He never complains, and I have never seen him in anything except the highest of spirits. Equally dedicated is his wife, Eve, whom he married during his years of darkness and is now beside him constantly, providing eyes and other help for the expression of a noble soul. The world is better off for such people. Their victory is our inspiration.

We call the inner substance of a person his character, or consciousness. This book will help you build your consciousness so that you may overcome difficulties, solve problems, and develop your true potential. There are many aspects of the human personality. Since its potential is limitless and is destined to reach perfection there is no end to the powers and characteristics which we possess. Work toward the develop-

---

* See *How to Relax in a Busy World,* by Floyd Corbin (Prentice-Hall, Inc., Englewood Cliffs, N. J., 1962).

ment of these powers within yourself. Here is a check-list for introspection and personal growth:

20 PERSONAL HUMAN POWERS

1. Will	11. Wisdom
2. Imagination	12. Courage
3. Love	13. Vision
4. Faith	14. Truth
5. Understanding	15. Awareness
6. Order	16. Resourcefulness
7. Discipline	17. Perseverance
8. Humility	18. Concentration
9. Humor	19. Patience
10. Enthusiasm	20. Strength

THE TIME OF YOUR LIFE

One of our human complaints is, "I haven't enough time!"

Where did it go? Isn't there just as much time now as there ever was? Don't we have all the time there is? Of course. We must take it, that's all. It is a matter of putting first things first. You must decide how you are going to use your time.

1. Take time for work.	3. Take time for others.
2. Take time for worship.	4. Take time for yourself.
	5. Take time for living.

Make each moment significant. Live each one fully as it comes along. What would you do if you were told that this present moment were your last one? You would certainly try to make it a good one, wouldn't you? You would endeavor to do all the things you had meant to do but never did. You would try to make everything right within yourself and in your relationship with other people as you strove to get right with God. You would endeavor to correct all past mistakes and to make your life as perfect as you could. In short, you would do the best you could to live in that moment your entire life the way you would have liked it to have been all along.

Since it is impossible to ever do this in a single moment, even if it were the last one, we must do it as we go along. That is why life is a daily proposition. All parts of it are equally important. The way we act when we are alone is just as important as what we do when we are before the multitude. The way we act at the office is as important as the way we worship in church. The hours spent in the world's activities are as important, but no more so, than the hours spent in prayer. Everything in life is related to everything else. We cannot indulge in secret vices. Everything we are, think, feel, say and do is woven into the fabric of our lives. It is impossible to be one thing and express another. Everything shows. Darkness in the heart cannot produce light in the world. Confusion in the mind cannot produce order in our lives. A bad disposition can never produce harmony. A clouded consciousness can never bring happiness.

Live in the here and the now. Make each moment a masterpiece of living. William Cullen Bryant sums it all up in "Thanatopsis":

> "So live that when thy summons comes to join
> The innumerable caravan that moves
> To that mysterious realm, where each shall take
> His chamber in the silent halls of death,
> Thou go not, like the quarry slave at night,
> Scourged to his dungeon, but, sustained and soothed
> By an unfaltering trust, approach thy grave
> Like one who wraps the drapery of his couch
> About him, and lies down to pleasant dreams."

We must travel across the plains of what is sometimes dull and monotonous daily existence in order to reach the mountains. Both are parts of life. We must experience them both. It is during this journey that we build up the strength to climb the mountains once we reach them. The children of Israel had to wander "forty years in the wilderness" before they were allowed to "enter into the Promised Land."

Make your life what you want it to be. Do it now, and continue to do it in the daily business of living. Life stretches endlessly before us, but don't think of how far you have to go; think of how far you have come. The primordial ooze in which we originated is far behind us and we have all already had numerous glimpses of the heaven which is our destination. We achieve our destiny of complete fulfillment by keeping eternally at it, "striving upward in the night," until we achieve the summit, standing on the pinnacle of understanding and enlightenment. This is the destiny of every one of us, and the assurance which gives meaning and purpose to our lives.

FIVE BASIC REQUIREMENTS FOR SUCCESSFUL LIVING

1. Guiding Purpose
2. Inner Strength
3. Sense of Values
4. Vital Faith
5. All-Embracing Love

God's work is done by everyone no matter what the particular occupation may be. The butcher, the baker and the candlestick maker all have their places in the great scheme of things. So do the artist, the musician, the actor, and the ditch digger, the minister and everyone else. Just be sure that your call comes from the Higher Self within you, that you have really heard it, and that it truly represents the expression of your highest and best. Nothing else is good enough for you. Nothing else can bring happiness, health, riches, fame or anything else. Do not deny the angel as it descends upon you. Do not sell your birthright for a mess of pottage. "Hitch your wagon to a star" and ride it to the farthermost planet. Compromise is not honored in the kingdom of God. The only requirements are clarity of purpose and depth of conviction. When we deny our dreams we necessarily deny ourselves. The Lord within is betrayed, and suffering and destruction are the result.

Gather your disciples together: Relaxation, Expectation, Recognition, Unification, Dedication, Intention, Identification, Conviction, Realization, Projection, Action and Cooperation *—and let nothing deter you as you go about this business of purposeful living. Call the roll of these inner disciples of the mind. Be sure they are all present, and examine them carefully as they answer. There is no place for weakness any place in life; certainly not in the residents of the kingdom of your mind. If one of these basic attitudes is weak, single it out for special training. Start to think in terms of strengthening this part of your consciousness. Eliminate everything that contradicts this attitude. Affirm! Affirm! Build the conviction that what you want to be is already true within you. Build the conviction that you can and will follow through until you obtain the kingdom of accomplishment. This is the entire purpose and meaning of life. We are here not just to exist, but to live!

* See the author's *Your Thoughts Can Change Your Life*, Prentice-Hall, 1961.

Daily Guide to Meaning and Purpose

Today I affirm meaning and purpose in my life. There is real significance in my being alive. I am here for a reason. I determine to find out what it is, and to devote my life to fulfilling my destiny. I know that God has need of me, and I dedicate myself to meeting that need. I am about my Father's business at all times, and in every way.

I know that "there are more things in heaven and earth than are dreamt of in my philosophy." I devote my life to exploring the mysteries and meaning of existence. I want to know about everything. I learn through living experience. I know that I am a Divine experiment, and I have every intention of seeing that it is a success. I am responsible for my life. I can do with it what I please. I determine to live it with meaning and purpose. Everything in God's universe helps me do exactly that.

I thrill to the meaning of life today. I am aware of many wonderful things. I am on the threshold of great experience. I know that something wonderful is about to happen at every moment of time. God has placed the full potential of all things deep within my being and has left me to discover them for myself. This is the work of eternity, but I have no time to lose. I get with it right now. I put everything I have into everything I do. I hold nothing back. I know that I receive as I give. I give everything to Life. Life returns everything to me.

Quietly and confidently I relate myself to the wonder and glory of living. It is given unto me to know all things. I wisely use that which is given me. I understand the meaning and purpose of life today. "Beloved, now are we the sons of God, and it doth not yet appear what we shall be." (I John 3:2) I do everything I can to help fulfill God's Plan for me. *And so it is.*

CHAPTER TWELVE

"THE TRUTH SHALL MAKE YOU FREE"

Along with a good percentage of the country's population, I like to watch and listen to the World Series and other athletic events on television and radio. I thrill to the clean competition and keen rivalry of the great teams pitted against each other.

The attributes which go to make a good athlete or an effective team are the same ones necessary to all of us if we are to live effectively in peace and fredom. Of primary importance is the principle of cooperation—the realization that it is necessary to work together if we are going to get anything done. Athletes have this drilled into them by their coaches from the very beginning. Some players readily learn this golden rule and become good "team" players. A club of team-minded players is always stronger and wins more games, and the players get more satisfaction and reward than when self-seeking individuals selfishly seek to be stars all by themselves.

The "All-Star" games of various kinds are a good example of what happens when individual performers attempt to play together without an integrated feeling of team-play. We have all seen teams made up of inferior players, but who had the "one for all and all for one" spirit, topple an aggregation which was made up of individual "grand-stand" players.

Sometimes we have to learn the lesson of team-play, just like many other of life's lessons, the hard way. In high school I was a pretty fair center on the football team—and I think I was a good team-player, simply because there isn't much else you can be in that position. On offense, the center's job is to pass the ball back to the backfield men so they can run, pass or kick, and then he must help to clear the way so that the backfield man can do something with it. When the center fails in either of these assignments, disaster results. On defense, most football players are good team-men because common sense shows you that you can't stop the entire opposing team by yourself, so self-survival forces the players to "gang-up" and work together for the common good. But it is often another matter on offense.

It was late in the football season of my senior year. Our team had done very well, and we were well on the way to the league championship. School and team spirit were running high as we faced our last week of scrimmage before the big game the next Saturday. It was the classic situation of two strong rivals pitted against each other for supremacy, and to us on the Cheney, Washington, high school football team it was every bit as important as the World Series. We wanted desperately to win, and the coach was drilling us hard and late on team-work.

During this crucial period a fierce desire began to assert itself in me. I wanted to make a touchdown. During four years of play I had passed the ball from center for hundreds of touchdowns, and had blocked out defensive players, clearing the way for many others. But I had never made a touchdown. Now, I was facing the final game of my high school career, and if I didn't make a touchdown in this game, I never would. The chances of recovering a fumble for a touchdown are always there of course, but since it hadn't happened during four years, I didn't think it would in Saturday's big game. The idea grew on me during the week, and I guess I made a lot of noise about it, and the coach and team sat on this nonsense pretty hard, but I persisted. To shut me up more than anything else, I think, the coach finally devised a play whereby the entire line would shift over to one side, thus making the center—me—eligible to receive a pass. He said that if we ever got far enough ahead and the situation was right in a game we could use it as a surprise play and maybe Curtis could make his touchdown, but he would skin me alive if it didn't work. We practiced the play a few times until it was firmly in our minds and we could execute it. I was satisfied; and nothing more was said about it as we concentrated on preparation for the big game.

Saturday was a typical football day—clear, cool weather, a championship game, a big crowd in the stadium and all the rest of that traditional situation. Both teams were keyed up to a fine fighting pitch. The going was tough. The two teams battled back and forth in mid-field throughout the first three periods of the game, but finally in the middle of the fourth quarter our team started a march and advanced to inside the ten-yard line when our quarterback was injured on the third down, and had to be removed from the game. I was given the job of calling signals for the all-important play which could win the game if it was successful.

Facing the Truth About Our Pride

I decided that this was the time for me to make my touchdown, so I called for the shift of the line so that I, the center, could become an end, and therefore be eligible to receive a pass. It almost worked. This unorthodox formation completely confused our opponents. I snapped the ball and ran out in the flat toward the goal line with no one paying any attention to me whatsoever. Why should they bother with the center? The tacklers were after the man with the ball! Visions of glory passed through my mind as I turned and saw the ball sailing straight toward me. All I had to do was catch it and fall across the goal line. I would have my touchdown! I—I—I—my—my—my—You guessed it. A very good team player became completely worthless when he started to think completely about himself. That's exactly what I did. I was making a grandstand play! I wasn't thinking about winning the game; I was thinking about making a touchdown!

Not content with this, I decided to make it look really heroic. All I would have needed to do was to stand still and let the ball fall into my arms. Instead, I decided to jump and make a desperate catch, the way our halfbacks had done all season when they made the touchdowns I envied so much. I got my hands on the ball, held it for a moment while I took a few steps toward the goal, then let it slither ignominiously through my fingers as I fumbled it, and it spun around on the three-yard line—a free ball. The opposing team recovered, and in so doing, recovered their morale, and working together beautifully as a team, started a march which took them down the field across the goal line and victory, with only seconds left to spare in the game.

I have since been grateful for this lesson, but it was anything but easy to face the coach, my teammates, and my friends after having let everyone down. Even then I knew that I had been completely in the wrong. Anyone could fumble the ball—it's done in every game by someone. I could be forgiven for that, but I didn't deserve to be forgiven for going all out for myself instead of the team. To me then it was more important that I make a touchdown than anything else. I put myself ahead of the team. My motive was not pure, and I suffered accordingly.

This is pretty much the road we all have to travel in life. If our motive is not pure, if we are out merely for ourselves and to heck with everybody else, sooner or later we will be caught up short and we will have to learn the lesson of cooperation the hard way.

Facing the Truth About Teamwork

Not only is it easier to get things done by teamwork, but it is actually a lot more fun. The home is a much happier place when all members of the family are working together. The office is certainly a better place to work in when we all apply ourselves to the job at hand. The governments of nations can make real contributions to the welfare of the people when all branches of the government, all parties and all departments keep the principle of cooperation active. And nations themselves have found that world cooperation is necessary if we are to co-exist in this modern world.

The headline-grabbers and the glory-seekers still exist, of course, but one of these days they will become as extinct as the dodo bird, and all men everywhere will cooperate on the level of personal, group, national and international teamwork to bring about peace and freedom in our currently troubled world.

We can only experience peace and freedom in our world when we first establish it in our minds and hearts. Jesus said, "And ye shall know the truth, and the truth shall make you free." (John 8:32) This is the promise of religion—to help us find Truth, to provide understanding and guidance by which we may live. We all need a religion whether we know it or not. The question is not so much "Which one?" as "What kind?" Each one of us individually plays a vital part in providing this answer.

Facing Up to Religious Truths

The scope of modern religion must be broad enough to encompass everything concerning man's life and his relationship to God. This is the approach of this book. It is an endeavor to blend together the affirmative principles in the inspired teachings of the wise men of all ages, in all idealistic philosophy, and in the vital living religions.

Jesus is quoted frequently because of the effectiveness of what he taught. He practiced what he preached. This is the only guide for the validity of any spiritual philosophy: *Can you live by it?* If you can't or don't, what good is it? But don't expect to have your religion ladled out to you with a silver spoon. Don't be too eager to subscribe to *all* the precepts of man-made religion. No one has all the answers. Religion is a personal matter. Seek Truth, then form your own religious philosophy. Stay free.

Although a part of my training has been in Religious Science, the Science of Mind, and I am a teacher of this philosophy and the minister of a Church bearing the name, I recognize no restrictions upon the area of its teaching. All roads lead up the mountain to God. "Truth is One; men call it by many names." You need not attach any name to the teaching of this book. I trust that it is aligned with Truth. It has been formed through many channels, but most of all from the One Source, through intuition, insight, inspiration and personal experience. Whether you are Christian, either Catholic or Protestant, Jew, Buddhist, Hindu, Moslem, eclectic, atheist, agnostic—or whatever, you will find something here for you to weigh, consider and use. I, for one, recognize no differences in religious beliefs. In this modern day, religion must move out of the realm of pure creed, formalism and ceremony into a practical guide for purposeful living. It is all a matter of understanding. I do not believe in separation; I believe in Truth, and that's the only name it needs. I am dedicated to teaching the Truth as it is revealed to me. This book is intended to be a step in that direction. Read it through completely, then study it carefully, as a whole and in parts, and practice the techniques and suggestions given. Make this book your constant companion. Using this book will require dedication and application from you, just as it has required them from me in writing it; but, I assure you, it is worth it.

The Mighty Army of the Dedicated

The world is full of people dedicated to serving God and helping humanity. I don't wish to imply that they are all in the field of religion and applied thought. Far from it. It just happens that this is my field and major interest, and so I use the examples with which I am most familiar. But there are dedicated servers in every walk of life. I have found that when a person lives in close contact with the Higher Self within him, he invariably becomes dedicated to service, giving his entire time, talent and energy for the glory of God and the good of others.

This book is dedicated to the purpose of helping you find and express your real self. It is designed to free you from the tyranny of the false ego so that you may discover and express your magnificent potential. Self-examination and a desire to change are the starting points, followed by cleansing ourselves thoroughly of everything that is holding us back. Tempers and bad dispositions must go. Selfishness must be turned into generosity. Hatreds and resentments must be dissolved by love. Fear must release its wasted energy into constructive faith. All of this is accomplished when we get on the constructive side of life.

Who Are Your Mentors?

There are many wonderful teachers who have contributed to my spiritual education thus far, and I know I am only beginning. Naturally, there are certain ones who stand out more than others. Every teacher attracts his own to him, and every student finds his right teacher—if he is dedicated to the quest. "When the pupil is ready, the Master appears." I have been fortunate in the number, frequency and intensity with which they have appeared in my life.

In *Your Thoughts Can Change Your Life*, I mentioned Dr. Ervin Seale, Dr. Raymond Charles Barker and Dr. Ernest Holmes, but four others stand out as shining stars, mainly because of their dedication to certain aspects of the whole picture of spiritual unfoldment. They are modern titans in the field of human evolution. Each is dedicated to developing the concept of the whole person. Together, they form a magnificent circle of completion. I love them dearly, and have found in their inspired teachings a rounding out of the total picture. My debt and devotion to them is complete.

Here they are, with the aspects of human growth which they represent:

I. Manly Palmer Hall, Founder of the Philosophical Research Society, Los Angeles, California: Knowledge, Wisdom and Understanding.

II. Brother Mandus, Founder of the World Healing Crusade, Blackpool, England: Meditation, Faith, Healing.

III. Dr. Baghat Singh Thind, Independent Sikh Teacher and Master of Hatha Yoga, Hollywood, California: Discipline, Exercise, Health.

IV. Flower and Lawrence Newhouse, Founders of the Christward Ministry, Vista, California: Devotion, Love, Beauty.

There are many others, but for me, these lead all the rest, mainly because of their unselfish dedication and the clarity and irrefutability of their teaching. Each one is well-known in his own right. Each has written numerous books, and each is vitally active as a teacher today. They are similar in that they each teach from the unmistakable authority of transcendent spiritual experience, each is unselfishly dedicated to the service of God and mankind, and each projects a vision of the larger scope of things which rises above personal human experience. You will note that together they represent twelve areas of the human consciousness just as this book deals with twelve areas of human experience and *Your Thoughts Can Change Your Life* deals with twelve basic mental and emotional attitudes. This is no accident. Twelve is the number of completion—symbolizing the disciples, which through service to the Indwelling Christ, complete the whole man.

YOU CAN DISCOVER NEW TRUTHS

When you are thoroughly familiar with this book, the emergence of your own magnificent potential will lead you to find your own teachers. The inner spiritual expansion which this book will give you will project itself into your world and you will attract whatever and whomever you need. But remember, things do not happen to you, they happen through you. The earnest seeker will explore many paths. The personal experiences and the philosophy of their teachings is fully explained in the various books by these four teachers, so I won't enlarge upon them here except to direct your attention to them and to acknowledge with gratitude their dedication and contribution to our lives.

"THE SICK SEVEN": HUB OF BONDAGE

Most of our problems arise from emotional involvement in matters that should be kept completely objective. Unbalanced emotional response causes all of these "Sick Seven" inner attitudes:

1. Hurry   4. Anxiety
2. Tension   5. Confusion
3. Pressure   6. Rejection
            7. Insecurity

Richard March was suffering from all of them when he first came to see me. He was all mixed up, his life was a mess, and he didn't know where he was going. Like so many people, he had come to me as a last resort. Having tried everything else, he had lost hope. He didn't really expect to be helped, but a friend whom I had helped persuaded him to make this one last try. Richard had all of the "Sick Seven" plus most of the other negative inner attitudes which we have talked about throughout this book. His body was sick, his disposition was bad, and he was broke and unemployed. We went to work to see what we could salvage. Resistance was great and progress was slow, but through simple instruction and steady prayer treatment we made progress.

"The world is a comedy to those that think, a tragedy to those that feel," opined Horace Walpole. Throughout the book we have seen that the tragedy can be avoided if we learn to feel correctly about the right things instead of the wrong ones. Richard was feeling intensely about the wrong things. He was bemoaning his fate one day, when I decided to have a good talk with him. I said, "Nothing is ever as bad as it seems to be when you are emotionally involved with it. Remember, as William James said, 'When there is an emotional bias you develop an intellectual blindspot.'

"It stands to reason that, since thought causes all things, *if you change your thought the situation will change.* This is the way to win all of your battles. *Reverse your thought.* To do this, you must first quiet your mind. 'Relax, let go and let God.' Completely relax and quiet yourself—then start to build a more complete life for yourself by starting to think more constructive thoughts, based upon a sound set of principles and values.

"Now, as you know, all of this is not as easy as it sounds, but you can do it, you must do it; everyone must. It is the work of a lifetime, perhaps of many lifetimes, but it is the most important job in the world, and we must keep eternally at it. We have unlimited power right inside of us. We could rebuild the world in a single day if we used this power wisely, but we get all bothered and bewildered and destroy things with our thoughts and feelings faster than even God can build them up."

"Where do I start?" Richard asked.

"Why, you know," I replied. "Start right where you are, and do it right now. You're already doing it; you're an entirely different person than you were a few minutes ago. You are relaxed now, and your attention, turned away from your problems, and turned toward answers and solutions is 'building more stately mansions' in your soul. Continue this. We become great and noble by keeping eternally at it. There is no short cut to growth; we must *become* that which we wish to be. This process of becoming is a slow one. Look at the innumerable rings around the trunk of a tree which has been cut down—each one indicating a year of growth, but no year was ever hurried. All growth is imperceptible while it is happening, but it is always going on. Our job is to cooperate with growth instead of resisting it."

"I know all that, Dr. Curtis," he replied, "But it's hard to follow through! It's easy to be quiet and relaxed here listening to you, but what about all of the problems and difficulties that come up every day? What about people?"

"Well, what about them?"

"They're—always causing trouble!"

"They are?"

"Why sure, you know how people are."

"How are they?"

"Well, you know, they're—they're—people!"

"Precisely. They're people. Even as you and I. Don Blanding's beloved nurse told him when he was a child, 'Honey, you'd better get used to likin' people 'cause they's the things they's the most of.' No, my friend, we can't blame other people for our problems, nor the weather, nor the government, nor taxes, nor germs,—no, nor God, either. Did you ever read *Julius Caesar*? Shakespeare says, 'The fault, dear Brutus, is not in our stars, but in ourselves, that we are underlings.' "

Richard thought for a long moment before he spoke. "You mean

I'm responsible for what happens to me because of something within me?"

"Of course," I affirmed. "Experiences happen through you, not to you. No two of us experience the same things even in the same situation. It is the 'set' of the mind and the heart that has a great deal to do with it. This 'set' is largely determined by how relaxed you are."

"Relaxation is that important, eh?"

"You bet it is. Never underestimate the first step in anything. It is always the most important. An Oriental proverb says, 'Start a thousand mile journey by taking the first step!' Relaxation is the first step in a balanced life, and unless your life is balanced you're going to run into difficulty sooner or later. Life is like a wheel; if it is wobbly at the center, it will wobble all the way through. Just look at the wheel. The rim may cover hundreds of thousands of miles at great speeds, the spokes may blur until we see right through them, but the center of the wheel never moves. That's a great lesson: *Never let life move you; you move it.* Follow the Biblical injunction, 'Be still and know that I am God.' (Psalm 46:10) *Relax at the center of your being first, then create constructively from there.*"

FIRST STEPS TOWARD FREEDOM OF THE MIND

Years ago, Dr. Baghat Thind taught me a simple technique of meditation which has been my constant companion through many troubled waters. I shared it with Richard March as I share it with you. It consists of only four simple steps:

1. Calm
2. Quiet
3. Peace
4. Silence

Progress through them into the complete relaxation of inner silence. The words themselves sound like the state of consciousness you wish to attain. Get by yourself, sit quietly and comfortably, shut out all distraction, get still inside, and move through these four steps to the very core of your being. The inner well-springs of strength will be released through you.

After nearly an hour together in the Silence, Richard March and I were changed people as we silently took leave of each other. On my way home I stopped my car along a country road, got out and walked into a wood nearby. I then climbed part way up a hill and seated myself on a ledge which commanded a beautiful view of the country. I was completely relaxed, filled with peace, and receptive to the beauty of Nature around me.

"How relaxed Nature is," I thought. "No stress, no strain, no fuss and feathers. Nothing is struggling to be anything other than what it is. Nothing is hurrying to get anywhere. The trees aren't trying to take anything away from other trees, and the sky and the sea aren't in competition with each other."

As my musing turned to reverie and meditation, I drank deeply from the well-springs of quiet and relaxation within me. As has long been my habit, I followed this period of meditation with definite prayer treatment about specific things in my life. Relaxation is actually a prayer in itself, and prayer leads to deeper relaxation. It is a magic circle. Try it. It works.

I didn't see Richard again for several months, but when I did, I knew that he had learned his lesson well—and was practicing it.

"Well!" I greeted him. "I haven't seen you for a long time, Richard. What have you been doing?"

"Raking leaves."

"Raking leaves? What do you mean?"

"Just what I said, Dr. Curtis. Something happened to me during that last session of ours. After we had that long period of silence, I decided that if anything was going to be done about Richard March, I was going to have to do it. You gave me the key: *I had to start inside myself.* Well, I started there, and it took me all this time to get out. I had a lot of sorting out to do, and I decided to take time to do it. It seemed that all my life I had been running to catch a bus. I decided to let somebody else catch it for a change. I had a lot of leaves to rake up—literally and figuratively.

"I decided to do nothing for awhile until I felt like it, and I haven't all this time—except to rake my lawn and rake my mind. Yesterday, for the first time, I felt I had them in the shape I wanted them in."

"Wonderful! Richard, I'm proud of you," I exclaimed.

"Wait a minute. 'You ain't heard nothin' yet!' Getting rid of the 'Sick Seven' was only part of it. This morning I got a telephone call from a company I've been wanting to work for for years. I've just been to see the manager. I am on the payroll as of right now. I report for work the first thing tomorrow!"

"Congratulations, Richard. I know you'll make a big success of the job," I said.

"I know I will, too," Richard replied. "I have to. I can't flub a chance like this one. But don't congratulate me, Dr. Curtis. You did it. You taught me how to rake leaves. You made a believer out of me. So long. See you in Church on Sunday!"

My friend laughed as he walked jauntily on his way. Another example of one who changed his life by changing himself.

Richard March could be you or any one of us. Life is a journey, and as long as we travel by trial and error we will be forced to go through the process of losing our way and finding it again. What we are interested in here is finding the right path and staying on it. The many techniques and suggestions in this book will help you do exactly that.

FREEDOM IS FOR EVERYMAN

There is a basic sameness in the human story. We all have the same basic instincts, urges, desires, needs, goals and ambitions. Shakespeare touched upon man's similarity to man in *The Merchant of Venice* when Shylock says,

"I am a Jew. Hath not a Jew eyes? Hath not a Jew hands, organs, dimensions, senses, affections, passions? Fed with the same food, hurt with the same weapons, subject to the same diseases, healed by the same means, warmed and cooled by the same winter and summer, as a Christian is? If you prick us, do we not bleed? If you tickle us, do we not laugh? If you poison us, do we not die? And if you wrong us, shall we not revenge?" (*Merchant of Venice*, Act III, Sc. 1)

Extend this concept beyond the comparison between Jew and Christian to include all people of every nationality, color and creed, and you will have a pretty good concept of the human situation.

Our one basic drive is to live. All other desires stem from this one. Everything we do stems from and is directed toward our desire to live life and to live it abundantly. The desire to live is a subjective drive. When we consciously cooperate with it, we remove obstructions and move steadily ahead to accomplishment and fulfillment.

SOME BASIC NEEDS OF MAN

Our human endeavors and problems fall into five major areas. Consciously or subconsciously we are working to achieve:

1. Health   3. Prosperity
2. Happiness   4. Freedom
            5. Self-expression

We set up these areas as goals for fulfillment because of our twelve basic needs. We need:

1. To love and be loved.   7. To be accepted.
2. To be understood.   8. To belong.
3. To have emotional security.   9. To be needed.
4. To experience variety and change. 10. To feel important.
5. To have self-esteem   11. To be alone.
6. To be recognized and appreciated. 12. To find spiritual fulfillment.

Again, these needs are subjective motivations. We are impelled and compelled by them whether or not we are consciously aware of it. Remember, we are spiritual, mental and emotional beings as well as physical ones. We are not talking here about sense-gratification. We are seeking to understand what makes us tick, and to consciously cooperate with the creative process. Go through this list carefully and recognize that all of these needs are asserting themselves in you simultaneously.

Realize that they are there and need to be fulfilled. In your treatment work, declare that they are fulfilled, and order the deeper mind to create a balanced life for you by meeting all of these needs. It is up to you. All of these needs will be met, and you will be a happy, healthy and properous person if you choose that they will be. Your over-all happiness, health, prosperity, freedom and self-expression will be the results of your balanced development in the acceptance of the fulfillment of your twelve basic needs. Work with this list until you understand it and yourself. There are really no conflicts or overlaps, even though there may seem to be. For instance, "To have self-esteem" and "To feel important" may seem synonymous, but they really are not. Your self-esteem is your affirmative feeling about yourself. Your feeling of importance is your acceptance of others' affirmative evaluations of you. "The need to be alone" may seem to conflict with some of the other needs, but it doesn't need to. Solitude is essential to your health on every level—but not too much solitude. Work for balance in all things.

Your over-all treatment objectives should include:

1. Perfect order	7. Understanding
2. Balance	8. Peace
3. Harmony	9. Freedom
4. Right Action	10. Fulfillment
5. Proper Relationships	11. Goodness
6. Adjustment	12. Wisdom

Treat yourself—that is, condition your mind to accept these attributes of complete adjustment and essentials for effective living. Notice that this list has to do with inner concepts and attitudes. Develop these, and whatever "things" you need will come to you automatically. The details of your personal life will be the results of your individuality expressing itself.

DISCOVER YOUR GREATEST NEEDS

Our basic characteristics and needs are the same, but our specific opinions, choices, desires, tastes, ideas, plans and procedures will be different. You may want and need something that does not interest me at all, and vice-versa. You may wish to travel while I may wish to stay home and work. You may want to have a new car every year while someone else may prefer walking or riding buses. We are all guaranteed "life, liberty and the pursuit of happiness" by the Constitution of the United States of America. This means that we have the freedom to do whatever we feel necessary to protect and fulfill these rights—as long as we do not infringe upon others in so doing. This book has been written to help you capture and enjoy some of the happiness you have been pursuing. We'll never have it if you just keep chasing it. Make friends with it. Live it. That's the message.

As we have said, even though we are all going in the same direction and are basically the same, details differ. After you have treated on the "basic needs" and the "basic objectives" lists, you will then want to treat specifically for some of the details and things which you need for effective objective expression. When you have done thorough inner work at the point of cause, most of the things you need will flow through your experience automatically, but there are occasions when you will want to treat for something. Make up your own list. This one is bound to have some points that will interest you—or someone:

1.	To work	7.	To be famous
2.	To have a good time	8.	To have power
3.	To travel	9.	To be successful
4.	To have nice things	10.	To have a home
5.	To be married and have children	11.	To have a new car
6.	To make money	12.	To maintain status

Don't be bashful. Make your needs, wants and wishes known. Treat on them. Be definite and specific. Accept them, but don't outline how much, when, or how it is to come about. Remember, there are always many more wonderful things on the way to us than we can accept with our limited human comprehension. Jesus said, "It is your Father's good pleasure to give you the kingdom," (Luke 12:32) and "Your Father knoweth what things ye have need of, before ye ask him." (Matt. 6:8)

It is all right to treat for things, but as someone has said, "be careful what you treat (pray) for, because you'll surely get it." Never underestimate the creative power of your own thought. It is through thought and feeling that the creative process is set in motion. Consciously directed thought and feeling to achieve a specific end or purpose is what we call treatment. Effective treatment involves moving our inner consciousness from "wishing" to conviction. Many people say, "I wish I could do this," or "I wish I could have that," without realizing that they can if they believe they can. Treatment is the process of arriving at the point where you are convinced that you can, and (in consciousness), do have the thing which you previously only wished for.

Choose wisely, however. Wishes are incipient demonstrations. The creative power of the mind is the most powerful force in the Universe. Direct it intelligently.

There is the legend of the couple of olden times who were granted three wishes—only three.

"Oh, I wish I had some sausages!" exclaimed the wife, and they appeared.

"You and your sausages!" remonstrated the husband, disgusted by his wife's foolish wish. "I wish you had those sausages on the end of your nose!" And that's exactly where they were.

Since they had only one wish left, it doesn't take much imagination to realize what they had to use it for.

Most of us are similarily profligate with our creative power. It is completely unnecessary to waste our lives trying to get sausages off the ends of our noses when we could be building more stately mansions in our souls and enjoying the riches of the kingdom.

Let's do exactly that. Let's change our lives for the better. Here are five points that will help.

HOW TO CHANGE YOUR LIFE FOR THE BETTER

1. Give up criticism and condemnation for brotherly love.
2. Give up sickness and weakness for strength and wholeness.
3. Give up lack and limitation for knowledge of God's abundance.
4. Withdraw attention from the false and unworthy and give it to the true and worthy aspects of life.
5. Exchange fear and resentment for faith, love, and the expectation of all that is good.

Now here are some definite things not to do, and some definite things for you to do. They all help.

Five Things Not to Do:

1. Don't get too tired.
2. Don't get bogged down.
3. Don't get depressed.
4. Don't be irritable.
5. Don't take yourself too seriously.

Five Things to Do:

1. Do save some time for people you love.
2. Do have some fun.
3. Do express the wonderful things within you.
4. Do laugh and be happy and the whole world changes.
5. Do take time to pray.

As a final check list to help you solve your problems and get the most out of life, work on the following points until they become part of your standard equipment.

TWELVE STEPS TO EFFECTIVE LIVING

1. Dissolve negative mental attitudes and avoid undue emotional stress.
2. Stop worrying.
3. Eliminate inferiority.
4. Improve your disposition and develop a pleasing personality.
5. Learn to make your work easy.
6. Count your blessings.
7. Forgive yourself and others.
8. Dissolve the false ego. Learn to get along with yourself and others.
9. Pray and meditate. Develop your contact and faith in God.
10. Learn to get the most out of your religion.
11. Keep interested in life, what you are doing, and in other people.
12. Obey the laws of common sense on every level.

Daily Guide to Peace and Freedom

I know the Truth and the Truth makes me free. Today I identify myself with the oneness and wholeness of life. I dissolve all bondage. I am free. I dissolve all blockage. I am free. I dissolve all doubt and suspicion. I am free. I am free from fear. I am filled with peace and love. I am attuned to the wonder and beauty of living. I am one with life.

Healing waves of peace flow over me and through me. I drink deeply from the well-springs of the Infinite. I am filled with the cleansing ambrosia of spirit. I am refreshed, renewed and refilled. I am born again. I burst out into my world with joy, enthusiasm and power. I am a free and wholesome individual. I am at peace within myself. Nothing disturbs me. I am God-centered. Nothing discourages me. I am joy-centered. Nothing confuses me. I am established in deep and perfect peace. Nothing hurts me. I am free from all painful attitudes, tendencies and experiences now and forever.

Quietly now, I lie down in the green pastures of my own soul. I immerse myself in the still waters. I am purified and cleansed by the detergent and astringent action of my own thought. I lift up my eyes unto the hills from whence cometh my help. I lift up my mind unto God. I can do all things through the inner power which strengthens me.

The inner peace of order, balance and right action are established in my soul. I endeavor to be and do my highest and best at all times. My life is my expression of God's life living itself through me. I am part of a magnificent wholeness which is perfect. I thrill with the challenge of life today. I live my life abundantly every step of the way.

My inner peace and freedom lead me to the portals of knowledge and wisdom. I get wisdom, but with all my wisdom I get understanding. It is this understanding which establishes and maintains me in perfect peace and freedom. *And so it is.*

INDEX

ELVIN POWERS SELF-IMPROVEMENT LIBRARY

ASTROLOGY

ASTROLOGY: HOW TO CHART YOUR HOROSCOPE Max Heindel	3.00
ASTROLOGY: YOUR PERSONAL SUN-SIGN GUIDE Beatrice Ryder	3.00
ASTROLOGY FOR EVERYDAY LIVING Janet Harris	2.00
ASTROLOGY MADE EASY Astarte	3.00
ASTROLOGY MADE PRACTICAL Alexandra Kayhle	3.00
ASTROLOGY, ROMANCE, YOU AND THE STARS Anthony Norvell	4.00
MY WORLD OF ASTROLOGY Sydney Omarr	5.00
THOUGHT DIAL Sydney Omarr	4.00
WHAT THE STARS REVEAL ABOUT THE MEN IN YOUR LIFE Thelma White	3.00

BRIDGE

BRIDGE BIDDING MADE EASY Edwin B. Kantar	7.00
BRIDGE CONVENTIONS Edwin B. Kantar	5.00
BRIDGE HUMOR Edwin B. Kantar	3.00
COMPETITIVE BIDDING IN MODERN BRIDGE Edgar Kaplan	4.00
DEFENSIVE BRIDGE PLAY COMPLETE Edwin B. Kantar	10.00
GAMESMAN BRIDGE—Play Better with Kantar Edwin B. Kantar	5.00
HOW TO IMPROVE YOUR BRIDGE Alfred Sheinwold	3.00
IMPROVING YOUR BIDDING SKILLS Edwin B. Kantar	4.00
INTRODUCTION TO DEFENDER'S PLAY Edwin B. Kantar	3.00
SHORT CUT TO WINNING BRIDGE Alfred Sheinwold	3.00
TEST YOUR BRIDGE PLAY Edwin B. Kantar	3.00
VOLUME 2—TEST YOUR BRIDGE PLAY Edwin B. Kantar	5.00
WINNING DECLARER PLAY Dorothy Hayden Truscott	4.00

BUSINESS, STUDY & REFERENCE

CONVERSATION MADE EASY Elliot Russell	3.00
EXAM SECRET Dennis B. Jackson	3.00
FIX-IT BOOK Arthur Symons	2.00
HOW TO DEVELOP A BETTER SPEAKING VOICE M. Hellier	3.00
HOW TO MAKE A FORTUNE IN REAL ESTATE Albert Winnikoff	4.00
INCREASE YOUR LEARNING POWER Geoffrey A. Dudley	2.00
MAGIC OF NUMBERS Robert Tocquet	2.00
PRACTICAL GUIDE TO BETTER CONCENTRATION Melvin Powers	3.00
PRACTICAL GUIDE TO PUBLIC SPEAKING Maurice Forley	3.00
7 DAYS TO FASTER READING William S. Schaill	3.00
SONGWRITERS RHYMING DICTIONARY Jane Shaw Whitfield	5.00
SPELLING MADE EASY Lester D. Basch & Dr. Milton Finkelstein	2.00
STUDENT'S GUIDE TO BETTER GRADES J. A. Rickard	3.00
TEST YOURSELF—Find Your Hidden Talent Jack Shafer	3.00
YOUR WILL & WHAT TO DO ABOUT IT Attorney Samuel G. Kling	3.00

CALLIGRAPHY

ADVANCED CALLIGRAPHY Katherine Jeffares	7.00
CALLIGRAPHER'S REFERENCE BOOK Anne Leptich & Jacque Evans	6.00
CALLIGRAPHY—The Art of Beautiful Writing Katherine Jeffares	7.00
CALLIGRAPHY FOR FUN & PROFIT Anne Leptich & Jacque Evans	7.00
CALLIGRAPHY MADE EASY Tina Serafini	7.00

CHESS & CHECKERS

BEGINNER'S GUIDE TO WINNING CHESS Fred Reinfeld	3.00
CHECKERS MADE EASY Tom Wiswell	2.00
CHESS IN TEN EASY LESSONS Larry Evans	3.00
CHESS MADE EASY Milton L. Hanauer	3.00
CHESS PROBLEMS FOR BEGINNERS edited by Fred Reinfeld	2.00
CHESS SECRETS REVEALED Fred Reinfeld	2.00
CHESS STRATEGY—An Expert's Guide Fred Reinfeld	2.00
CHESS TACTICS FOR BEGINNERS edited by Fred Reinfeld	3.00
CHESS THEORY & PRACTICE Morry & Mitchell	2.00
HOW TO WIN AT CHECKERS Fred Reinfeld	3.00
1001 BRILLIANT WAYS TO CHECKMATE Fred Reinfeld	4.00
1001 WINNING CHESS SACRIFICES & COMBINATIONS Fred Reinfeld	4.00
SOVIET CHESS Edited by R. G. Wade	3.00

COOKERY & HERBS

____CULPEPER'S HERBAL REMEDIES *Dr. Nicholas Culpeper*	3.00
____FAST GOURMET COOKBOOK *Poppy Cannon*	2.50
____GINSENG The Myth & The Truth *Joseph P. Hou*	3.00
____HEALING POWER OF HERBS *May Bethel*	3.00
____HEALING POWER OF NATURAL FOODS *May Bethel*	3.00
____HERB HANDBOOK *Dawn MacLeod*	3.00
____HERBS FOR COOKING AND HEALING *Dr. Donald Law*	2.00
____HERBS FOR HEALTH—How to Grow & Use Them *Louise Evans Doole*	3.00
____HOME GARDEN COOKBOOK—Delicious Natural Food Recipes *Ken Kraft*	3.00
____MEDICAL HERBALIST *edited by Dr. J. R. Yemm*	3.00
____NATURAL FOOD COOKBOOK *Dr. Harry C. Bond*	3.00
____NATURE'S MEDICINES *Richard Lucas*	3.00
____VEGETABLE GARDENING FOR BEGINNERS *Hugh Wiberg*	2.00
____VEGETABLES FOR TODAY'S GARDENS *R. Milton Carleton*	2.00
____VEGETARIAN COOKERY *Janet Walker*	4.00
____VEGETARIAN COOKING MADE EASY & DELECTABLE *Veronica Vezza*	3.00
____VEGETARIAN DELIGHTS—A Happy Cookbook for Health *K. R. Mehta*	2.00
____VEGETARIAN GOURMET COOKBOOK *Joyce McKinnel*	3.00

GAMBLING & POKER

____ADVANCED POKER STRATEGY & WINNING PLAY *A. D. Livingston*	3.00
____HOW NOT TO LOSE AT POKER *Jeffrey Lloyd Castle*	3.00
____HOW TO WIN AT DICE GAMES *Skip Frey*	3.00
____HOW TO WIN AT POKER *Terence Reese & Anthony T. Watkins*	3.00
____SECRETS OF WINNING POKER *George S. Coffin*	3.00
____WINNING AT CRAPS *Dr. Lloyd T. Commins*	3.00
____WINNING AT GIN *Chester Wander & Cy Rice*	3.00
____WINNING AT POKER—An Expert's Guide *John Archer*	3.00
____WINNING AT 21—An Expert's Guide *John Archer*	4.00
____WINNING POKER SYSTEMS *Norman Zadeh*	3.00

HEALTH

____BEE POLLEN *Lynda Lyngheim & Jack Scagnetti*	3.00
____DR. LINDNER'S SPECIAL WEIGHT CONTROL METHOD *P. G. Lindner, M.D.*	1.50
____HELP YOURSELF TO BETTER SIGHT *Margaret Darst Corbett*	3.00
____HOW TO IMPROVE YOUR VISION *Dr. Robert A. Kraskin*	3.00
____HOW YOU CAN STOP SMOKING PERMANENTLY *Ernest Caldwell*	3.00
____MIND OVER PLATTER *Peter G. Lindner, M.D.*	3.00
____NATURE'S WAY TO NUTRITION & VIBRANT HEALTH *Robert J. Scrutton*	3.00
____NEW CARBOHYDRATE DIET COUNTER *Patti Lopez-Pereira*	1.50
____QUICK & EASY EXERCISES FOR FACIAL BEAUTY *Judy Smith-deal*	2.00
____QUICK & EASY EXERCISES FOR FIGURE BEAUTY *Judy Smith-deal*	2.00
____REFLEXOLOGY *Dr. Maybelle Segal*	3.00
____REFLEXOLOGY FOR GOOD HEALTH *Anna Kaye & Don C. Matchan*	3.00
____YOU CAN LEARN TO RELAX *Dr. Samuel Gutwirth*	3.00
____YOUR ALLERGY—What To Do About It *Allan Knight, M.D.*	3.00

HOBBIES

____BEACHCOMBING FOR BEGINNERS *Norman Hickin*	2.00
____BLACKSTONE'S MODERN CARD TRICKS *Harry Blackstone*	3.00
____BLACKSTONE'S SECRETS OF MAGIC *Harry Blackstone*	3.00
____COIN COLLECTING FOR BEGINNERS *Burton Hobson & Fred Reinfeld*	3.00
____ENTERTAINING WITH ESP *Tony 'Doc' Shiels*	2.00
____400 FASCINATING MAGIC TRICKS YOU CAN DO *Howard Thurston*	3.00
____HOW I TURN JUNK INTO FUN AND PROFIT *Sari*	3.00
____HOW TO WRITE A HIT SONG & SELL IT *Tommy Boyce*	7.00
____JUGGLING MADE EASY *Rudolf Dittrich*	2.00
____MAGIC FOR ALL AGES *Walter Gibson*	4.00
____MAGIC MADE EASY *Byron Wels*	2.00
____STAMP COLLECTING FOR BEGINNERS *Burton Hobson*	2.00

HORSE PLAYERS' WINNING GUIDES

____BETTING HORSES TO WIN *Les Conklin*	3.00
____ELIMINATE THE LOSERS *Bob McKnight*	3.00

___HOW TO PICK WINNING HORSES *Bob McKnight*		3.00
___HOW TO WIN AT THE RACES *Sam (The Genius) Lewin*		3.00
___HOW YOU CAN BEAT THE RACES *Jack Kavanagh*		3.00
___MAKING MONEY AT THE RACES *David Barr*		3.00
___PAYDAY AT THE RACES *Les Conklin*		3.00
___SMART HANDICAPPING MADE EASY *William Bauman*		3.00
___SUCCESS AT THE HARNESS RACES *Barry Meadow*		3.00
___WINNING AT THE HARNESS RACES—An Expert's Guide *Nick Cammarano*		3.00

HUMOR

___HOW TO BE A COMEDIAN FOR FUN & PROFIT *King & Laufer*	2.00
___HOW TO FLATTEN YOUR TUSH *Coach Marge Reardon*	2.00
___JOKE TELLER'S HANDBOOK *Bob Orben*	3.00
___JOKES FOR ALL OCCASIONS *Al Schock*	3.00
___2000 NEW LAUGHS FOR SPEAKERS *Bob Orben*	3.00
___2,500 JOKES TO START 'EM LAUGHING *Bob Orben*	3.00

HYPNOTISM

___ADVANCED TECHNIQUES OF HYPNOSIS *Melvin Powers*	2.00
___BRAINWASHING AND THE CULTS *Paul A. Verdier, Ph.D.*	3.00
___CHILDBIRTH WITH HYPNOSIS *William S. Kroger, M.D.*	3.00
___HOW TO SOLVE Your Sex Problems with Self-Hypnosis *Frank S. Caprio, M.D.*	3.00
___HOW TO STOP SMOKING THRU SELF-HYPNOSIS *Leslie M. LeCron*	3.00
___HOW TO USE AUTO-SUGGESTION EFFECTIVELY *John Duckworth*	3.00
___HOW YOU CAN BOWL BETTER USING SELF-HYPNOSIS *Jack Heise*	3.00
___HOW YOU CAN PLAY BETTER GOLF USING SELF-HYPNOSIS *Jack Heise*	3.00
___HYPNOSIS AND SELF-HYPNOSIS *Bernard Hollander, M.D.*	3.00
___HYPNOTISM *(Originally published in 1893) Carl Sextus*	5.00
___HYPNOTISM & PSYCHIC PHENOMENA *Simeon Edmunds*	4.00
___HYPNOTISM MADE EASY *Dr. Ralph Winn*	3.00
___HYPNOTISM MADE PRACTICAL *Louis Orton*	3.00
___HYPNOTISM REVEALED *Melvin Powers*	2.00
___HYPNOTISM TODAY *Leslie LeCron and Jean Bordeaux, Ph.D.*	5.00
___MODERN HYPNOSIS *Lesley Kuhn & Salvatore Russo, Ph.D.*	5.00
___NEW CONCEPTS OF HYPNOSIS *Bernard C. Gindes, M.D.*	5.00
___NEW SELF-HYPNOSIS *Paul Adams*	4.00
___POST-HYPNOTIC INSTRUCTIONS—Suggestions for Therapy *Arnold Furst*	3.00
___PRACTICAL GUIDE TO SELF-HYPNOSIS *Melvin Powers*	3.00
___PRACTICAL HYPNOTISM *Philip Magonet, M.D.*	3.00
___SECRETS OF HYPNOTISM *S. J. Van Pelt, M.D.*	3.00
___SELF-HYPNOSIS A Conditioned-Response Technique *Laurance Sparks*	5.00
___SELF-HYPNOSIS Its Theory, Technique & Application *Melvin Powers*	3.00
___THERAPY THROUGH HYPNOSIS *edited by Raphael H. Rhodes*	4.00

JUDAICA

___HOW TO LIVE A RICHER & FULLER LIFE *Rabbi Edgar F. Magnin*	2.00
___MODERN ISRAEL *Lily Edelman*	2.00
___SERVICE OF THE HEART *Evelyn Garfiel, Ph.D.*	4.00
___STORY OF ISRAEL IN COINS *Jean & Maurice Gould*	2.00
___STORY OF ISRAEL IN STAMPS *Maxim & Gabriel Shamir*	1.00
___TONGUE OF THE PROPHETS *Robert St.John*	5.00

JUST FOR WOMEN

___COSMOPOLITAN'S GUIDE TO MARVELOUS MEN Fwd. by *Helen Gurley Brown*	3.00
___COSMOPOLITAN'S HANG-UP HANDBOOK Foreword by *Helen Gurley Brown*	4.00
___COSMOPOLITAN'S LOVE BOOK—A Guide to Ecstasy in Bed	4.00
___COSMOPOLITAN'S NEW ETIQUETTE GUIDE Fwd. by *Helen Gurley Brown*	4.00
___I AM A COMPLEAT WOMAN *Doris Hagopian & Karen O'Connor Sweeney*	3.00
___JUST FOR WOMEN—A Guide to the Female Body *Richard E. Sand, M.D.*	4.00
___NEW APPROACHES TO SEX IN MARRIAGE *John E. Eichenlaub, M.D.*	3.00
___SEXUALLY ADEQUATE FEMALE *Frank S. Caprio, M.D.*	3.00
___YOUR FIRST YEAR OF MARRIAGE *Dr. Tom McGinnis*	3.00

MARRIAGE, SEX & PARENTHOOD

___ABILITY TO LOVE *Dr. Allan Fromme*	5.00
___ENCYCLOPEDIA OF MODERN SEX & LOVE TECHNIQUES *Macandrew*	5.00
___GUIDE TO SUCCESSFUL MARRIAGE *Drs. Albert Ellis & Robert Harper*	5.00

___MAGIC IN YOUR MIND *U. S. Andersen*	5.00
___MAGIC OF THINKING BIG *Dr. David J. Schwartz*	3.00
___MAGIC POWER OF YOUR MIND *Walter M. Germain*	4.00
___MENTAL POWER THROUGH SLEEP SUGGESTION *Melvin Powers*	3.00
___NEW GUIDE TO RATIONAL LIVING *Albert Ellis, Ph.D. & R. Harper, Ph.D.*	3.00
___OUR TROUBLED SELVES *Dr. Allan Fromme*	3.00
___PSYCHO-CYBERNETICS *Maxwell Maltz, M.D.*	2.00
___SCIENCE OF MIND IN DAILY LIVING *Dr. Donald Curtis*	3.00
___SECRET OF SECRETS *U. S. Andersen*	5.00
___SECRET POWER OF THE PYRAMIDS *U. S. Andersen*	5.00
___STUTTERING AND WHAT YOU CAN DO ABOUT IT *W. Johnson, Ph.D.*	2.50
___SUCCESS-CYBERNETICS *U. S. Andersen*	4.00
___10 DAYS TO A GREAT NEW LIFE *William E. Edwards*	3.00
___THINK AND GROW RICH *Napoleon Hill*	3.00
___THREE MAGIC WORDS *U. S. Andersen*	5.00
___TREASURY OF COMFORT *edited by Rabbi Sidney Greenberg*	5.00
___TREASURY OF THE ART OF LIVING *Sidney S. Greenberg*	5.00
___YOU ARE NOT THE TARGET *Laura Huxley*	4.00
___YOUR SUBCONSCIOUS POWER *Charles M. Simmons*	4.00
___YOUR THOUGHTS CAN CHANGE YOUR LIFE *Dr. Donald Curtis*	4.00

SPORTS

___BICYCLING FOR FUN AND GOOD HEALTH *Kenneth E. Luther*	2.00
___BILLIARDS—Pocket • Carom • Three Cushion *Clive Cottingham, Jr.*	3.00
___CAMPING-OUT 101 Ideas & Activities *Bruno Knobel*	2.00
___COMPLETE GUIDE TO FISHING *Vlad Evanoff*	2.00
___HOW TO IMPROVE YOUR RACQUETBALL *Lubarsky, Kaufman, & Scagnetti*	3.00
___HOW TO WIN AT POCKET BILLIARDS *Edward D. Knuchell*	4.00
___JOY OF WALKING *Jack Scagnetti*	3.00
___LEARNING & TEACHING SOCCER SKILLS *Eric Worthington*	3.00
___MOTORCYCLING FOR BEGINNERS *I. G. Edmonds*	3.00
___RACQUETBALL FOR WOMEN *Toni Hudson, Jack Scagnetti & Vince Rondone*	3.00
___RACQUETBALL MADE EASY *Steve Lubarsky, Rod Delson & Jack Scagnetti*	3.00
___SECRET OF BOWLING STRIKES *Dawson Taylor*	3.00
___SECRET OF PERFECT PUTTING *Horton Smith & Dawson Taylor*	3.00
___SOCCER—The game & how to play it *Gary Rosenthal*	3.00
___STARTING SOCCER *Edward F. Dolan, Jr.*	3.00
___TABLE TENNIS MADE EASY *Johnny Leach*	2.00

TENNIS LOVERS' LIBRARY

___BEGINNER'S GUIDE TO WINNING TENNIS *Helen Hull Jacobs*	2.00
___HOW TO BEAT BETTER TENNIS PLAYERS *Loring Fiske*	4.00
___HOW TO IMPROVE YOUR TENNIS—Style, Strategy & Analysis *C. Wilson*	2.00
___INSIDE TENNIS—Techniques of Winning *Jim Leighton*	3.00
___PLAY TENNIS WITH ROSEWALL *Ken Rosewall*	2.00
___PSYCH YOURSELF TO BETTER TENNIS *Dr. Walter A. Luszki*	2.00
___SUCCESSFUL TENNIS *Neale Fraser*	2.00
___TENNIS FOR BEGINNERS *Dr. H. A. Murray*	2.00
___TENNIS MADE EASY *Joel Brecheen*	2.00
___WEEKEND TENNIS—How to have fun & win at the same time *Bill Talbert*	3.00
___WINNING WITH PERCENTAGE TENNIS—Smart Strategy *Jack Lowe*	2.00

WILSHIRE PET LIBRARY

___DOG OBEDIENCE TRAINING *Gust Kessopulos*	4.00
___DOG TRAINING MADE EASY & FUN *John W. Kellogg*	3.00
___HOW TO BRING UP YOUR PET DOG *Kurt Unkelbach*	2.00
___HOW TO RAISE & TRAIN YOUR PUPPY *Jeff Griffen*	2.00
___PIGEONS: HOW TO RAISE & TRAIN THEM *William H. Allen, Jr.*	2.00

*The books listed above can be obtained from your book dealer or directly from
Melvin Powers. When ordering, please remit 50¢ per book postage & handling.
Send for our free illustrated catalog of self-improvement books.*

Melvin Powers

12015 Sherman Road, No. Hollywood, California 91605

_____AMATEUR HORSE BREEDER *A. C. Leighton Hardman*	4.00
_____AMERICAN QUARTER HORSE IN PICTURES *Margaret Cabell Self*	3.00
_____APPALOOSA HORSE *Donna & Bill Richardson*	3.00
_____ARABIAN HORSE *Reginald S. Summerhays*	3.00
_____ART OF WESTERN RIDING *Suzanne Norton Jones*	3.00
_____AT THE HORSE SHOW *Margaret Cabell Self*	3.00
_____BACK-YARD FOAL *Peggy Jett Pittinger*	3.00
_____BACK-YARD HORSE *Peggy Jett Pittinger*	3.00
_____BASIC DRESSAGE *Jean Froissard*	2.00
_____BEGINNER'S GUIDE TO HORSEBACK RIDING *Sheila Wall*	2.00
_____BEGINNER'S GUIDE TO THE WESTERN HORSE *Natlee Kenoyer*	2.00
_____BITS—THEIR HISTORY, USE AND MISUSE *Louis Taylor*	3.00
_____BREAKING & TRAINING THE DRIVING HORSE *Doris Ganton*	3.00
_____BREAKING YOUR HORSE'S BAD HABITS *W. Dayton Sumner*	4.00
_____CAVALRY MANUAL OF HORSEMANSHIP *Gordon Wright*	3.00
_____COMPLETE TRAINING OF HORSE AND RIDER *Colonel Alois Podhajsky*	4.00
_____DISORDERS OF THE HORSE & WHAT TO DO ABOUT THEM *E. Hanauer*	3.00
_____DOG TRAINING MADE EASY & FUN *John W. Kellogg*	3.00
_____DRESSAGE—A Study of the Finer Points in Riding *Henry Wynmalen*	4.00
_____DRIVING HORSES *Sallie Walrond*	3.00
_____ENDURANCE RIDING *Ann Hyland*	2.00
_____EQUITATION *Jean Froissard*	4.00
_____FIRST AID FOR HORSES *Dr. Charles H. Denning, Jr.*	2.00
_____FUN OF RAISING A COLT *Rubye & Frank Griffith*	3.00
_____FUN ON HORSEBACK *Margaret Cabell Self*	4.00
_____GYMKHANA GAMES *Natlee Kenoyer*	2.00
_____HORSE DISEASES—Causes, Symptoms & Treatment *Dr. H. G. Belschner*	4.00
_____HORSE OWNER'S CONCISE GUIDE *Elsie V. Hanauer*	2.00
_____HORSE SELECTION & CARE FOR BEGINNERS *George H. Conn*	4.00
_____HORSEBACK RIDING FOR BEGINNERS *Louis Taylor*	4.00
_____HORSEBACK RIDING MADE EASY & FUN *Sue Henderson Coen*	4.00
_____HORSES—Their Selection, Care & Handling *Margaret Cabell Self*	3.00
_____HOW TO BUY A BETTER HORSE & SELL THE HORSE YOU OWN	3.00
_____HOW TO ENJOY YOUR QUARTER HORSE *Williard H. Porter*	3.00
_____HUNTER IN PICTURES *Margaret Cabell Self*	2.00
_____ILLUSTRATED BOOK OF THE HORSE *S. Sidney* (8½" x 11")	10.00
_____ILLUSTRATED HORSE MANAGEMENT—400 Illustrations *Dr. E. Mayhew*	6.00
_____ILLUSTRATED HORSE TRAINING *Captain M. H. Hayes*	5.00
_____ILLUSTRATED HORSEBACK RIDING FOR BEGINNERS *Jeanne Mellin*	3.00
_____JUMPING—Learning & Teaching *Jean Froissard*	4.00
_____KNOW ALL ABOUT HORSES *Harry Disston*	3.00
_____LAME HORSE—Causes, Symptoms & Treatment *Dr. James R. Rooney*	4.00
_____LAW & YOUR HORSE *Edward H. Greene*	5.00
_____LIPIZZANERS & THE SPANISH RIDING SCHOOL *W. Reuter* (4¼" x 6")	2.50
_____MANUAL OF HORSEMANSHIP *Harold Black*	5.00
_____MOVIE HORSES—The Fascinating Techniques of Training *Anthony Amaral*	2.00
_____POLICE HORSES *Judith Campbell*	2.00
_____PRACTICAL GUIDE TO HORSESHOEING	3.00
_____PRACTICAL GUIDE TO OWNING YOUR OWN HORSE *Steven D. Price*	3.00
_____PRACTICAL HORSE PSYCHOLOGY *Moyra Williams*	4.00
_____PROBLEM HORSES Guide for Curing Serious Behavior Habits *Summerhays*	3.00
_____REINSMAN OF THE WEST—BRIDLES & BITS *Ed Connell*	4.00
_____RESCHOOLING THE THOROUGHBRED *Peggy Jett Pittenger*	3.00
_____RIDE WESTERN *Louis Taylor*	3.00
_____SCHOOLING YOUR YOUNG HORSE *George Wheatley*	3.00
_____STABLE MANAGEMENT FOR THE OWNER-GROOM *George Wheatley*	4.00
_____STALLION MANAGEMENT—A Guide for Stud Owners *A. C. Hardman*	3.00
_____TEACHING YOUR HORSE TO JUMP *W. J. Froud*	2.00
_____TRAIL HORSES & TRAIL RIDING *Anne & Perry Westbrook*	2.00
_____TRAINING YOUR HORSE TO SHOW *Neale Haley*	4.00
_____TREATING COMMON DISEASES OF YOUR HORSE *Dr. George H. Conn*	3.00
_____TREATING HORSE AILMENTS *G. W. Serth*	2.00
_____YOU AND YOUR PONY *Pepper Mainwaring Healey* (8½" x 11")	6.00
_____YOUR FIRST HORSE *George C. Saunders, M.D.*	3.00
_____YOUR PONY BOOK *Hermann Wiederhold*	2.00

*The books listed above can be obtained from your book dealer or directly from
Melvin Powers. When ordering, please remit 50¢ per book postage & handling.
Send for our free illustrated catalog of self-improvement books.*

Melvin Powers
12015 Sherman Road, No. Hollywood, California 91605